THE FAILURE OF UNION
CENTRAL AMERICA, 1824-1960

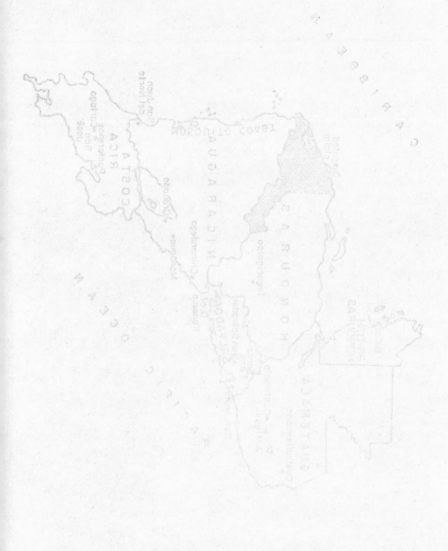

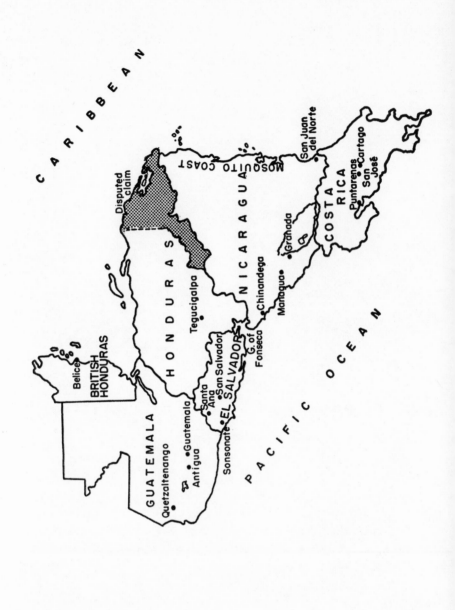

THE FAILURE OF UNION

CENTRAL AMERICA, 1824-1960

By

Thomas L. Karnes

Chapel Hill

THE UNIVERSITY OF NORTH CAROLINA PRESS

To Virginia

Preface

The numerous movements to combine the five republics of Central America into one federal union have been
the subject of a vast quantity of literature. Most of this
writing, produced by Central Americans, portrays the
glories that such unification might bring in contrast with
the tragedy that has so often been the Central American
experience. Much of the production has been emotional
rather than critical, and until very recently, almost none
has been documented. Often the authors have been participants in some of the unification conferences and have
seen fit to concentrate their studies on the events that they
knew personally. As a consequence, only two books, the
new and able volumes by Alberto Herrarte and Ricardo
Gallardo, have exhibited any interest in a survey of the
entire federation story.

United States authors have largely played the same
theme but with more willingness to blame the foreign
policy of the United States for the failure of union. The
reader of these books and articles in English should be-
ware of two historiographic booby traps. First, in Central
America the forces of liberalism have had all of the trum-
pets—most of her historians were Liberals, and Liberals
favored federation. Therefore, any method or person sup-

porting the movement received a good press at home. United States writers relying on Central American secondary sources were often misled by this inequitable and partisan distribution of accounts. Secondly, the Yankee must avoid the heedless assumption that the Central American effort to confederate paralleled the United States experience, that therefore it was automatically "good," and, just as mechanically, that it must succeed. Not much investigation is necessary to see the error of this comparison. The most obvious differences existed in the size, wealth, and political experience of the Central American and North American peoples at the end of their colonial eras. Less apparent but of great practical importance were the absence in Central America of some of the most significant sources of the strength which helped establish the power of the federal government of the United States over the individual states after 1787. I refer to the fact that in Central America no single government waged a war against the mother country for independence; no central war debt existed to be amortized by a strong central government; there were no centrally owned lands to be played off against the states or made into new states beholden to their creator; and, for three hundred years no frontier had been open in Central America. Central America's cohesive ties must be sought in her own environment.

Although I may not have succeeded in avoiding less obvious pit-falls, I have tried to shun these clearly marked biases. While I have relied completely upon primary sources when I could, I have been at times forced to borrow heavily from some of the secondary works. The prejudice of the latter is manifest enough, but the shortcomings of the former can be even more critical. Acts of God and man have reduced the archives of Central America to a minimum for many periods and events. I regret that as a result I have relied more heavily upon the records in Guatemala and Costa Rica than I would have wished.

One other bibliographic problem is that the coverage of individual attempts at confederation varies greatly. Some conferences caught the public eye and received wide press and official attention; others, of similar importance, were mentioned only in a few memoirs or state papers years later.

Within the limits imposed by these problems in research, this book is intended to provide the first survey in English of all of the known attempts to combine the Central American states, from the time of independence until the present. Since all attempts failed finally, I have felt it my responsibility to summarize them with the purpose of explaining why the ideal has not come about rather than to repeat the commonplace that federation would be good for Central America. In some respects the story is dismal: failure follows failure after failure because the Central Americans behave like other people and refuse so often to get along with one another. But there is a positive aspect of the story which may be Central America's most important contribution to a world frightened by its radioactive shadow. This lesson lies in the irrepressible optimism of the Central American people. The significance is not that they failed and failed and failed, but that they tried and tried and tried.

I wish here to acknowledge several debts. Professor John J. Johnson of Stanford University first suggested Central American confederation to me as a subject of study, but as my graduate advisor he aided me in an immense number of other ways. He possesses the ideal teacher's virtues of impatience, irascibility, a hard earned knowledge of his field, and the willingness to do battle with any agency or person for the sake of a student. His wife,

Maurine, once suggested that the best way to thank him would be to try to follow the same policy. This I hope to do.

In the past few years I have revised this manuscript many times, stimulated greatly by discussing much of what is obscure or bewildering in Central America's history with Professor William J. Griffith of Tulane University. His years of Central American experience helped me to encounter people and documents that might have escaped me. Moreover, we have argued so many points completely through that I am not always sure which good ideas are mine. I know the bad ones are not his.

The road from manuscript to book is long, rough, and often tricky. William R. Hogan, Chairman of the History Department at Tulane, frequently operated surveying level and caterpillar tractor with equal ardor and skill to smooth and straighten my path.

I must not conclude without adding to the list of my creditors Dr. Robert Wauchope, Director of the Middle American Research Institute, Mrs. Edith B. Ricketson, Librarian of that agency, and the librarians and staffs of the Archivos Nacionales of Costa Rica, the Archivo Nacional of Guatemala, and several private and public libraries in Central America.

I wish to acknowledge my indebtedness to the University Council on Research of Tulane University for aid in the publication of this book, and to the Ford Foundation for a grant under its program for assisting American university presses in the publication of works in the humanities and the social sciences.

Contents

Contents

co, but Mexican troubles soon made the idea unpopular. Lacking all but the barest of political experience, the Central Americans were forced to decide what would be their relationship, not only with Mexico, but with Spain, Colombia, major powers like Great Britain, and most of all with each other. The repeated consideration of these numerous choices, and the attempts to obtain concurrence of all five of the states in a single form of government, has engaged much of the political energy of the Central American republics since that time.

The many attempts to establish a single government for all Central America have seemed promising for two reasons. First, the very apparent similarities of the republics cause the most casual observer to suggest the likelihood of successful unification. Second, it is usually hypothesized that for about three centuries the Central Americans made up a cohesive political unit of the Spanish Empire and with such firm roots might be expected to continue to function as one body after independence. While both of the premises contain much truth, the degree of error involved is critical.

A first significant difference among the states is revealed by a survey made in 1824. The estimated population was:[2]

Guatemala	660,580
El Salvador	212,573
Nicaragua	207,269
Honduras	137,069
Costa Rica	70,000

To question the accuracy of the figures would be reasonable but fruitless. It seems fair to conclude, however, that Guatemala probably contained more people than the other

2. Rodrigo Facio, *Trayectoria y crisis de la federación Centroamericana* (San José, C.R., 1949), p. 67.

four states combined. Granted that most of these Guate-malans—Indians—played no part in politics, it would have to be assumed that such would be the case in each state. The extent of illiteracy was substantial in all of Central America, and the undoubted political disinterest of the Guatemalan Indian would be partly balanced by the equal disinterest of the *mestizo* in the other nations.

The measure of participation, however, is much less important than the fact that the first Central American constitution provided that every resident be counted for purposes of representation. Thus the states began their independent history with an unhealthy disbalance in congress. It helps explain their desire for a bicameral legislature based upon population *and* equality of the states, just as is the Congress of the United States.[3] This disproportionate ratio was reflected in a chronic fear in Central American history—the fear of Guatemala's numbers—significantly aggravated by Guatemala's colonial tradition of power, wealth, and authority. In terms of numbers and strength there was little similarity between Guatemala and her four sister republics.

Particularly was this apparent to the Costa Ricans. Recognizing clearly their poverty and general backwardness, they also saw the ineffectiveness in federal affairs of such a tiny population. To balance Guatemalan size, they often sought measures which would give them assistance from foreign nations such as Great Britain or Colombia.

A second distinction among the Central Americans that should be noted is that, contrary to common belief, they are not racially homogeneous. The variations in ethnic composition of the states now, and it must be assumed, in the 1820's, were very great. Precise calculations do not

3. What different decisions might have been made at Philadelphia in 1787 if Virginia had more people than the other twelve states combined?

exist, but a reasonable estimate would be that Guatemala is 70 per cent Indian and the balance white or *mestizo*. In Nicaragua and Honduras the majority of the people are mixtures of white, red, and to a lesser extent, black, coupled with very small quantities of pure strains of those same colors. El Salvador is almost completely *mestizo*, and Costa Rica claims to be about 80 per cent white.[4] In this last state the pre-conquest Indians were few and very backward. They were forced off the central plateau area fairly easily without greatly influencing the race of the conqueror. Guatemala, on the other hand, contained hundreds of thousands of Indians, peopling some of the highlands so densely that the Spanish had little real impact upon them. In the three middle provinces, the ratios of white to Indian were much closer, miscegenation was the rule, and only small numbers of either race could claim a "purity."

Such variations in degrees of racial mixture may mean very little. They are emphasized here only to point out that racial homogeneity is an insecure premise on which to base a successful confederation of the Central American people.

Population disparity and racial distinctions are only two of several differences which blur the outward resemblances among the people of the five states. Another popular assumption which must be qualified is that all of the people speak Spanish. In Guatemala, alone, there are Indian tribes speaking some nineteen different languages, and they are often so set apart from the white man's culture that Spanish is unknown.

4. The figures used are from official publications of the states concerned. No attempt is being made here to differentiate the people culturally but on racial grounds only. Great error is, of course, possible.

Also, Central American society does not have the uniformity that is alleged. It is true that the wealthy coffee grower of Guatemala lives much the same life as the planter in El Salvador, and their social attitudes are not likely to differ much from those of the Fruit Company executives or prosperous importers. But these people of the international set, with their comfortable or luxurious living standards, have little or nothing in common with their tenants, the Indians in the village, the illiterate *mestizo* laborer or the semi-civilized Mosquito Indian of the Caribbean coast. Poor and backward as these latter groups have been, they had no role on the political stage. Yet by the 1830's some of them constituted important factions in determining the progress or failure of confederation.

Religion, finally, has not always served as a uniform substructure of the political community in the Central American states. Notwithstanding the great predominance of Catholicism, one cannot safely conclude that it is a unifying agency in political thought. Quarrels within and concerning the church have rent Central America repeatedly. Church leaders have opposed and favored federation. They have done this as churchmen, and they have done this as office-holders. Their active participation in legislatures early in the nineteenth century was a commonplace. On occasion priests have even opposed one another in congressional debate over confederation. Powerful as the Catholic hierarchy might be in Central America, it has had no singleness of purpose in regard to uniting the states.

In sum, these preliminary observations on commonly accepted similarities of Central American states are not made to argue that confederation is not feasible but to question the widely accepted convictions that unity can come because the people are "so much alike."

The other major premise which underlies much of the

talk of confederating the Central American states stems from their long colonial history presumably under one government. Unified for so long, is it not likely that they can more readily confederate again? This assumption also needs examination.

Spain permitted the conquest of Central America from three different headquarters and three different directions at virtually the same time. *Conquistadores* from Panama, Mexico, and the island of Santo Domingo, ambitious and jealous of each other, tried to stake out claims for personal empires. This senseless rivalry resulted in bloodshed as well as conflicts of political authority that Spain never solved. Before 1543 jurisdiction of Central America was divided among the *audiencias* of those three colonies, but the New Laws of 1542 decreed the establishment of a separate Central American *audiencia* at Gracias a Dios in present-day Honduras. Yucatán, Chiapas, and Panama were considered part of Central America in this arrangement.

The boundaries were not static. After much switching, Spain permanently assigned Yucatán to the Audiencia of New Spain in 1560, and seven years later transferred Panama to Peru. Meanwhile the government of Central America was often shifted, its location usually being Guatemala, but at times moving as far as Panama with jurisdictional changes accompanying the geographic.[5] The last adjustment to be made occurred at the moment of independence when Mexico annexed Chiapas, an action that still rankles in Guatemala.

Years of feudal warfare among *conquistadores,* followed by significant alterations in boundaries and authority, could not create a Central American feeling of unity

5. This concise narrative generally copies C. H. Haring, *The Spanish Empire in America* (New York, 1947), pp. 79-83.

but, on the contrary, fostered localism and personalism of an enduring sort.

The tenuous political structure had a parallel in church organization. While religious orders sent numerous friars to Central America, the Spanish Crown waited until 1743 before establishing a religious authority in the region. In that year Guatemala's Bishop Pedro Pardo de Figueroa was named the first archbishop in Central America and given jurisdiction over the bishoprics of Ciudad Real in Chiapas, León in Nicaragua, and Comayagua in Honduras. This action did not appear to link those territories more closely, but it did serve to make those *towns* more strongly pro-church and ultimately centers for the defense of conservative regimes, whether they be Spain, Iturbide's Mexican Empire, or tory-dominated republics after independence. The unifying influence of the colonial church was severely limited to the personal power and prestige of archbishop and bishop. In effect it followed municipal rather than provincial lines. Where imposing power was daily displayed, there the church was the strongest. It is not coincidence that the provinces without their own bishops, Costa Rica and El Salvador, were the most outspoken against centralized government when independence came.

The existence, hundreds of miles away, of an archbishop whom they had never seen, did not link the provincials and village Indians any more closely to the officials in Guatemala. The attachment of the devout was to the church as represented by the parish priest, and it was he who guided the affiliation of the flock. There was no way to predict the directions that this guidance might point.

Decentralization of political and religious authority was further exaggerated by the meagerness of communications. Provincial capitals were all poor, isolated towns, weakly linked to one another by mule trails. The most distant, Cartago in Costa Rica, was about one thousand miles from Guatemala City. In the dry season, rapid messengers might complete the one way trip in a month and a half. For all but the most determined, travel simply ceased during the extended rainy season, generally from June to November. Communication with Mexico City was even worse, and it was a major factor in the ease with which the rule of the viceroy at that city could be ignored by Central Americans.

Within each province the conditions were better only in that distances were shorter. Populations centered in the temperate highlands when at all possible, and Spanish defensive policy strengthened this wish of the people. Cartage of agricultural and mineral production to seaports and supervision of the important customs collections thus became difficult tasks. (This is a problem that is not yet solved in Central America.) The modest glamor and trappings attendant to a captaincy general and an archdiocese made provincial tours of duty depressing to officials, and in that way, also, weakened the bureaucratic hold.

The evidence is scant, then, that this Audiencia of Guatemala was any more than an arbitrary unit of the Spanish Empire.[6] Faced with, and perhaps favored by, this fact, the provinces grew very slowly under the necessity of making their own decisions and solving their own problems, calling upon the capital for guidance only when it suited their purposes.

Such were the conditions in Central America when events in Europe compelled the breakup of Spain's empire across the Atlantic.

6. Contemporaries used the terms *"audiencia,"* "kingdom," and "captaincy general" in an interchangeable fashion as a general reference to the government of Central America.

Chapter II

Independence

INDEPENDENCE came to the Central Americans because of events in Europe. As elsewhere in Latin America perplexity and surprise accompanied receipt of the news that Napoleon had invaded the mother country and, in 1807, deposed the Spanish ruler Charles IV and his son Ferdinand VII. The authorities in Guatemala, as well as many of the citizens, swore allegiance to Ferdinand and asked to send delegates to the Cortes of Cadiz, the last remnant of Spanish authority at home. The liberal, French republicanism of this body soon became apparent. Furthermore the Cortes looked with disfavor upon the many self-governing *juntas* arising in America. Ignoring the king, the men at Cadiz just as clearly opposed the independence of the colonies. Even with Americans in attendance, little consideration was given to lifting the many restrictions on commerce, manufacturing, agriculture, and office-holding of the Creoles. There evolved, at that time in Central America, dual forces thinking of freedom; outright republicans, typical of the decade and to be found all over America; and secondly a more conservative faction, not republican in ideology but fearing the new-found "radicalism" of the ruling forces in Spain. Uneasy alliances between the two groups could occasionally be made against the same Spanish oppressions, though not so easily against the same Spanish rulers.

By 1811 the men of the Cortes, including as delegates two Central American clergymen, Antonio de Larrazábal of Guatemala and Florencio del Castillo of Cartago, were completing work on a new Spanish constitution. About the same time the beleaguered government transferred to Guatemala a new Captain General and Governor, José de Bustamante y Guerra, and the implementation of Spain's liberal constitution of 1812 fell to the lot of this vigorous conservative. Aided by the Guatemalan Archbishop, Ramón Casáus y Torres, Governor Bustamante opposed the document and the liberalizing tendencies of the council in that city. Even before the promulgation he had noticed increasing signs of republicanism, and his reactionary attitude brought home to many Central Americans the blessings possible with independence.

In November of 1811 momentary success was achieved in San Salvador by a revolt under the leadership of Manuel José Arce, Juan Manuel Rodríguez, and two priests, José Matías Delgado and Nicolás Aguilar. But when the other principal Salvadorean towns—Sonsonate, San Miguel, and Santa Ana—remained loyal, the uprising collapsed. Bustamante dismissed several officials, punished the ringleaders, and restored quiet to El Salvador.

Nicaragua was the scene of other rebellions in the same year. The immediate cause was the misrule of the long-time *intendente,* José Salvador, but as in El Salvador, there were more fundamental objections to Spain's mercantilist regime, now tottering from the force of the French invasion. The Nicaraguan Bishop, Nicolás García Jerez, became the new *intendente* and suppressed the movements quickly, except in Granada. Creoles there overthrew the recognized council and ruled independently of colonial officials for some five months. Deserted by the other towns, the Granadans' defeat at the hands of Spanish troops was doubly bitter. Bustamante broke a promise of amnesty to the rebels, and the leaders were severely punished. Though death sentences were commuted to life exile, estates were confiscated, and seeds of independence had been planted beside seeds of town hatred.

Other revolts were attempted with little accomplishment. Tegucigalpa in 1812, Belén convent in Guatemala in 1813, and San Salvador again in 1814 were the sites of critical disorders, while other places saw disturbances that were not classified as attempts to overthrow authority. By 1814 the manifest acts for independence of Central America ended, and in that same year Ferdinand VII was restored to the throne of Spain. He promptly annulled the Constitution of 1812 and gave his support to Bustamante's persecutions. Until 1821 there was no further struggle of significance between Spain and its colonists in Central America. There had been no civil war, and little blood had been shed, but the people in a position to achieve independence were now actively planning it. Indeed, some of the leaders such as Manuel José Arce spent years in jail for these early unsuccessful efforts. They were now awaiting the right opportunity.

The events of the years 1811 to 1820 greatly help to explain the turbulence which followed independence in 1821. Old antagonisms were heightened as new ones arose. Each province supported its share of distrust of the others, but upon Guatemala fell most of the censure. Men in the pay of Spain, whether Creole or peninsular, received the brunt of the social and economic complaints, although the measures causing the discontent normally originated in Spain. The city of Guatemala, especially in the minds of provincial commercial and agricultural groups, represented the control which was becoming more abhorrent. Among many of the more sophisticated Central Americans developed the realization that Guatemala might easily usurp Spain's role if the metropolis were ever overthrown.

The evidence is strong. In 1814 a provincial deputation of Nicaragua protested to the Spanish regency that Guatemala treated them harshly in economic matters. Restrictions on tobacco cultivation they described as capricious, and the recent ban on trade with New Granada hurt badly. As a remedy they requested that Nicaragua be made a captaincy general of equal rank with Guatemala, with its own *audiencia* and jurisdiction over an *intendencia* of Costa Rica.[1]

Costa Ricans protested, also, that taxes levied at Guatemala were ruinous to commerce and remembered that it was the *audiencia* that had destroyed the Panama commercial link.

The city of San Salvador posed the greatest threat to Guatemalan domination and equally feared Guatemala! City as more repressive than the mother country. Some of this ambition was political, some economic and some religious. There is good reason to believe that the last of these was the most important. From early colonial times San Salvador province urged its elevation to a bishopric, equal in status with Guatemala, Chiapas, Nicaragua, and Honduras. This demand became very great among Salvadoreans when in 1743 Guatemala was raised to an archdiocese. On the basis of population Salvador should have had its own bishop before either Honduras or Nicaragua, but the Crown ruled otherwise. In the decade after 1811 the chief candidate for the expected opening was the strong Liberal leader, José Matías Delgado. He openly ad-

1. Sofonías Salvatierra, *Contribución a la historia de Centro-américa* (Managua, 1939), II, 354-60.

vocated the separation of El Salvador from Guatemala in civil matters the better to achieve ecclesiastical independence.[2] Following the failure of the rebellions of 1811 many of Delgado's followers were severely punished by officials in Guatemala only to have the penalties greatly softened by authorities in Spain. It is of major importance that by 1820 many Central Americans were as opposed to membership in a political organization headed by Guatemala as they were to remaining in the Spanish Empire.[3]

The stage was set for a violent expression of these rivalries, and all that was needed to unleash them was the removal of the dying Spanish power.

It is reasonably correct to say that there was no Central American war for independence. Success came in part by default, but this should not conceal the work and suffering of small groups of Central Americans in the post-Napoleonic era. Pitched battles did not occur. In 1818 Bustamante was replaced by an older and milder Captain General, Carlos Urrutia y Montoya. Evidently of a kindly nature, Don Carlos was much more popular than his predecessor and reinstated some of the rights and privileges that had been lost to towns and citizens in the years just passed. Then in January, 1820, troops in Spain under Colonel Rafael Riego mutinied and marched upon Madrid rather than go to America to put down the Creole armies. Other uprisings occurred, and soon King Ferdinand was made a virtual prisoner and forced to restore the Constitution of 1812.

In Central America these events gradually became known (Bustamante had been quite successful in keeping

2. Mary P. Holleran, *Church and State in Guatemala* (New York, 1949), p. 64.
3. Perhaps unwittingly Spain abetted distrust by granting imposing and empty titles to Cartago and León for supporting the authorities when Granada revolted in 1811.

the citizens unaware of the progress of the South American revolts), and attitudes crystalized. Freedom of the press was one of the outgrowths of these developments, and an independent newspaper appeared in Guatemala for the first time. Political parties presented slates of candidates for local offices in 1821. The issue at stake between the factions was not the clear-cut question of independence alone. Rather, it was a struggle to control Guatemala, and those other portions of Central America that mattered, whether independence was achieved or not. But independence could not be long delayed, with Spain gradually being driven from the continent to the south, and the freer air after 1820 made political discussions more pronounced and passionate than ever before in Central American events.

Members of the two chief factions that arose were initially named Cacos and Gazistas, politically meaningless terms with a touch of slander in their connotation. Most Cacos favored independence, and their most important members were Creoles, One of the leaders was the previously mentioned José Matías Delgado, but probably the physician and editor Dr. Pedro Molina was more influential. The first issue of his *El Editor Constitucional* was dated July 24, 1820, and for more than a year this weekly paper reported local and world news of importance, including the debates in the Spanish Cortes. An outspoken advocate of liberty, Molina felt that the liberals in Spain had little interest in American freedom but were allied with pro-Spanish elements in Guatemala. He deplored the fact that Spain's constitution did not give equal rights to colonials. He bitterly attacked the Holy Alliance in his pages and urged the abolition of the small amount of slavery that then existed in Central America. Another favorite target of Molina and his followers was Spain's commercial policy, and the paper spoke frequently of the benefits that would accrue from "free trade" and the abolition of monopolists.

While *El Editor* reflected some of the heterogeneity of the Cacos, and therefore was not as rabidly liberal as its opponents assumed, it gradually became the leading voice for separation from Spain. In August of 1821 Molina altered the paper's name to *El Genio de la Libertad,* to keep up, as he said, with the changes of the times and the matters with which the paper treated.[4]

Quickly, in opposition to *El Editor,* the organ of the Gazistas appeared, *El Amigo de la Patria.* The intellectual leader of the group and regular contributor to *El Amigo,* if not its editor, was José Cecilio del Valle. Valle was one of America's most brilliant men, a scientist and philosopher, who could see that the weaknesses of his society were profound and would not disappear with mere freedom from Spain. Thus, on the question of independence he was much less radical than Molina, and his great influence continued long after Central America became free. The pages of *El Amigo* also reflect interest in liberty and constitutional rights, but there is more concern with property and its protection than can be found in Molina's writings. Valle believed that progress would come by evolutionary changes in the archaic feudal institutions of Spain. Social injustice was a great evil and a rightful concern of government. Public welfare, in fact, was government's primary consideration, and Valle discusses in *El Amigo* the problems of poverty and poor communications in Central America.[5]

When local elections were held in 1821 the issue was

4. Pedro Molina, *Escritos,* Editorial del Ministerio de Educación Pública (Guatamala, 1954), III, 743.

5. Virgilio Rodríguez Beteta, *Ideologías de la independencia* (Paris, 1926), pp. 48-58.

not whether to break from Spain but rather how rapidly social and economic change was to take place. The question was reform within the framework of Spanish society, and independence might or might not accompany the outcome. In Guatemala the Gazistas were victorious but by small margins, helping to influence the opposition to become a more outspoken party of freedom in the hope that such a step would assure more votes in the future.

These elections and the freeing of the press brought about ardent political discussions that stirred the people of Central America just as rumors began arriving from Mexico of the new phase of its war for independence. Official news of the Plan of Iguala proposed by Agustín Iturbide reached Guatemala on May 9 of 1821. By then it was apparent that Spain's power was waning, dissipated on a dozen fronts, and many Central Americans first faced the realization that some stand would have to be taken. As usual the lead was taken in Guatemala; Captain General Urrutia, old and increasingly inactive, did not favor freedom for the colony, but did little to prevent it, and was prevailed upon by leading Creoles to delegate his authority to the Spanish Inspector General of the Army, Gabino Gaínza. Gaínza at first opposed any step toward independence and spoke out against Iturbide, but public opinion strengthened against his stand. When he received word on September 13 that the neighboring provinces of Tehuantepec and Chiapas had accepted the Iguala agreement, he realized that some action would be necessary to appease his people.[6]

Urged on by the Cacos as well as many Gazistas, Gaínza convoked a meeting of important civil and church officials on September 15, 1821, and before the day was

6. In this manner Chiapas permanently transferred allegiance from Guatemala to Mexico.

out they had declared Guatemala independent of Spain. While there were Spanish troops in Guatemala City, they were under the orders of Gaínza and did not oppose the measure. Since the mother country had no forces to spare for an attack, the movement remained completely bloodless. The existing government remained in office, and Gaínza directed the provincial governors to do the same.

Away from the city of Guatemala the citizens as well as the regional officials faced a more complex problem. Concerned over what action Spain might be able to take, they also were not sure what their relationship was to Guatemala. Mexico began exerting pressure on separate Central American towns in an effort to add them to the nation which had been proclaimed on September 27 when Iturbide had entered Mexico City. Within each province, and what was worse, within each town, majority views were hard to observe, so divided was the public by economic, political, or religious interests. In most towns *juntas* were chosen to try to determine courses of action.

The *junta* of San Salvador was managed by the liberal leaders, José Matías Delgado and Manuel José Arce, and this agency proclaimed independence on September 29 for the *intendencia* of San Salvador. Among the signers of this declaration was the Spanish *intendente,* Pedro Barriere. Delgado and Arce next proposed to León and Comayagua that the three towns (and, presumably, the *intendencias* that they ruled) should form a republic in opposition to Iturbide. This is probably the first formal suggestion for a Central American confederation. The authors of the plan said that these provinces would make a respectable nation and that perhaps Yucatán, Granada, Cartago, and Tegucigalpa also could be persuaded to join. The alternatives to this, they felt, were anarchy or domination by Mexico or Guatemala.[7] Although often opposed by San Miguel and Santa Ana, San Salvador and San Vicente generally controlled the area roughly equal to present-day El Salvador. It is clear that in this small area there already existed a real fear of its neighbors, for any Central American government would have to be framed so as to provide protection for the weaker members.

Some of the same feeling existed in Nicarauga. The *diputación* of León, which had been created in 1813 by Spain, declared its independence of Spain *and* Guatemala on September 28. By Nicaraguans this action was presumed to include Costa Rica since Spain had placed that government under León. In Nicaragua, as in the other provinces of Central America, the declaration was not a radical step in the year of 1821. Two of the most conservative men in all of the Guatemala kingdom were signers of the act: Miguel González Saravia, the *intendente* of Nicaragua, and Nicolás García Jerez, bishop for the same area. Correctly estimating the muddled situation, they retained the leadership in a delaying action until, as they said, "se aclaren los nublados del día y pueda obrar esta provincia con arreglo a lo que exigen sus empeños religiosos y verdaderos intereses."[8] By mid-November it was clear to this faction that their true interests lay with Iturbide as the closest agency in America to the Spanish tradition that they would uphold. But León could no longer speak for all of the *intendencia*. The people of Villa Nicaragua voted independently to adhere to Iturbide's plan, but the much more important city of Granada felt differently and, with some inconsistent advice from Gaínza

7. Rafael Heliodoro Valle, ed., *La anexión de Centro América a México* (Mexico, 1924-27), I, 160.

8. Costa Rica, Secretaría de Educación Pública, *Documentos históricos posteriores a la independencia* (San José, 1923), I, 15-16.

in Guatemala, decided to act separately of León and remain loyal to Guatemala.

The most isolated and least informed province, Costa Rica, lacking even a press, played a cautious and often neutral role. Some of this could be attributed to isolation, of course, but there was exhibited surprising political wisdom by a few of its leaders. Among these were the Alvarado brothers, who at that moment were residing in Guatemala. José Antonio was a priest, a sincere republican soon to serve in an advisory *junta* created by Gaínza, and in which capacity he became famous for defending Costa Rica from the designs, as he saw them, of Guatemala. His younger brother was Pablo, a school teacher, with a background of rebelliousness against authority and a zeal for liberty in all its forms. These men observed conditions in Guatemala and reported them to their native province. Pablo, in particular, urged destruction of any tie with Spain. He wrote to the *ayuntamiento* of Cartago that Spain had turned them all loose, that Costa Rica should declare its freedom, and that, to avoid civil war, it should join a large republic, preferably Santa Fé de Bogotá (Colombia).

Only partially following this advice, the Costa Rican town councils met individually, deposed the Spanish governor, and declared independence from Spain as of November 1. As in the other provinces there was not unanimity among the towns, but led by Rafael Barroeta and José María de Peralta, the various councils acted together long enough to conclude a provisional pact. On November 5 Costa Rica severed its links with León, amid protests from the latter, but then early in December two towns, Cartago and Heredia, declared their allegiance to Mexico.

A similar but more severe split tore Honduras. The town of Comayagua, dominated by the *intendente*, José Tinoco, declared its independence from Spain and an inclination to join Mexico. Tegucigalpa favored continuing under the jurisdiction of Guatemala. While no immediate clash occurred, both cities sought allies and armed themselves for civil war. Comayagua sent agents to Mexico for help against a possible attack by Guatemala and warned San Salvador not to interfere in the internal affairs of Honduras. Tegucigalpa claimed that it was being coerced into the Mexican Empire by its rival city and sought aid from Gaínza.

This official had meantime acted in accord with the Guatemalan declaration of independence which required the convening of delegates from all of the old captaincy general in Guatemala City on March 1, 1822, while in the interim, he and the other Spanish officials would continue to govern. This reasonable approach was largely nullified by Iturbide's ordering of Mexican troops to Central America and as far as Panama "to protect those who wish to join the Empire." It was a positive action that impressed many of the undecided people. Gaínza then asked all of the Central American towns to hold *cabildos abiertos* to decide upon annexation to the Mexican Empire as a unit. Many of the results were never reported to Guatemala, and there was a strong minority opposing Mexican ties, but a substantial majority voted in favor of annexation to the Empire.[9]

The vote changed the position taken by Gaínza. In October of 1821 he had warned Central Americans that they would be swallowed up by Mexico and that joining Iturbide would be foolish. By December he was describing the evils of isolation. Several towns joined Mexico by their own action, and the trend was nearly complete when on December 29 Guatemala City and Quezaltenango united themselves with Mexico. On January 9 Gaínza could an-

9. Valle, *La anexión,* II, 24-27.

nounce the union of all of Central America with the Empire. Henceforth all choice in the matter ended. Gaínza warned that he would enforce the will of the majority, and the question of annexation would no longer be a subject for public discussion—even on the street corners. Officially, then, from January of 1822 Central America was a part of Mexico, by means of a more or less democratic process.

The motives of the various groups who favored this step should be briefly examined. In a sense it was Spain and not the Central Americans who broke the colonial relationship, and for several years many of the Central Americans retained a hope that Spain might reacquire its empire. In the meanwhile, conservatives—in the sense of preserving tradition and tolerating as little change as possible —rightly understood that the Mexican Empire would come closer to protecting established rights and privileges than any other form of government likely to reach Central America. Agustín I was tarnished and a rascal, but he knew where his strength lay and would not precipitate drastic reforms. Ideas of the French Revolution permeated Central America, and republicanism was accompanied by demands for abolition of all social, political, and religious inequities. It is not strange, then, that churchmen, like Archbishop Ramón Casáus of Guatemala and Bishop García Jerez of Nicaragua favored the union. Political leaders of the old regime, Gaínza, Saravia, Tinoco, and lesser appointees, technically served under the viceroy of Mexico until 1821 and could well assume that they, too, might be best advised to move cautiously. It was an ideal period for the shrewd leader, though, and great was the temptation to pick up a lesser crown or, at least, one of the new offices sure to develop.

But others joined the conservatives in favoring the

Mexican bond. Much of the correspondence and many speeches made in the councils indicated a feeling of political ingenuousness which required the tutelage of experienced statesmen from outside Central America. The most dramatic example was the Salvadorean effort to join the United States, but many earnest citizens in the more backward provinces of Honduras, Nicaragua, and Costa Rica advocated joining Mexico or Colombia for a period of apprenticeship. Among other peoples was the fear of war —invasion by France or Spain, or what was worse, civil war. The only military strength apparent in all of the isthmus belonged to Iturbide.

By no means all Central Americans were willing to accept the new relationship, and some endangered themselves by resistance to Gaínza's decrees. Chief among these anti-imperialists was a liberal faction largely centered in the city of San Salvador but to be found in some number in every province. They refused to consider themselves members of the Mexican Empire and were not reluctant to commence civil war. Although opposed by a few Salvadorean towns, San Salvador, led by José Matías Delgado and Manuel José Arce, declared its complete freedom from Mexico and Guatemala. When Santa Ana and Sonsonate reiterated their allegiance to Mexico, Arce took command of a miltary force to attack those two cities. Gaínza ordered out Guatemalan troops to oppose Arce by capturing San Salvador itself. These soldiers, under the command of Colonel Manuel Arzú, overran the city and then lost it by pure carelessness. Throughout most of 1822 El Salvador continued divided with much of the province favoring complete independence but threatened with invasion from Guatemala.

In the other provinces the situation was less critical, although surely no less puzzling to the citizens. For example, Quezaltenango refused to recognize its old allegiance to Guatemala City but, like that place, affirmed its loyalty to Mexico. The same attitude was assumed by León and much of Honduras. These regions looked with pleasure on the expected arrival of the Mexican army, anticipated about the middle of 1822. Most districts sent delegates to Mexico City to serve in Iturbide's congress assembling in May, but they found much futility and even danger—within two months the Emperor was imprisoning his congressional enemies—and above all they found little consideration for Central American affairs.

Under the command of Brigadier General Vicente Filísola a greatly reduced Mexican army of five or six hundred men finally reached Guatemala City in June of 1822. Filísola carried Iturbide's orders to send Gaínza to Mexico and to take his place as military head of all of Central America. His was to be a difficult assignment. Word of Iturbide's declining popularity at home reached Central America with the reports of the deputies; towns in the same province faced each other with increasing tension over the Mexican question; Costa Rica resumed flirting with Colombia; and to many Filísola's expedition resembled an invasion. His immediate task was to settle the dispute between Guatemala and San Salvador. He opened negotiations that continued for weeks in the hope that he could obtain the peaceful annexation of all of El Salvador to Mexico. The agreements went unratified partly because of Iturbide's stubbornness and partly because of the many conditions that Delgado, in the role of political chief of El Salvador, kept adding. One of these stipulations was, coincidentally, the creation of a bishopric for San Salvador, a post which Delgado had long expected for himself.[10] Completely losing patience with the affair, Itur-

10. Manuel Montúfar, *Memorias para la historia de la revolución de Centro América* (Guatemala, 1853), p. 17.

bide ordered Filísola to make an immediate attack upon San Salvador. As a last gesture Delgado revealed the pathetic effort of the Salvadorean congress to forestall invasion. He declared that an emissary had been sent to the United States seeking annexation, and in the meanwhile El Salvador considered itself a part of the republic of the north. He said that the step was taken in order to protect the rights of the citizens so ruthlessly crushed by a Mexico intent upon dominating everything to the isthmus. A few days later he warned Filísola that even if the United States rejected annexation, it would take cognizance of what Mexico was doing and act accordingly.[11] By late February of 1823 Filísola had subdued all of El Salvador that had opposed Mexico. The conquered he treated fairly as he hastily returned to Guatemala, ignoring en route a request for help from Saravia who had found in Granada a parallel to the San Salvador affair.

The sudden departure for Guatemala City was prompted by a change in the position of Filísola's Emperor. Conspiracies had broken out in Mexico against Agustín and congress had become increasingly resistant to his will. On October 31 he dissolved that body and ruled through a committee of his selection. Several old heroes of independence raised provincial armies in support of a form of federalism, and Iturbide's position was placed in greater jeopardy yet by the appearance on the scene of the champion of all Mexican opportunities, General Antonio López de Santa Anna. Coupled with the liberals, the combination

11. Valle, *La anexión*, II, 400 and 412. The Unites States made no reply. James Buchanan to Elijah Hise, June 3, 1848, in William R. Manning, ed., *Diplomatic Correspondence of the United States. Inter-American Affairs* (Washington, 1933), III, 33. In September of 1823 Arce and Rodríguez visited Washington to pursue the matter but returned home on hearing of Iturbide's fall. Henry Clay to William Miller, April 22, 1825, in William R. Manning, ed., *Diplomatic Correspondence of the United States Concerning the Independence of the Latin American Nations* (New York, 1925), I, 239.

was too much for Iturbide, and in February of 1823 he was helpless to oppose a federalist pronouncement calling for the end of the Empire. It was at this juncture that Filísola feared for his position in El Salvador, and probably, as well, for his future. To return home seemed the wisest course, and withdrawing by way of Guatemala City he received news of the abdication of the Emperor.

Chapter III

Dios, Unión y Libertad

WITH the overthrow of Emperor Agustín I in March, 1823, the ties of Central America and Mexico were broken. Mexican affairs had been so turbulent that even without knowledge of Iturbide's abdication, Filísola clearly anticipated some upheaval and, about ten days after that event, called for the provinces to elect deputies for a Central American congress. This decree, dated March 29, 1823, was issued in accordance with the second article of the Act of Independence of 1821 and had the effect of nullifying the annexation to Mexico.[1]

In most of the provinces there was temporary peace. The bitterest struggle, a war brought about by the separation of Granada from the rest of Nicaragua, had reached substantial proportions, with the *intendente*, Miguel Saravia, leading forces from León against its neighboring city. But the decree from Filísola seems to have put an instant end to the war, and he recalled Saravia to Guatemala. Saravia's absence contributed to the truce, and by April a *junta gubernativa* created in León was claiming to represent all of Nicaragua.[2]

1. Vincente Filísola á la División Auxiliar de su mando, March 29, 1823. In Genaro García, ed., *Documentos inéditos ó muy raros para la historia de México* (Mexico, 1911), XXXV, 93. Filísola was acting on behalf of the Guatemalan authorities according to some writers.

2. José Dolores Gámez, *Historia de Nicaragua* (Managua, 1889), p.

In May a provincial assembly for Honduras proclaimed its desire for peace and unification with the rest of Central America. Guatemala and El Salvador were pacified as much by Filísola's calm and deliberate actions as by the continued presence of his troops.

Costa Rica's turmoil lasted a few weeks longer than that of the other provinces. In part this was simply evidence of the traditionally poor communications with the most distant area of Central America, but it was also evidence that important elements of Costa Rican society held sharp hostility to any foreign regime. Since independence, there had existed rancorous disagreement between imperial and republican factions. This was aggravated by groups in Nicaragua that attached themselves to Iturbide and undertook to re-establish over Costa Rica the old Spanish tobacco monopoly. Aided firmly by the Bishop of León much of the trouble could be layed at the door of Saravia. This interference, as Costa Ricans viewed it, widened the rift between San José on the one hand, and Cartago and Heredia on the other. The first alleged that the others were under the complete influence of the clergy, meaning the Bishop, and that this was the reason that they had affirmed their loyalty to Iturbide. By March there was again apparent strong sympathy among republicans for joining Colombia or for establishing a separate sovereign state.[3] An assembly of delegates from the towns was called, and on March 17, 1823, Costa Rica declared itself an independent province reserving the right of the Costa

---

350. There was also such a *junta* in Granada. Alejandro Marure, *Bosquejo histórico de las revoluciones de Centro América* (Guatemala, 1837), I, 56.

3. Junta gubernativa to Intendente of Panama, March 15, 1823, No. 828, f. 6, Archivos Nacionales of Costa Rica. Hereafter ANCR.

Ricans to federate with some American power if later agreed upon.[4]

As always, the Ticos were hampered by the tardy arrival of news from the provinces and were late in grasping the meaning of Filísola's victory in San Salvador and the gains of Saravia in Nicaragua. The information was intoxicating to the imperialists of Costa Rica; in Cartago they overthrew the government and chased the republicans to San José and Alajuela.[5] Using these two towns as assembly points, the latter regrouped under the leadership of Gregorio José Ramírez and Lieutenent Cayento Cerda, a Salvadorean, to attack the imperialists. They moved out of Cartago to defend themselves and engaged the Josefinos at Ochomogo, a high point between Cartago and San José. The few casualties were the first to result from civil war in Costa Rica. The battle ended somewhat indecisively, but agreement was reached to move the capital to San José, and in that sense the republicans had won. By now the impact of the Mexican revolution against Iturbide was apparent in Costa Rica, and the last gesture toward alliance with Mexico had been made.[6]

In the remaining weeks before the Central American Constituent Assembly was to meet at Guatemala, various *juntas* continued to be active in seeking an acceptable form of government or in establishing blocs that might strengthen their positions in the future republic. For example, some of the leaders at León called upon Costa Rica, Comayagua, Tegucigalpa, and Granada for delegates to a provincial deputation. Nothing came of this, but an alarmed

4. Marco Tulio Zeledón, ed., *Digesto constitucional de Costa Rica* (San José, 1946), p. 17.

5. Rafael Obregón Loría, *Conflictos militares y políticos de Costa Rica* (San José, 1951), pp. 4-6.

6. Ricardo Fernández Guardia, *La Independencia y otros Episodios* (San José, 1928), pp. 109, *et passim*.

Granadan *junta* asserted itself by establishing a similar body and claiming that *it* had representatives from the important Nicaraguan towns and that the *junta* would act independently until it heard from Guatemala.[7] Filísola wrote to all of the provinces that Mexico was suffering badly from anarchy and that the same conditions would prevail in Central America unless agreements for unified action were achieved.

It might have happened. Fortunately for the Central American welfare no individual leaped at the chance to set himself up as dictator. Filísola was in the best position to establish a personal strong-man rule and, barring that, could probably have prevented such political assertions by anyone else. While his role as military ruler of Central America for Iturbide had technically disappeared with the overthrow of the Emperor, he more than any single person could assume a pretense of authority. Confusion and lack of communication were on his side. He had a few hundred of the best troops in Central America, and there were many persons of importance who supported him. But he made no bid for power and let the Central American people determine their own future.[8] Recognizing his lack of popular support, he abstained more and more from local affairs and made preparations to leave Central America. With his troops he departed in August, 1823, for Mexico, to render service as a general under Santa Anna.

In the fifteen to eighteen months that the individual provinces of Central America had been attached to Mexico

7. Diputación provincial of León calls for delegates, April 17, 1823, No. 668, f. 16, and Cleto Ordóñez to *junta*, May 12, 1823, No. 449, f. 3, ANCR.

8. Some contemporaries of Filísola were very critical of his conduct, and reference is made to this in the works of Bancroft, Marure, Chamorro, and others. It would seem that he could easily have set himself up as dictator had he wished.

nothing had been done to improve the conditions of any of the parties involved. Marure calls the relationship an unhappy one. The Empire had in no wise united the provinces. Filísola's call for a congress, whether the result of expedient, good will, or local pressure, was not ordered by the Mexican government but was a local decision. Anarchy and petty, internal war had been the rule. The traditional suspicions of the villager were intensified by the issue of allegiance to the Empire. Town rivalries were exaggerated as many citizens found it appropriate to move to those communities where majority views on Mexico more closely approximated their own. Because independent action was the order of the day, more people had had the opportunity to participate in political affairs than ever before, and self-reliance was visibly increased by the necessity of day-to-day decision making. Often, conservative modifiers were to be found in the *ayuntamientos* and deputations, men who had held office in the colonial regime and whose experience or personalities retained position for them in the trying period of post-independence. Troublesome often, dangerous occasionally, they soon realized that it might be easier to cast their lots with America, and the number returning to the peninsula was not large. As independence was assured, and the prospect for reconquest vanished, such men normally adapted themselves to the new atmosphere and assumed roles as the logical leaders of conservatism and its political parties.

The Mexican interlude had done even more. The new ruling groups were ready to attempt the united action implicit in Filísola's decree, but if, as many Central Americans were predicting, the provinces could not go forward together, they would at least have had the exacting experience of self-analysis that the Mexican period had enforced.

It is not correct to say with Bancroft that "Central America, after a fifteen months' connection with Mexico, was again in the same position it had occupied at the separation from Spain."[9] The position was similar in that the Central Americans again had to decide upon their form of government, but the Central Americans could never be the same again. The Mexican issue had cut cleanly through provincial boundaries. Party lines were being strung out in new and dangerous fashions; a Liberal in El Salvador was for decades to come to find more in common with a Liberal from Nicaragua than with a Conservative from his home town.[10] Suspicion was everywhere. Some saw Spain behind Iturbide's empire; others feared a resurgent Mexico or a rampant Colombia. Imperialists, temporarily in eclipse from Mexico's failure, feared the tyranny of liberal masses in political control for the first time. Certain of the roots of these divisions existed from colonial times, but in a year and a half distrusts were exaggerated, alignments strengthened, and decisions made that were to become Central America's curse.

While true revolution did not come to Central America in 1823 as it might have, partisanship nevertheless grew most bitter as the new liberal leaders were forced to prove themselves in village debate before assembling in Guatemala.

In El Salvador the dominant motif was increasing hatred for Guatemala. In Nicaragua and Honduras no one town or coalition could completely control, and the result was to be years of civil war. Honduras suffered the additional fate of being a battle ground for others because of its central location. Isolated Costa Rica reinforced its

9. Hubert Howe Banfroft, *History of Central America* (San Francisco, 1887), III, 67.

10. This is a phenomenon by no means dead in the twentieth century.

tendencies of late colonial times toward localism, neutrality, and a realization that it was better to be separated from the quarrels of the other four. In Guatemala there was perhaps less division among the towns because of the vigor of the capital, but even there were planted the seeds of a critical split. It was in the midst of this spirit of faction that the first Central American Congress was convened.

Nearly three months after Filísola summoned them, the first delegates met in Guatemala City on June 24, 1823. He and his troops had not yet left for Mexico, so they lent their numbers and color to the opening ceremonies, but there were many conspicuously absent. Distance, internal factors, and the presence of these same soldiers ordained a delay in the arrival of the delegates from Costa Rica, Nicaragua, and Honduras. If the province of Chiapas still felt attachment for Central America, it was unable to express this interest, and neither now nor later did it take part in the sessions or send deputies.

The provinces had followed the stipulations of the act of independence of 1821 which authorized one delegate for each fifteen thousand persons and directed that the existing electoral *juntas* make the selections. The total allotment was sixty-four—Guatemala, twenty-eight; El Salvador, thirteen; Honduras, eleven; Nicaragua, eight; and Costa Rica, four—but this figure was not achieved until October. In the meantime, blessed by the archbishop, a near-quorum of forty one Guatemalans and Salvadoreans began the task of ruling the Central American people.

Calling itself the National Constituent Assembly, this body was at the same time the government of Central America and the agency charged with drafting a constitution for the permanent republic of Central American states. For the next year and a half—until January of

1825—the assembly carried this double burden. Inexperienced men, trying to arrange the neat balance of powers that a federal system requires, daily faced the questions of the mere existence of Central America. It was too severe a test for the young land. Yet at the same time the delegates were acting for regions that were still on provisional bases. Not one of the five provinces had organized its permanent government, and three years were to elapse before all five states had promulgated their individual constitutions.[11]

Obviously there was a scarcity of trained men. In each provincial capital, experience was at a premium to help organize the new state firmly and soundly, but to protect its interests each province needed exceptional men in Guatemala for the tug of war at the federal level. Thus, teachers, priests, and publicists were thrust into the political cockpit, bringing with them some measure of education but also their abstractions, untested theories, and prejudices. Then in each arena, at home and in the capital, these men and their ideas came face to face with men of property and position, the traditionalists who served only to prevent the change that his opponent would bring about.

In these lights the constitution of the Central American people was a solid achievement. The first routine work was readily accomplished. With José Matías Delgado acting as president, the assembly declared the provinces independent from Mexico and "any other power," calling themselves the Provincias Unidas del Centro de América.[12]

11. Marure, *Bosquejo*, I, 120. The government operated in a centralized fashion while organizing the *federal* type of government. Pedro Joaquín Chamorro, *Historia de la Federación de la América Central* (Madrid, 1951), p. 46.

12. The Mexican interlude was summarily dismissed. The meetings of June, 1823, were considered extensions of the sessions that brought independence in September of 1821, and the incorporation of Central America into Mexico was classified the *de facto* result of violent and illegal measures.

They were unable to persuade Chiapas to join with them, but the citizens of that state were specifically invited to enter the confederation whenever they felt it advisable. A three-man executive power was provisionally chosen. All Liberales, Manuel José Arce and Juan Vicente Villacorte were from El Salvador, while Dr. Pedro Molina was a Guatemalan. Arce was in the United States so his place was taken by Antonio Rivera Cabezas. The presidency was to rotate monthly among the three, and Molina assumed the position first.[13]

The election of the provisional executives served to reopen the question of party alignments. Though discredited, the imperialists were not destroyed. In general they became the party of opposition to the Liberales and were called Serviles, Moderados, or Conservadores. This can be too simple, however, for there were outstanding examples, such as Mariano Gálvez and Cirilo Flores who had supported annexation to Mexico but otherwise were ardent Liberales. Nor can one be sure that the members of the assembly were always precise in their usage of the numerous party epithets. It is reasonable in the interest of narrative to conclude that for the first few years of its existence, the Central American government held two major political groups: one, the Liberales, federalists and states' rightists; and two, the Serviles, more conservative and generally centralists in the significant matter of government structure. The momentary weakness of the latter is exemplified by the election of three Liberales to the executive branch. Nevertheless, the party gained converts, partly from fear of a radical program and partly because of the espionage system that the triumvirate employed—worse, said Filísola,

13. Decree of Asamblea Nacional Constituyente, July 10, 1823, Guatemala, *Documentos inéditos* (no pagination) located in the Biblioteca Nacional of Costa Rica.

than any attempted by Robespierre and Marat.[14] Soon the Serviles were to acquire most of the fence-sitters and become the more numerous party.[15]

Most of this strength lay in Guatemala, however, with a heavy proportion springing from the capital city itself. Federalism as an ideal logically developed in the remoter areas, and there was a marked cleavage between Guatemalan conservatives who advocated centralism and the liberal elements from the other provinces who favored a federation. It was not numbers or overwhelming popular demand that determined that the government would be federal in structure, nor was it majority wish that brought about the liberal nature of the new nation. It was the spirit of the times, the enthusiasm of the reformer, the memories of too much privilege that carried the day—and not too many days—for the Liberales.

Attempts were made to effect typical liberal reforms. Religious freedom was urged by the administration, though the number of non-Catholics must have been very small. This measure had no success. The religion of the people was to be the Roman Catholic to the exclusion of all others. Freedom of the press made no greater progress, though books written in foreign languages were exempt from such censorship. There was more enthusiasm for the destruction of nobility, and titles of distinction were ordered abolished. The "Citizen" of the French Revolution replaced "Majesty," "Highness," "Excellency," "Lordship," and "Don," and while it is obvious that the last term continues in common usage, liberal officials diligently strove

14. Chamorro, *Historia,* pp. 46-47. Chamorro reports that the terms *serviles* and *liberales* were earlier used in the Spanish Cortes of Cadiz.

15. They gained additional support from bureaucrats turned out of office by the triumvirate. Anyone tinged by the Mexican experience was likely to be included.

in speech and correspondence to supplant it with the more egalitarian "Citizen."[16]

The Central Americans studied the "Declaration of the Rights of Man," and many, but by no means all, of the Liberales favored a total change in society, but this was to be no French Revolution. There was little of an organic alteration, no change in class structure, no sweeping confiscations; there was little more drastic than the deposing of various priests who had too stoutly supported Iturbide. Perhaps severe reforms were not needed. Perhaps it was felt that the establishment of independence was a long enough step for the moment and that the newly created government could bring about improved conditions successfully and gradually. There is a certain innate conservatism in the measure designed to attach all or parts of Central America to the United States, Mexico, or Colombia, evidence of a lack of confidence in political facility not easily reconciled with the radical activity of true revolution. Furthermore, as the weeks passed, the party divisions crystallized with the Serviles obtaining a clear majority that was retained throughout the life of the Constituent Assembly.[17]

16. Decrees of A. N. C. July 15 and 30, 1823. Further French influence was to be seen in the three-striped flag, consisting of wide, horizontal bars, top and bottom blue, the middle one white. In the center of the last was an equilateral triangle containing five volcanoes bathed by the two seas. The sun was rising behind them, and over all was a small rainbow under which floated a liberty cap, flashing rays of light. The confederation's motto was "Dios, Unión y Libertad."

17. Among the deputies were forty-six classified as Serviles and only eighteen as Liberales according to one of the latter; Pablo Alvarado to Gobierno Superior de Costa Rica, November 3, 1823, Provincia Independiente, Exp. 1125, ANCR. The terms "Liberal" and "Conservative," though often used or implied, had little meaning in Central American politics, certainly as of 1824. While they might differ consistently on such things as the relationship of church and state, they were not normally doctrinaire. Professor William J. Grif-

The condition of the treasury presented a critical problem for the young government. Several old sources of income dried up with independence, and much movable wealth and even tax records had disappeared—presumably to Mexico. The government could not pay its debts and was dangerously in arrears to the army. Most of the troops had been disbanded, but one disgruntled officer, Captain Rafael Ariza y Torres, organized an insurrection that broke out on September 14, 1823, among the soldiers and badly frightened the assembly.[18] Though Ariza assured the assembly that he was loyal to the government, they feared him, and the executive called upon Quezaltenango, Chiquimula, and San Salvador for help. The assembly gave Ariza the promotion he sought, while Guatemalan citizens fought his troops in the streets. The position of the government was made to look even weaker when many of the assembly fled the city.

Although it appeared that Ariza had temporarily vanquished the authorities, he recognized the limitations of his future. The Guatemalan public had not supported him and, in fact, had posed the only resistance. But placing him and his rebels in greater jeopardy was the impending arrival from San Salvador of some 750 volunteers under

fith of Tulane University has suggested to me that there were no consistent party names in the early 1820's and that subsequent historians retroactively supplied "Liberal" and "Conservative" for later nineteenth-century readers. Some justification can be found for writing of "Guatemalans" and "provincials," but that distinction was temporary as well as being dangerously simple. Making the picture even more complex is the conclusion drawn by Miss Susan Strobeck in "The Political Activities of Some Members of the Aristocratic Families of Guatemala" (master's thesis, Tulane University, 1958). This careful study of voting patterns indicates that, contrary to usual opinions, the aristocrats, a well-defined group in early Central America, did not vote solidly but were found in strength on both sides of every political question. I have adopted a principle of uniformity that the Central American of the 1820's would not have recognized.

18. The first Central American barracks revolt.

the command of a peninsular, José Rivas, veteran of the Salvadorean defense against Mexico. Neither the government nor Ariza desired a showdown, and each exhibited fatal weakness. Stimulated by the vote of new delegates who, reaching Guatemala only recently, had played no part in selecting the executive, the Servile faction felt an increase in strength proportional to the growing feebleness of the liberal executive branch. Thus the triumvirate was forced to resign, and in their place the assembly named Manuel José Arce, José Cecilio del Valle, and Tomás O'Horán. The first two were still absent from the country, and as substitutes José Santiago Milla and Juan Vicente Villacorta were designated. The last named was unhappy over being required to serve as a substitute in the same task from which he had just been deposed and looked upon this as touching his honor. He was mollified, however, and grudgingly continued to serve.[19]

The new trio was considerably less liberal than the old and reflected the reascendancy of the Serviles. Merely making the foreign-born O'Horán eligible for one of the posts required new legislation that the Liberales opposed. Knowing the political allegiance of the oncoming Salvadoreans, the new executive sent orders for the troops to halt about thirty-five miles from the capital. Captain Rivas was told that he could bring 150 men into the city but that the rest would have to return home. Liberales in congress who had run from Ariza now came back to work, and the recent rebel in his turn departed for Antigua. When the government ordered his pursuit, he went into exile in Mexico. His executive officer was less fortunate—captured, he was quickly hanged.

Captain Rivas was acting as the agent of the state of El Salvador, and his orders were to remain in Guatemala

19. Marure, *Bosquejo,* I, 75.

until he was convinced that the government and, in particular, the Liberales in the assembly were functioning freely and safely. Rivas sent two delegates ahead to the city to determine whether liberties were being suppressed. They decided in the affirmative, and the troops marched on against the wishes of the Serviles. On October 12, 1823, they entered the capital city. Five days later about two hundred soldiers arrived from Quezaltenango. Originally ordered by the government because of the Ariza uprising, they were just in time to serve as something of a counterbalance to Rivas' Salvadoreans. The new troops from "the heights," including about fifty Mexicans left behind by Filísola, clearly were in support of the Serviles, and the two armies faced each other in the streets. There was no fixed battle. Guatemalans were divided in their loyalty and certainly not desirous of having their town become a battle site. It was rumored that Rivas was only a tool of Salvadoreans who wanted the capital moved to that state. If he was bluffing, he was called. The government, changing the odds, rounded up a ragged outfit of nearly one thousand: militia, deserters, old "Volunteers of Ferdinand VII," and the Quezaltecos. Turning over to this group its meager artillery, the assembly now felt strong enough to serve notice on Rivas and his "foreign" soldiers.

Old scores were settled as the Salvadoreans met some of the same Mexicans so recently after they had fought during Filísola's invasion. Small groups of either force insulted, molested, and occasionally killed their opponents when they could be found in street or plaza greatly outnumbered. For several days Guatemalans moved in terror until the executive presented a plan that was reasonably acceptable to both armies. A small sum of money was presented to Rivas for expenses incurred on the way home, and a system of proportionate departure of the two military factions was agreed upon. A platoon of Salvadoreans left town on one road at the same moment that a platoon of the Quezaltecos was homeward bound on another. There was much suspicion and good reason for distrust. Little tricks were played by both parties to delay their complete evacuation, but finally the city was cleared of the most belligerent soldiers, and the assembly could work in peace for the first time in nearly two months.[20]

Thus ended the first real crisis of the newly united provinces. The circumstances were largely accidental and the issue unimportant, but the incident revealed grave weaknesses in the government. It was obvious that even a small detachment of unfriendly troops could put officials in a panic in the absence of any regular army. Pedro Joaquín Chamorro emphasizes that this brief period saw the planting of seeds of disorder that were to flower so profusely in the years to come.[21] There were to be many times in the future when the public did *not* oppose the *caudillo* but made it easy for him to work his way with the administration. This was not the beginning of factionalism, yet it endorsed the most malignant kind. There had always been rivalries among the provinces. Now there had been invasion, and the differences were sharpened, sensitized. To the government it meant that prompt agreement on a permanent constitutional form was essential.

Toward this end the work was hastened. The Serviles now had a clear working majority, but it was concentrated largely in Guatemala. These members realized that Guatemala would likely dominate any form of government cre-

20. Pablo Alvarado to Gobierno Superior de Costa Rica, November 3, 1823, P. I., Exp. 1125, ANCR. Alvarado was an eyewitness of these events and reported them at length to his constituents.
21. Chamorro, *Historia,* pp. 51-56.

ated (this, of course, was equally recognized in El Salvador) so could afford to accept some sort of compromise.
Nevertheless, the Serviles made an effort to get support
for a centralized government by polling the towns on the
single issue of centralism versus federalism. Liberales an-
grily resisted the discussion and the vote. They maintained
that a federal system had been agreed upon from the earliest days of the assembly. Some states had drawn up
fundamental laws incorporating the idea, and as late as
October, 1823, a committee of the assembly had recommended this basis for the permanent republic.

The federalist strength lay primarily in the towns of
San Salvador, Granada in Nicaragua, and San José in
Costa Rica. This widely distributed opposition—and it
was vigorous—meant that a centralized constitution would
not likely go into effect. Guatemalan Serviles calculated
that they must acknowledge the sovereignty of the states,
or there would be no Central American nation. Not yet
was there a leader or a body of partisans willing to unite
the region by armed might. All too often this was to be
tried in the decades to come.

The constitutional issue facing the Central American
people in 1823 was duplicated in most of the new Latin
American republics of the 1820's, and nowhere was the
question easily solved. Central America's tragedy was that
failure to keep the provinces together doomed the old
"Kingdom of Guatemala" to an exaggerated, destructive
fragmentation. Roots of federalism are generally considered to be deepest in Brazil, Argentina, Mexico, and Venezuela. Had cooperative action failed in any of them, the
resulting independent states would still have been of de-
fensible area. Separatism in Central America brought

with it province-sized nations, smaller than any non-insular republics in the Western Hemisphere.

Federalism was to fail in Central America, and the result was five tiny states. Could a centralized nation have overcome the separatist forces and have preserved a single nation, unified and strong? It was never attempted and so cannot be judged. Central America destroyed itself in the rancors that grew from making decisions. While local suspicions might cause a Nicaraguan to fear and distrust a Honduran, for example, real bitterness and hatred, of a kind that could lead to war, came out of the months of argument over the position of the states in the republic. Even when there was official agreement that the federal type should be copied, the issue seems not to have been closed. Debates were still waged in the provinces and it would appear that much pointless and personal strife was provoked and magnified by the question.

Neither Liberales nor Serviles were doctrinaire in their beliefs. To both factions centralism meant continuation of the old and still existing condition, namely that Guatemala was the center of government. It was the metropolis of colonial times, it was headquarters for the Mexican contingent during the adherence to Iturbide's empire, and its citizens dominated the assembly hearings of the United Provinces. So the great debate was not waged over political philosophy and ideal government but simply, what was to be the role of the city of Guatemala?[22]

It was a combination, then, of enormous pressure from the provinces for federalism and the not completely reluctant Guatemalan decision to accept this minority view that led to the publication in December of 1823 of the

22. An enlightened discussion of this problem can be found in Rodrigo Facio, *Trayectoria y Crisis de la Federación Centro-americana* (San José, 1949), pp. 61-63.

bases for constitution with a federal framework. Through-out most of 1824 the assembly's committee continued to govern Central America, to prepare drafts of the constitu-tion, and to encourage the states to complete their constitu-tions in accord with the federal plan.

Acceptance of the bases of government did not mean harmony. Salvadoreans tried to persuade Costa Ricans to join in a movement to transfer the assembly sessions to San Salvador, presumably as a prelude to making that city the capital of the new republic. Always there was the fear of intervention or reconquest by Spain. Modern schol-arship generally scoffs at the danger, but the enunciation of the Monroe Doctrine in December, 1823, was a North American symptom of a threat that the Central Americans felt most intensely. Some of the Liberales claimed that they were forced to submit to indignities and grievances in order to prevent the dissolution of the congress and the complete victory of the Serviles aided by the Holy Alliance. The rumor was current that Simón Bolívar was about to be crowned king in Colombia, whereupon he would call a congress in the isthmus for the purpose of "seducing these provinces by means of the Royalists" and turn them over to the Colombian monarchy.[23]

Meanwhile, the states were organizing their own gov-ernments to harmonize with the federal plan. Even this relatively uncomplicated task was beset with difficulties, and many months passed before all of the states completed their work. The constitution of El Salvador was decreed

23. As early as 1822 Bolívar had urged several nations to dis-cuss a confederation at Panama. Finding this step premature, he post-poned a similar action until December of 1824, and the result was the Congress of Panama of 1826. Central America participated. Vicente Lecuna and Harold A. Bierck, Jr., eds., *Selected Writings of Bolívar* (New York, 1951), II, 456-59, and Juan de los Santos Madriz to Secretary of Junta of Costa Rica, February 5, 1824, P. I., Exp. 1074, ANCR.

in June, 1824; Costa Rica's in January, 1825; Guatemala's in October, 1825; and Honduras' in December of the same year; disorders in Nicaragua delayed the promulgation many months. The events in Nicaragua that created the delay need concern us but little. There was a miserable succession of outbreaks with issues and sides badly confounded. Though town fought against town, there was much repartitioning. The Liberales (or mobs, according to Dunlop),[24] in León and Granada, made war upon the administration and the army. Serviles from Managua, Chinandega, and Rivas came to the aid of the latter. Rival *juntas* in León and Managua claimed to speak for all of Nicaragua and suffered states of siege for their boasts. Hundreds of Nicaraguans were killed, and property suffered vast damage in the bitter struggles.

It was in the course of this catastrophe that party lines seem to have acquired the geographical inclination so stereotyped in Nicaraguan history. The siege of León being directed primarily against its liberal leaders, many Serviles residing in that town found it advisable to move. For this group Granada proved to be more hospitable, and the century-long rivalry of these two communities is generally recognized as bearing a liberal versus conservative aspect.

In the capacity of conciliator a Guatemalan Colonel, Manuel de Arzú, was sent to Nicaragua in October of 1824 by the executive power which now included the properly selected Manuel José Arce and José Cecilio del Valle. Lacking a military force, Arzú attempted to arbitrate the dispute but found that method futile and his own life endangered. His failure, as well as his acknowledged support of Valle led to the demand for military interven-

24. Robert G. Dunlop, *Travels in Central America* (London, 1847), pp. 160-62.

tion by Arce, and that chief at the head of some five hundred Salvadoreans marched on Nicaragua in January. His authority and show of strength sufficed to bring an armistice without battle; he then disbanded the two Nicaraguan forces and sent the principle leaders into exile. Temporarily peace came back to Nicaragua, and the organization of the state was achieved in April, 1826.

Not completely concealed from the Central Americans were the ominous signs that the Nicaraguan civil war delineated. The natural rivalry between two important leaders was heightened as Valle and Arce appealed to factions in Nicaragua that might support one or the other as the most obvious candidate for the Central American presidency.[25] These men had brought quiet to Nicaragua, but nothing had been settled, and town rivalry continued unabated in a fashion that wracked the nation for decades to come. Another consequence of the chaos was that the fertile province of Nicoya (today Guanacaste) detached itself from Nicaragua to escape the wars and joined Costa Rica.[26] It developed in importance as Costa Rica's western frontier, a profitable land of opportunity and the source of many disputes between the two southernmost states of Central America.

Finally it should be noted that the Nicaraguan anarchy was ended by Arce with soldiers from his native El Salvador, not an army representing Central America. Too soon, perhaps, for us to expect any other police power, it dramatized once again the absence of real federal authority. But more serious than this weakness was the augmented state rivalry that came from using "nationals" from one province

25. Arce resigned from the executive power for "personal reasons" when he left for Nicaragua.

26. Gámez, *Nicaragua,* p. 370. Most Nicaraguans did not object to the transfer at that time. The government was weakened so greatly by civil war that it could not prevent the action.

to put down those of another. Even conceding that no federal army was in existence at the time, the executive power made a blunder in not acquiring forces that could give an appearance of being interprovincial. As Pedro Joaquín Chamorro wrote, "Cuanto germen disociador iba acumulando la Federación de Centro América."[27]

Among these distractions the Constituent Assembly continued to hold its committee meetings and completed a constitution November 22, 1824. Framed primarily by Pedro Molina, José Francisco Barrundia, José Matías Delgado, and Mariano Gálvez, it was a clear adaptation of the federal principle with some obvious resemblance to the constitution of the United States.

The republic was to be called the Federation of Central America and was to be popular, representative, and federal. The introductory paragraph of the Central American constitution reads strikingly like the preamble of the United States' constitution and is dotted with some of the precepts of the Declaration of Independence.[28] Their constitution provided for a distribution of powers among an executive, a legislature, and a judiciary. The concept of this separation was, of course, widely recognized by this time and need not have been copied from the United States. There was a president and vice-president, elected by the people in a complex sifting process vaguely like our electoral college. Their renewable terms were for four years.

The legislative branch was made up of a congress based on population and a senate composed of two men from each state. There was a supreme court and a lesser

27. Chamorro, *Historia*, p. 56.
28. In this prologue the Central Americans restored the "protection of property" that Jefferson omitted from Locke's writings. The "pursuit of happiness" was ignored.

judicial system, and there was a long bill of rights. The president of Central America had no right of veto over the legislation of the Congress. The senate could not initiate laws; its chief function was to sanction—or refuse to—the acts passed by congress. Its concern with such bills was to determine whether they were constitutional and *"conveniente"* to the nation. If a majority of the ten senators ruled in favor of a measure, it was sent to the president for enforcement. If the majority opposed, the bill was returned to congress for reconsideration. Two-thirds of that body could then put the law into effect, with the senate merely confirming by an automatic sanction.

The senate had numerous other powers, several in the field of advising the president as well as reviewing certain types of decisions made by the supreme court.

Concern with individual liberty was manifest; guarantees of protection against the state were much more numerous and specific than in the Bill of Rights of the United States, and there was a significant concern with the rights of the accused and of prisoners awaiting sentence. Slavery was abolished with enthusiasm. (A related clause making Central America an asylum and haven for every foreigner brought trouble in 1825 with the neighboring Belice establishment from which some one hundred slaves escaped into the young republic. An almost noble debate was waged in the Central American government over the return of these slaves to their British owners before more practical considerations compelled their restitution. Some honor was preserved by the fact that not all of the slaves were sent back.)

There was no religious liberty for the native. The constitution prohibited the public exercise of any but the

Roman Catholic Church; foreign Protestants could worship as they chose so long as it was not openly. Some reduction in clerical influence was visible, however, in the provisions that the president and supreme court justices could not be priests of any type and only one of each state's two senators could be an ecclesiastic.

In order to implement the constitution during the period of transition to the new government, several liberal reforms were put into effect by decrees. Economic monopolies were removed, freedom of the press was put into practice, and plans were drawn for free public schools. The Inquisition and special privileges for the clergy were eliminated. Restrictions were devised to reduce the flow of novitiate priests and nuns into religious service, and Papal Bulls needed the approval of the federal government before promulgation. As an obvious consequence of the liberalism of the time, these reforms forced the clergy even more into the ranks of the Serviles and brought into focus dangerous religious issues.

Criticism of the constitution of the first Central American Federation abounds. Because the government ultimately collapsed, historians of that period have regularly blamed this document for the failure. The usual accusations are that it was too idealistic for an untutored people or that the foreign constitutions, North American, British, or French, were copied too slavishly. The first of these charges is probably true, but the same comment has been made concerning virtually all of the early Latin American codes. It is possible that the relative degree of idealism and backwardness in Central America was less favorable than elsewhere, but a reasonable judgment would be most difficult to make.

Foreign principles of government were apparent, and

there is room for serious research to learn what copying was deliberate and how much was simply derived, like our Declaration of Independence, from the climate of the times. It is a weak argument to affirm that the Central Americans copied any document too closely. Such an assertion is impaired when one attempts to decide just which prototype was used. A better grounded belief is that the Central American constitution was a hodgepodge of ideas, some borrowed, some indigenous, some suitable, some not. For this the framers should not be blamed; it is the basis of most organic law.

In pragmatic fashion certain specific provisions should be examined. Article sixty-five declared that when the circumstances of the nation permitted, a federal district would be created, presumably in a more central location than Guatemala City. This important step was never taken. Throughout most of the life of the federation the capital remained in that town in spite of occasional protests from the other provinces. The government of El Salvador was especially anxious for a new site and succeeded in 1834 in having the capital moved to Sonsonate and then to San Salvador where it remained until 1839.[29] But this transfer was too late to benefit the nation greatly. Separatism was already widespread, and the selection of San Salvador was little improvement over Guatemala. No true federal district existed, although one was intended, for the national government found that in San Salvador, as in Guatemala, there was constant irritation and strife caused by the proximity of the provincial officials.

For this oversight the framers of the constitution are not completely at fault. A federal district was planned (and the language authorizing it is no more vague than that to be found in the United States' constitution provid-

29. Bancroft, *History*, p. 120.

ing for its federal district), but "circumstances" just never "permitted."

A second source of trouble emanating from the constitution was the relationship of the congress to the president. While in Central America as elsewhere in Latin America, the executive branch grew steadily in power, this tendency was not apparent in the years immediately after independence. More obvious was the fear of the despot, and so the Central Americans built safeguards into their law to make the congress clearly supreme. Once the congress passed a law and obtained the sanction from the senate (normally received without much trouble), the president was required to put the law into effect within fifteen days. He could not return a measure for reconsideration, he could not veto it, he could not nullify it by pocket veto, he could not weaken it by delays in execution. He was, in the words of Rodrigo Facio, merely decorative.

Precisely why such restrictions were favored by both Serviles and Liberales is not immediately clear, but it must be assumed that this role was reasonably satisfactory to both parties. Each faction must have believed that its security lay with a strong congress based upon population. While the Liberales distrusted a powerful executive reminiscent of the Spanish king, the Serviles could also oppose him because their strength lay in the congress through the city and state of Guatemala with its population so top-heavy in relation to the other provinces. Since the senate was weak and not to be construed as resembling that of the United States in its authority, the only true protection for the states could have been the president. Thus the Liberales, generally equated with Federalists, were sacrificing states' rights on the altar of liberty. Any concept of nationhood, of Central Americanism, had to find its embodiment in the executive; emasculating that branch meant that there was no Central America.

A last charge against the constitution that must be considered is that its basic federal philosophy was ill-advised. This argument holds that the Central Americans, blindly copying the United States because it was successful, adopted its general organic structure without concern for the fact that the two lands were poles apart in so many important elements. Much of this is beside the point. The simple question is whether the federal form of government *that the Central Americans set into motion* was suitable for *them*. Here the Yankee is bothered by terminology. Federation to the Central American did not then or now mean what it does in the United States. The correspondence, the protests, the legislative suggestions of the Federalists of 1824 indicate that the government that they created was a confederation, far looser than John C. Calhoun ever proposed.

The men advocating this kind of federation (and the reader is reminded that they were almost always Liberales) referred to their provinces as "sovereign states" and argued in congress the right of a state to oppose a federal tax levy. Article ten of the constitution declared that each one of the states was "free and independent in its internal government," a clause open to the widest interpretations. Documents and correspondence of the provinces indicated varying concepts of autonomy with the expression "free state" commonly used, and Costa Rica's constitution, promulgated very shortly after that of the federal government, was entitled "Fundamental Law of the Free State of Costa Rica." The head of each state was called the *"jefe supremo."*

Thus, while some Central American statesmen may have felt that their government was a federation somewhat like the United States, the organism that they drafted not only was not like it, but the Liberales, at least, did not mean for it to be. A stronger centralization might have been more "suitable," but it would not have been acceptable.[30] Provincial minds were taking the first step toward nationhood, and any balance that they struck between unity and localism was going to be weighed heavily in favor of the latter. Human experience would indicate that political solidarity normally requires outside dangers or pressures. The Central Americans had not yet felt this, and they had even missed the cohesive influence of a common military enemy when they obtained independence. Now, free, there were dangers, but they were vague and diversified, and the enemy was not an armed outsider. It is interesting to note that when asked for a stronger government for protection against foreigners, the Liberales charged the Serviles with contriving a foe just to weaken the rights of the states.

It is hard to escape the conclusion that the form of government put into effect was in its broad outlines the only one possible. Minor changes, interpretations, judicial decisions or usage might refine the document in one direction or another, but basically Central America planned for and received an association of states.

Does this then mean that no one government for the five states of Central America was possible? It seems to the writer that the federation as promulgated could have succeeded in the short run and strengthened ties for a future firmer government—if more authority had been given to

30. Cleto González Víquez, "Carrillo y Costa Rica ante le Federación," *Revista de los Archivos Nacionales de Costa Rica,* I (San José, Julio-Agosto, 1937), 492-521.

the president as the realization and personification of Central American nationality, and if the people of Central America had wanted to unite badly enough to overcome suspicion and fear by occasional compromise. This is all speculative, of course, but centuries of going in separate directions were not to be remedied by a document, no matter how ideal or suitable.

The important task of electing the first president occupied the Central Americans early in 1825. For several months the Liberales had been campaigning for Manuel José Arce, while with somewhat less enthusiasm, the Serviles supported José Cecilio del Valle. These leaders possessed distinguished records from late colonial times. Arce was sent to prison by Spanish officials for his part in an uprising in 1814, and he was an outstanding spokesman among Salvadorean Liberales. Valle, very able, was one of the very few Central American intellectuals. He represented his region in the congress of Emperor Iturbide and, like Arce, had been part of the executive power in the provisional government.

A potential electoral vote of eighty-two had reached only seventy-nine because of complications in creating Guatemalan districts, and four other votes were nullified. Valle led forty-one to thirty-four out of the seventy-five resulting. Since the constitution required an absolute majority, the question then arose as to whether Valle's forty-one should be based upon the authorized eighty-two votes or upon the actual seventy-nine cast. In the latter case Valle would be the unquestioned winner, but in the former Valle would fall one short of the necessary majority.

Sensing the lack of Serviles' enthusiasm for his opponent, Arce made a deal. Long an advocate of a bishopric in San Salvador, a post that would have gone to a relative, José Matías Delgado, Arce backed down. Though stating that he still believed in a promotion on the religious scale for his province, he agreed to refer the matter to the next congress, where, with the Serviles ruling, the clerical issue could be settled to their satisfaction as well as that of the archbishop of Guatemala. This chicanery arranged, the congress announced that Valle lacked a majority, and the election was in its hands. By a congressional vote of twenty-two to five Manuel José Arce thus became the first president of Central America.[31] Both Valle and José Francisco Barrundia declined the vice-presidency, and it was then passed on to Mariano Beltranena.

Following Barrundia's example, which Arce bitterly condemned as creating a whimsical and capricious fashion, distinguished Liberales such as Mariano Gálvez declined the Ministry of Hacienda and Pedro Molina that of Relaciones.[32] At the very beginning of his term Arce thus found a minimum of cooperation from many individuals and groups that had been most active against Spain or Mexico. Nevertheless, by April, 1825, the senate and the superior court of justice had been elected and had taken their positions in Guatemala City. Though weak and divided, the Central American government was a functioning reality.

Diplomatic recognition was highly desired by the young republic especially from lands outside Latin America. The

31. This bargain reveals some of the futility of the terms "Serviles" and "Liberales" that I have chosen to use. Almost all of the congressmen in the first group voted for Arce, so-called liberal. The only protest defending the rights of Valle, so-called conservative, came from the Costa Rican delegation which boasted of its liberalism. Pablo Alvarado to Secretary General of Despatch, July 7, 1825, P. I., Exp. 1301, ANCR. An interesting comparison was alleged with the recent victory in the United States of John Quincy Adams. *El Indicador,* Guatemala, Sept. 22, 1825, microfilm in Middle American Research Institute Library, Tulane University.

32. Alberto Herrarte, *La Unión de Centroamérica* (Guatemala, 1955), p. 157.

United States obliged quickly on August 24, 1824, and followed this with a treaty of commerce and friendship which went into effect in 1826.[33] At about the same time Latin American sister republics were accomplishing the same ends with Mexico and Colombia being the first.[34] Great Britain and the Netherlands dispatched commercial agents in 1825 and 1826 but did not deem it wise to grant recognition immediately for reasons aside from the Central Americans' ability to assume the obligations of a sovereign state. Spain delayed recognition for many years in Central America just as it did with the rest of Latin America because of the reluctance of Ferdinand VII to accept the dissolution of his empire. In the end, that nation, France, and the Papacy reserved recognition, and only in the late 1830's, during the period of Central American dismemberment, did they gradually establish diplomatic relations with the individual states.

The economic position of Central America was chaotic. There was virtually no public treasury at the time of independence, and by the inauguration of Arce the excess of expenses over income had brought the nation to the point of financial collapse. An unusual factor in creating extraordinary costs had been the maintenance of the Mexican troops during their occupation duty, but more critical was the attack upon the existing tax structure left from colonial times. A partly logical step (for the complaints of the Creole businessmen had much to do with separation from the mother country), but a dangerous one for the new regime, was the abolition of almost all of the old sources of revenue. Forced loans and direct assessments were temporary expedients to meet governmental costs,

33. Graham H. Stuart, *Latin America and the United States* (New York, 1955), p. 295.

34. George A. Thompson, *Narrative of an Official Visit to Guatemala from Mexico* (London, 1829), p. 265.

but they were detested by the public and, of course, not satisfactory systems of taxation.

A consistent source of income was expected to be from the monopoly on tobacco. This had been introduced in late colonial times by Spain and was accompanied by much complaining and smuggling in the Guatemalan "Kingdom." Never popular with the Spanish colonials, it bore the additional handicap that all of the Central American provinces could grow tobacco, and the quota and marketing systems created small, favored groups. In spite of this unpleasant background independent Central America accepted the fact that a tobacco monopoly brought a steady return, and so the practice was continued. Collection of this revenue was put into the hands of the states with the attendant varieties of enforcement, collection, and successful contraband that such arrangement accordingly fostered. In the first few years the gross receipts to the federal government were about 200,000 to 300,000 pesos annually.

Second to the realization from tobacco in the first year or two, but gradually outstripping it as a tax source, was the collection of the customs duties. This, too, was carried over from Spanish administration, was partially nullified by the smuggling habits of the citizens, but was somewhat less unpopular. The government officials recognized that substantial portions of merchandise went untaxed and resolved to seek funds to plug the holes in the coastal patrol.

In sum it can be said that the federal income augmented by the contributions from the states, could not meet the demands of a young nation nor service the public debt. It was then decided by Arce and the congress to seek a large foreign loan to provide an initial stability that was then lacking in the nation's economy.

The presence in Central America of various commercial and semi-official agents of foreign powers made it possible for the federal government to negotiate tentatively with European investors for substantial, long-term loans. The states of Honduras and Costa Rica attempted to borrow individually and found offers in spite of the fact that the national government opposed such debts and was expected to contribute shares to each state from the residue of the large loan then under consideration. It was a period of investors' enthusiasm for Latin America as a whole, with the British taking the lead. Several English houses were reported interested in entering into a transaction with the Central American government, including some who already were   under contract with other Latin American nations. On December 15, 1824, Manuel Julián Ibarra, Secretary of State, and John Bailey, Guatemalan agent for the London firm of Barclay, Herring, Richardson and Company, signed an agreement for a loan generally reckoned at 7,142,047 pesos before commissions and discounts. However, after deducting the share for Bailey, the Guatemalan House of Aycinena, and the very substantial discount made by the lending agency, the Central Americans expected to net about 5,000,000 pesos. The loan was to bear 6 per cent interest per year. The problems of British stockholders in raising a small portion of the money need not concern us in this chapter; it suffices to say that Central America received but one-third of a million pesos, though indebted for nearly three times that amount. Bankruptcy of Barclay, Herring, Richardson and Company and increasing British suspicions of Latin American solvency brought the federation only small and irregular advances that were dissipated on salaries, army, and other urgent current expenses and were not channeled into the increased customs security and the industrial and educational developments of longer range value that were the original purpose of the loan.[35] George A. Thompson, English traveler and agent of George Canning, arrived in Guatemala in 1825, witnessed many of these events, and is frequently quoted as observing that if the full loan had been made promptly, the Central American Federation might have been saved. Certainly the scarcity of funds had a crippling effect and contributed demonstrably to the lack of respect for the central government. There was no banking system of any kind, and local credit was arranged through merchants.

The economic position of the various states was no better than that of the federation. In the mid-1820's Nicaragua faced frequent civil war; Costa Rica continued to be thinly populated and commercially very backward; the Honduran conditions were similar, aggravated by a dispute with the federal government over the right of the states to obtain foreign loans. Conditions in the two northern states were somewhat better financially, as they had generally been in colonial times. But there was little prosperity anywhere on the isthmus, and businessmen were frightened and made overly cautious because of the danger of forced loans and capital levies.

A critical financial adjustment emerged. Only Guatemala gave sizeable monetary support to the federation, and at times, some of the states contributed nothing. Most of the costs of government, civil and military, came from that province, even when the expenditure was made in one of the other states. Even congressmen had to rely

35. A great deal of information concerning this important loan is contained in the diplomatic correspondence exchanged between the British Foreign office and the British Consul to Central America, Frederick Chatfield, in the 1830's and 1840's. The matter is discussed in some detail in Chapter V.

upon the Guatemalan treasury for their salaries, and there was much irony in the correspondence of deputies who hated Guatemala, complaining that they had to live on funds advanced by that province while awaiting payment from their own legislatures. This inequality could not long continue, and there was developing the menacing prospect that the state of Guatemala might consider itself, and actually become, stronger than the entire nation of Central America.

There was other evidence that the economic picture was very dark. The amount of silver and gold brought to the mint for coinage dropped sharply after independence, and in 1824 and 1825 it accounted for less than one-fourth of the production of the colonial year 1818. Miners were finding it more profitable to smuggle the specie out of the country in exchange for merchandise in the British possessions than to run the risk of selling it to a bankrupt treasury. Thompson reported that foreign trade had badly declined in the first years after independence, especially with the loss of the Spanish market, but by 1825 Central America's exports were almost to the pre-independence level. The chief items were still indigo and cochineal, the two reaching a combined value of probably two million pesos annually in overseas markets. More than half of Central America's imports came from Great Britain— items largely composed of textiles and light hardware.

Thus an incipient commerce of some promise was opposed by an undetermined tax system, a constitutional confusion over states' rights, a bad balance among the states' finances, a nondescript communications system, and a sudden money panic in the British Isles. The obstacles were too great to overcome.

The advantages of ties with the other new republics of Spanish America were apparent to the Central American citizens, and participation in conferences of the former Spanish colonies was a popular goal. It appears that José Cecilio del Valle was one of the first men in all of America to see the advantages of cooperation and even urged a "federation" to unite and enrich the states of America. When Simón Bolívar, as the head of the government of Peru, called for such a congress in December, 1824, the Federation of Central America quickly responded and appointed Dr. Pedro Molina and Antonio Larrazábal as delegates. Only four Latin American states were in attendance: Peru, Colombia, Mexico, and Central America. The last three named prevailed upon Bolívar to invite the United States of North America, but one delegate died en route, and the other arrived too late. England and the Netherlands had observers at the sessions.

The meetings in Panama lasted from June 22 to July 15, 1826. Two treaties were concluded: one to create a league of perpetual union with various measures for mutual help, the other to establish and maintain permanent military and naval forces with each of the nations providing specified quotas. No agreements were ratified sufficiently to go into effect. It was planned that in peace time similar conferences would be held every two years at Tacubaya, Mexico, and the Panama sessions officially moved to that village. The two Central Americans journeyed to Tacubaya alone and, after several months of waiting for the other representatives, decided to return home.

The importance of these meetings to Central America was slight. Participation ended with the final session. It should be noted, however, that the other republics shared the Central American fear of the Holy Alliance, and delegates talked of establishing an army that not only might oppose invasion but could bring to Latin America something of the European unity that they believed sprang from the Congress of Vienna. The still vague boundaries and the nascent nationalism had not yet permitted definitive ideas of what might be the extent of any of the inchoate states. Representatives spoke of confederacies and even federations of some or all of the Spanish peoples in America. The ideas were boundless, the words glib and obscure. Curiously the meetings helped to clarify the picture of Central Americans' behavior. The most backward of Spain's holdings could not be expected to possess more political sophistication, more ability to chart its future course than the larger, stronger, more densely populated captaincies and *gobiernos*.

Domestic political events worsened in 1826 to the point of civil war. Arce's ambition to be the first president had caused him to seek support beyond that of his original following of Liberales and in getting that help antagonized many of the latter group. Friction increased over the lack of a federal district: the capital of the state of Guatemala was briefly in Antigua, but officials determined to move back to Guatemala. In so doing they dispossessed private citizens from their property over the protests of the Arce administration. The power and wealth of the state government under Chief of State Juan Barrundia appeared to threaten Arce, and there were numerous jurisdictional quarrels magnified by the logical rivalry of the two leaders.

Within the congress of the federation there were attacks on Arce for alleged misuse of the funds from the British loan, as well as for his moderate relations with the clergy, anathema to the Liberales. Delegates from El Salvador were of a mixed mind concerning their countryman but did fear that the Guatemalan influence upon him could be nothing but evil. Their chief clergyman, José

Matías Delgado, had a running quarrel with Archbishop Ramón Casáus in Guatemala over the establishment of a bishopric in San Salvador. Delgado had achieved the post through the action of the Salvadorean legislature, an improper and presumptive act in the opinion of the archbishop and the Papacy. At times Arce and Delgado maintained their long friendship by continued cooperation, but even these two fell out ultimately and added to the dangerous confusion of El Salvadorean-Guatemalan affairs.

Relations between Guatemala and the federal government approached complete disintegration in 1826. Arce attempted to build a national army responsible to him, but at the same time Guatemala was protesting that it bore the entire financial burden of the five provinces and ceased its cash contributions. On charges that Arce was making illegal arrests in Guatemala, Chief of State Barrundia imprisoned the head of the federal guard, and was in his turn arrested by President Arce. During Barrundia's temporary absence, the acting *jefe* was Cirilo Flores, who, forced by his legislature to move the state capital to Quezaltenango, was shortly killed by an Indian mob for his liberal anticlericalism.[36]

Arce's opponents viewed the murder and subsequent attacks on the state deputies as a device of the president, especially as he set aside the state government and assumed control of Guatemala as well as the federation. It was now the Salvadoreans' turn to be frightened. Their delegates ceased sitting in the congress when the government was not moved from Guatemala City, and by early 1827 Salvadorean forces were organizing for an attack on Arce. Federal intervention in Honduras provoked mobilization of that province.

36. Mary P. Holleran, *Church and State in Guatemala* (New York, 1949), p. 90.

At the head of the army of the federation Arce repulsed the invasion, but his entry in El Salvador was similarly defeated on at least three occasions. Desultory war continued for several months during which Arce's position gradually weakened as dissatisfaction became more prevalent in the provinces. A stalemate ensued. It was not to be broken until the rise to leadership of the first Central American *caudillo,* Francisco Morazán, who emerged from the Honduran provincial ranks onto the national scene in the late 1820's.

In the first years of its existence the republic of Central America had made little progress. Arce's federal regime merely succeeded in avoiding complete disintegration. It did little for the citizens. The burdens of society were shouldered by the states individually, increasing their separatist feelings. There was almost no federal treasury, and only Guatemala among the states was able to meet its financial obligations. Commerce and industry were stagnate. The steady incomes brought by coffee and bananas were yet unimagined.

To raise revenue for roads, schools, and hospitals a few monopolies were reinstituted on such items as tobacco and *aguardiente.* But returns were small, and in general, customs duties and loans were counted upon to finance the responsibilities of state. There was little domestic capital. Reliance was upon the foreign loan, heavily discounted, frequently defaulted. The result of the cycle was fewer lenders, higher interest rates, more defaults.

A scarcity of funds brought varied and cumulative evils. One army officer complained that his troops sold their weapons for food, and thus his militia could not be counted upon for service.[37] A military career was so un-

37. Rafael Escalante to *junta* of Costa Rica, February 7 and October 7, 1827, Secretaría de Guerra, No. 9668, ANCR.

desirable that desertions had to go unpunished. The heavy incidence of smallpox, typhoid, leprosy, and goiter kept worker productivity low, giving the states less taxable income to use for the eradication of such pestilences. The town of Cartago reported that it had no doctor.

The governments did little for education. A few schools were opened through the initiative of municipalities with public subscription the most common form of support. Too often such weak institutions were forced to close occasionally from lack of funds. The great majority of the citizens were illiterate but enthusiastic for education. Coupled with highway construction, the establishment of an adequate educational system seemed to most Central American observers the chief needs of the land. (A century and a quarter later the same comment can accurately be made.)

The damage done by the civil war of 1826-29 should not be exaggerated. The troops involved were usually few in number, little of the land was ravaged, and, at times, whole provinces were untouched by military events. The simple economies were not badly disrupted, and one must conclude that most of the Central American peasants continued their normal activities in reasonable safety.

Danger from the outside was difficult to assess. Threats of Spanish counterattacks were made so often that they were treated as mere cries of "wolf" designed to strengthen some group or cause. Nevertheless, a small barracks revolt in Costa Rica produced an authentic menace. The leader of the attack, an exiled Colombian named José Zamora, was captured and subsequently testified that he was a lieutenant colonel in the Spanish army. He and his thirty-one followers, including a priest from Heredia, had been especially commissioned by the crown to create trouble and unrest in America.[38] The North American act-ing-consul, William Phillips, felt that reannexation by Spain was a distinct possibility because of the pro-Spanish groups in Guatemala, and he reported to Henry Clay that the province was the "headquarters of Ferdinandism and as much a colony of Spain as Puerto Rico."

But no invasion ever came, even from the twenty-eight French warships that Arce alleged were gathered at Martinque. Except for trivial border skirmishes, Central America was free for a generation from the peril of foreign invasion.

By 1829 the Central American atmosphere was one of distrust, disillusionment, and partisan strife, encumbering a backward, agarian society of modest potential. In retrospect we can see that there was room for a strong man. It was not to be Manuel José Arce, opportunistic politician and unsuccessful general; it could not be José Cecilio del Valle, Central America's brightest light but indecisive and lacking a leader's conviction; it might have been one of the Barrundia brothers, José Francisco or Juan, but they had a way of disqualifying themselves and withdrawing from the biggest jobs. A strong man finally pushed his way into this vacuum, a man who could lead, who could win battles, and who had a vision to unite Central America. This was Francisco Morazán.

38. Zamora was put to death. The unique punishments adminis-tered to the others make interesting commentaries on the times. Some were sent to a federal prison in Libertad, El Salvador, to be con-fined until Spain recognized Central American independence. The rest of the men, plus one common thief, were sent to Guatemala to fill the vacancies in the Costa Rican quota for the federal army. Manuel Aguilar to Ministerio General of El Salvador, February 10, 1826, No. 65, Sección General, ANCR; Costa Rica, Secretaría de Educación Pública, *Documentos Históricos Posteriores a la Independencia* (San José, 1923), I, 278.

Chapter IV

Francisco Morazán

CENTRAL America's first hero was Francisco Morazán. Possessing qualities of leadership in abundance, he exhibited them early in his life. On that question, at least, his biographers can agree.[1] The need for a symbol who would cross the confining boundaries of the five republics, plus his undoubted importance, has made Morazán the chief subject of eulogy and diatribe among the writers and statesmen of his land. When speaking of the nation of Morazán, one means Central America. He was born in Honduras, ruled in Guatemala and El Salvador, fought winning and losing battles in all of the provinces, and died in Costa Rica. No man, then or since, came so close to being a Central American. Reviled and loved by fanatic groups, Morazán's advantage was that he belonged to the same political persuasion as most of the Central American historians. Thus he has been compared variously with Washington, Bolívar, Napoleon, and Garibaldi. He was

1. Eduardo Martínez López, *Biografía del General Francisco Morazán* (Tegucigalpa, 1899); Arturo Mejía Nieto, *Morazán, presidente de la desaparecida república centroamericana* (Buenos Aires, 1947); Rafael Reyes, *Vida de Morazán* (San Salvador, 1925); Robert S. Chamberlain, *Francisco Morazán, Champion of Central American Federation* (Coral Gables, Florida, 1950); varying and briefer views of Morazán can be found in Marure, Bancroft, and Montúfar, as well as reports of several Central American travelers.

painted as an outstanding field general and dedicated statesman. Attempts to describe the history of his time often end, unfortunately, with debate solely over the merits of Morazán. But for good or for evil, Francisco Morazán represents to the five republics today the dream of Central American confederation, and references in the press to any new plan will invariably recall the "ideal of Morazán" even if the writer does not favor it. The era of Morazán's power (roughly the 1830's) was a turbulent one, and it is the irony of his career that it was this personification of Central Americanism who presided over its dissolution.

Morazán was born near Tegucigalpa, Honduras, in the early 1790's and was probably a *mestizo* of Corsican descent. His simple background and education gave him no preparation for important duties, but he was energetic and popular. He first appeared on the political scene in 1824 when he served as Secretary General of Honduras under the Liberal Chief of State, Dionisio Herrera. Having the same political leanings as his *jefe,* Morazán soon became a state senator. But the army attracted him and by 1827 he had a small command of Hondurans against one of the numerous interventions by President Arce's federal forces. Defeated and captured, Morazán soon escaped into Nicaragua where he organized a force and won small but decisive victories over Arce's followers. Moving back to Honduras he was now strong enough to drive out the federal army and assume acting political control of the state. Within a year he had won sufficient small victories to acquire partisans in Guatemala and El Salvador. On April 12, 1829, he compelled the surrender of General Arzú's federal army, and Guatemala City fell to the Honduran. Though there remained many large areas still loyal to the federal forces, this battle ended Arce's regime and gave

Morazán temporary control while a new government was created. Morazán and his faction called themselves Liberals, and as the federal congress and senate reassembled they bowed to Morazán's authority.

This legislature declared null and void all of the acts passed since September of 1826, when in the opinion of the Liberals, the last legal assemblies had adjourned. Morazán then installed José Francisco Barrundia as president of the republic on the basis of being the senior senator. Punitive steps were taken against Arce's party, now generally called Conservatives. Some of their property was confiscated, and any government salaries drawn since 1826 were forfeited. Some officials who were taken prisoner were permitted to buy their way into exile. The more important men, Arce, Vice President Mariano Beltranena, the President of Guatemala, Mariano Aycinena, and the historian Manuel Montúfar, among others, were threatened with death but ultimately were banished, in theory for life.

The church was similarly attacked. Fearing Morazán's avowed liberalism and knowing that the position of the church would be endangered by his success, most of the orders as well as the higher clergy vigorously opposed him. With his victory came their punishment. The first step was to direct Archbishop Ramón Casáus to remove certain unacceptable clergymen and to mint large amounts of the church silver. Then suddenly in July, 1829, Morazán decreed the expulsion of Casáus and almost all of the members of the three chief brotherhoods, Franciscans, Dominicans, and Recollets. The friars were seized by soldiers at night, hurried to ports on the Atlantic, and put on board a ship for Havana. Barrundia and the party upheld this summary action on the grounds of intrigue against the new government. A few of the men died en route to their

new posts, but whether this was because of ill treatment
or merely the unusual conditions faced by men so long
cloistered, it is difficult to say.[2]

Using this alleged conspiracy as an excuse, the government leaders now turned fully upon the church. they confiscated holdings of all of the orders except the Bethlehemites
who had played no part in politics. The recruitment of nuns
was prohibited, and the number of priests was sharply reduced. Steps similar to these were taken by the individual
states so that much tithing was eliminated along with many
religious holidays. In May of 1832 complete religious freedom was declared by congress and the states. It was confirmed by Article 11 of the Federal Constitution of 1835
which declared that the people of the republic could worship God according to their consciences. The anticlerical
activity was greater in Guatemala than in the other states,
for the church had been stronger there, and the new political chief, Mariano Gálvez, was a thoroughgoing Liberal.
He transformed a number of convents into public schools,
hospitals, prisons, and barracks. He suppressed the University of San Carlos because of its influence in religious
training, reduced church holidays in number, and prohibited religious processions in the streets. Then he initiated
steps to permit civil marriages and divorces, but these
policies proved unpopular and did not become standard
practice in Gálvez' time.

These reforms had but slight theological importance.
The Liberals themselves were primarily Catholics and

2. Casáus became archbishop of Havana and remained in that
city until his death in 1845, though frequently invited to return to
Guatemala after the overthrow of Morazán in 1839. On these events
see Mary W. Williams, "Ecclesiastical Policy of Morazán and other
Liberals," *Hispanic American Historical Review*, III (May, 1920),
119-43. Needless to say, exiling the clericals greatly agitated the Morazán controversy. Chamorro calls it Morazán's greatest mistake. *Historia*, p. 271.

not fighting for the right to introduce other denominations. Their purpose was simply to weaken the secular position of the church in Central American affairs. Evidence of this can be seen in the desire of the government (the liberal government) to acquire for itself the *patronato nacional* or national patronage from the pope. This right, which had been held by the rulers of Spain from the time of Columbus, would have given a great deal of authority to the federal government in ecclesiastical matters. The ruling party had little intention of eliminating the church, but knowing how deeply it was ingrained in the people, they simply sought to control it for their own uses. The church had been in charge of education and thus held the ability to attack the Liberals on grounds of atheism. Its holdings were vast, its income great. It was allied with the Conservatives and the Spanish and was a strong force for monarchism. The domination of this powerful enemy meant to Morazán income he badly needed, buildings to be utilized, and the weakening of the Conservative party.

Between 1826 and 1830 Central America had undergone three years of civil war and one year of drastic reform. They exacted a toll. Contemporary reports revealed the chaotic times. Persecutions and confiscations continued under Morazán, though somewhat lessened. Revolution broke out in Honduras against his regime, and the conspirators rejoiced over anticipation of help from Spanish or British intervention. Morazán took personal command in his native state and crushed the uprising. He dispatched a personal representative to Nicaragua who suppressed what was called in Mexican papers "frightful anarchy." The republic of Chile recalled its consuls from Central America because of the scandals and "immorality" in Guatemala. Costa Rica seceded from the federation from

1829 to 1831 on the grounds that the national government had ceased functioning during a quarrel between
Costa Rica and El Salvador.

These disturbed conditions aided Morazán when he
ran for the federal presidency in 1830. He was the strongest military leader in the nation and the logical individual
to be given the task of unification. Barrundia did not seek
the post but campaigned for Morazán. A Salvadorean Liberal, Mariano Prado, was elected vice president. In the
wide scattering of votes opposed to Morazán, José Cecilio
del Valle was a poor second.

As president now in name, Morazán found no need
for new policies. The elections merely had confirmed the
already recognized fact that Morazán was the true power
in Central America, but while his basic ideas remained
unchanged, he now could put more measures into effect.
The decrees and legislation that he introduced were designed to improve the sorry lot of so many of the people.
The undertakings were well meant and to a great extent
reflected reforms being attempted elsewhere in the world
at the same time. There is justification, however, to the
criticism that many of his plans were ill-conceived and
unsuited for his people.

Universal education was to Morazán the panacea for
his nation's numerous ills. Toward this end government
universities were created in San Salvador and León in
1830 and 1831. Lacking funds, equipment, and teachers
for the primary grades, the administration fell under the
spell of the Lancasterian dream of education so popular
in the early nineteenth century in Latin America as well
as in the United States. This scheme, claiming to require
only one professional teacher for a thousand or more
pupils, was, like most short cuts to education, doomed to

failure. The financial savings proved illusory when balanced over the years, and the system was too slow in a frontier or rural society where children were urgently needed at home as workers.

Another innovation of great moment was an attempt to reconstitute the legal framework of the republic. As early as 1824 Valle had led a movement to draw up a code of laws to replace the Spanish system. The next year a commission was created for this purpose and headed by Valle who, according to his own statement, did all of the work. In 1834 the state of Guatemala adopted the Livingston codes, written for, but never accepted by, the state of Louisiana. Its ancestor was Anglo-Saxon common law; its immediate parents were Edward Livingston, distinguished United States Senator from Louisiana, and the eminent British jurist, Jeremy Bentham.[3] It was acceptable to Guatemala's Chief of State Mariano Gálvez, and Morazán urged its adoption there prefatory to its use in the entire Central American republic.[4] But the code proved unsuited for the Central American climate. Trial by jury was distrusted as it is in much of Latin America today. Gálvez argued that there were not enough jurists in the state to man the numerous districts created. To many the principle of habeas corpus proved incomprehensible. A number of new prisons was needed. They were built by forced Indian

3. John Bowring, ed., *The Works of Jeremy Bentham* (Edinburgh, 1843), X, 559, and XI, 23. Bentham's influence upon Central America is as yet but vaguely known. He loathed bicameral legislatures (once telling Andrew Jackson how to eliminate the senate), and may have been responsible for the great power given the lower house in Central America. He strongly urged Valle to support a centralized rather than a federalized Central America. After Bentham's death in 1832, Valle persuaded the congress to declare a three-day period of mourning throughout Central America. One can not help wondering what was the public's reaction.

4. Mario Rodríguez, *The Livingston Codes in the Great Crisis of 1837-1838*, MARI Publication, No. 23 New Orleans, 1955).

labor, and the result was increased antagonisms toward the reforms.

The misapplication of these various basic concepts of education and law was of important significance in the final overthrow of the Liberals. It was notoriously difficult to alter the way of life of the Indian. In the 1830's this obstacle was fortified by interested parties who could profit by dissensions arising from these reforms. Furthermore, strengthening the army, tightening the tax collection methods, and similar business-like changes frightened many folk.

Never was Morazán free to pursue his program without discord. Conservatives found that they could persuade Indians of the menace of the administration. Interstate jealousies were always such that the federal regime could not be sure of the loyalty of any one state. When the right leadership became available, Indians and Conservatives were to unite in force and dominate first Guatemala and then all of the states. But in the meantime, while the Liberals were in the saddle, Conservatives sought allies among the Spanish and English in order to harass Morazán.

In 1831 a well coordinated plan was initiated to annihilate the Liberal party. From his asylum in Mexico former President Arce was to attack the Los Altos area in Guatemala. Honduras was to be weakened by the seizure of the Atlantic ports of Omoa and Trujillo. The governor of the first, Ramón Guzmán, seized the fort and ran up the Spanish flag. Then he dispatched ships to Cuba for aid from the exiled Archbishop Casáus. Another Conservative force, allegedly organized in British Honduras, took Trujillo and marched into the interior. Meanwhile, Arce plotted with the new chief of El Salvador, José María Cornejo, against the federal authorities. In the face of threatened invasion by Morazán, Cornejo ordered him to leave El Salvador, and the state seceded from the federal union. By March, 1832, the Federalists had everywhere won. Arce was defeated and driven back to Mexico, the Honduran revolts were suppressed, and the reinforcements from Cuba were captured. Morazán's army took San Salvador and brought the secession to a close.

The numerous quarrels between states and national government served often to obscure an important factor that must be re-emphasized. That was the old fear of Guatemala. While Morazán was no Guatemalan, and probably treated the states with reasonable equality, the other states could easily identify the federal government with the strongest and richest of the states especially since it was the headquarters of Morazán's regime. States assumed for themselves the customs duties intended for the national government, and increasingly individuals refused to pay. Demands grew for the creation of a federal district outside of Guatemala; in 1834 these were acceded to by moving the administration to Sonsonate and later to San Salvador, both in the especially jealous state of El Salvador.

Coincidental with this shift were proposals to alter the constitution with the smaller states seeking, among other things, equal representation in the congress. About 1830 Costa Rica received its first printing press and the resultant newspapers. At the outset they editorialized for constitutional reforms, and in Costa Rica that meant more states' rights and those more clearly prescribed. They protested that they were fervent Federalists but wanted many changes before they could adhere unquestionably. They seemed to prefer what we would call a loose confederation, for they were smug in their belief that there was no turbulence at home, while its existence in the remainder of

Central America brought burdensome duties and expenses in unfair proportions.

Gradually all of the states appealed for political reform, believing it the solution to the empty treasury that so plagued them all. Gámez wrote that the Centralists said that federal system of government was intrinsically bad; the Federalists sought more power for the general government; radicals demanded any change for its own sake; and the ultramontanists blamed the nation's low status upon the weak position of the church. Then, he concluded, all of the groups could agree in their dislike for the customs duties.[5] Individual towns made suggestions for reform, commissions were organized for similar purposes, and every newspaper editor volunteered his ideas and services to bolster the stagnating republic. A curious theme observable in many presentations was the voicing of the need for unity. Politicians and writers alike deplored the lack of common purposes. What Central America needed, they said, was a public opinion that could agree on mutual desires and goals. Of course, there was no unity. There had been no real enemy at the time of independence, and there had been none of the consolidating forces of revolutionary war. Perhaps that was the gist of the problem. The states were simply too young and immature to have acquired consolidated political views. In the wonderful language of Domingo Sarmiento, "Central America had made a sovereign state of each village." The congress, finding it impossible to satisfy every faction, ignored most of the requested changes and in 1835 drafted a new constitution that generally clung to the philosophy of the document of 1824. Most changes were minor; probably the most significant was the declaration of religious toleration. But

5. Gámez, *Nicaragua*, p. 432.

the states were not satisfied, and only Nicaragua and Costa Rica ratified the document.[6]

The states thus lost a chance to strengthen the central government—if that was what they wanted. It is more likely that they sought the cheapest government, a federation with all of its benefits and few of its responsibilities. The unquestioned military supremacy of Morazán kept them together in the mid-1830's, but this use of force brought increased complaints of intervention.

Late in 1833 a presidential election was held with Valle running against Morazán. The former won, but fell ill before he could take office, and on his death another election was called. This time Morazán won an easy majority and was sworn in for his second term beginning February 14, 1835.

The re-election of Morazán and the expectation that this would bring about more reforms made the Conservatives restive. Morazán's recent encouragement to foreign colonists was used to incite the poorer classes and the Indians by indicating that the nation was being turned over to the foreigners. Since most of the colonists were non-Catholic, the Conservatives could argue that the administration was attempting to destroy the ancient Central American culture.[7]

The best opening for the Conservatives was created in Guatemala, however, over matters that did not necessarily concern the entire republic. Once more the size, relative wealth, and power of that state badly exaggerated its influence on national affairs. Chief of State Gálvez had carried out reforms to a greater degree than had been the

6. A discussion of the proposed changes is to be found in Chamorro, *Historia*, pp. 390-401.
7. The Liberals gave encouragement and better terms to foreign colonization projects than did the Conservatives when in office.

case in the other states. The Livingston codes, for example, were scarcely applied outside Guatemala. Attacks upon the powers of the church, and secularization of many of its functions were more stringently administered there. The loss of the capital to San Salvador was not happily accepted in Guatemala City, and many people blamed the local officials for this change. Petty quarrels added to the discord, and there was a falling out among many of the Liberals including the most important of all, Gálvez and José Francisco Barrundia. By 1837, the minor uprisings, which had never quite ceased since 1826, were becoming more than the federal forces could manage, and it was at this time that the first case of Asiatic cholera appeared in Central America.

This dread disease came to middle America first, like most foreign imports, by way of Belice or British Honduras. Its trail from Europe was easy to follow, and in August and September the officials of Guatemala observed with great fear the progress of the pestilence from the Atlantic coast to the highlands. Governor Gálvez declared a quarantine on imports as well as persons from the British zone, and the Federal Republic respected this order. Nevertheless, the plague moved into the Petén peninsula and then into all of Guatemala. The peak of illnesses and fatalities was reached in April of 1837, but the disease was present in Guatemala for about a year. Gálvez' government seems to have done its best, considering the limited medical knowledge and the ignorance of many of the citizens. The state put out bulletins of advice; block superintendents were appointed to enforce standards of cleanliness; taverns were closed; and travel between towns almost came to a standstill.[8]

8. The British Consul to Central America, Frederick Chatfield, reported that there was "no medical practitioner native or foreign, of

The frightful epidemic engendered the greatest fear in the Indian villages, and it was rumored there that foreigners and the Gálvez government had poisoned the streams in the state for the purpose of killing off the natives and the more easily turning Guatemala over to the enemy. Squier, Crowe, and Bancroft, among others, relate in their accounts that the Catholic clergy were responsible for these charges and therefore for fomenting the civil war that followed. Frederick Chatfield reports that he was captured by Indians near San Salvador when he stopped at a river for a drink while on one of his regular horseback rides. The Indians accused him of poisoning the river and told him that all Englishmen were poisoners.

It would be incorrect to say that this was all part of a plot by the Conservatives. Some of these men were most active in fighting the cholera and aiding the government, and they signed and circulated decrees to the public protesting the absurdity of the rumor. They appealed, in fact, to the masses to follow the orders of the government in sanitation measures. Nevertheless, the government was increasingly harassed in its efforts, as mobs began to put officials and medical personnel to flight while attempting to carry out their duties.

It was not a long step from these mob activities to open revolt. Many people felt that Gálvez was using the reforms of the Liberal party to strengthen himself in office. He now began appointing justices to office throughout the state, no longer permitting the people to elect them. He burned Indian villages and dispersed their families, contrary to law, to put down objectors. His troops were

---

common education in this Republic." He estimated the deaths at about 1500. Chatfield to Palmerston, June 26, 1837, F. O. 15/19, MARI Microfilm, Tulane University.

guilty of excesses and demanded the restorations of their old pre-Independence privileges. Barrundia split with Gálvez and accused him of dictatorship, while the latter retorted that Barrundia created anarchy with his charges.

Neither man had control over a new force which now arose to trouble Central America. This young man was the ablest of the many mob leaders finding glory and loot in the turmoil of Guatemala. He was Rafael Carrera, a semi-literate Indian or *mestizo* of considerable energy and cunning. Rafael had been a drummer boy in the federal army of 1826-29. Like so many of the Indians he hated the liberal reforms, but unlike most of his class, he exhibited enough leadership to organize a band of followers.[9] Supported from the first by some of the local clergy, he demanded the abolition of the Livingston codes, the elimination of the capitation tax on Indians, and the restoration of the archbishop and the religious orders. His type of guerrilla warfare enticed all kinds of partisans including many who were interested only in the prospect of plunder. By 1838 he had risen to the position of military head of the Guatemala Conservatives with troops of Indian soldiers who were fanatically loyal to him.

Carrera's forces and Morazán's federal army fought a number of small skirmishes which the latter usually won. He might have achieved a conclusive victory in 1838 or 1839 if he had not been faced with uprisings in the other states. But Morazán was never able to concentrate all of his strength against Carrera, and with many Guatemalans actively aiding, including several hundred rebel troops from Antigua, the Indian took Guatemala City with little opposition on the first or second of February, 1838. Almost immediately the Gálvez government dissolved. To

9. It was a current rumor that Gálvez' men burned Carrera's village, abused his wife, and destroyed his house.

one eye-witness the occupation of the square by Carrera and his 4,000 was like the return of Alaric. Drunk, half naked, elated, they cheered the restoration of the Catholic religion and death to the foreigners. Many carried bags the better to haul away more loot. Carrera himself was soon attired in the uniform of a Spanish general, stolen from the home of Gálvez. At his side rode Barrundia and many other state leaders, plus three priests who seemed to have the greatest influence over him.

Liberal and Conservative alike now felt the urgency of clearing the city of the "horde," and they cooperated to buy Carrera off when he threatened to burn the town and kill all of the foreigners. The state of Guatemala then gave him the title of *comandante general*, $1000 for himself, some 1,000 muskets, small guns, and ammunition, and $10,000 to be divided among his troops.

For the moment the state was free from the Carrera menace, but it had strengthened him in the eyes of the populace and in his absolute military power. He would be back.

During the brief occupation of the capital, localism was able to assert itself in three western districts of Guatemala. With some encouragement from Chiapas of Mexico, Quezaltenango, Totonicapán, and Sololá created a new government called Los Altos and asked to become the sixth state of the Federal Republic of Central America. To this Morazán's government agreed but stipulated that the federal power would be used to protect any town that did not wish to leave the Guatemalan jurisdiction.[10] While the state did not exist long as a political entity, its very

10. Bancroft said that the new state government was in the hands of Liberals exiled from Guatemala City. Bancroft, *History*, p. 158. Chatfield commented that the Indians would not permit "whites" in the government. Chatfield to Palmerston, February 22, 1838, F. O. 15/20, MARI Microfilm, Tulane University.

creation was symptomatic of Central America's chronic regionalism as well as the crippling disturbances of the era. How real were these political differences? Was there a point to the constant bickering, the partisan strife that split off into sub-parties, the military skirmishes that substituted for caucuses? Frederick Chatfield, a keen observer of these years, but not known for his partiality toward Central America, wrote that Central American revolutions were hard to trace: "Not caused by a desire to support any defined system of government, to promote principles or enforce the observance of recognized laws, but simply serving as a pretext for the gratification of passions and interests of individual members of the community." The troubles sprang not from the people, who were docile, but from the private objectives of public functionaries.[11]

In this chaos the Central American Federation disappeared. With considerable reluctance the southern states viewed the Guatemalan affairs as final proof of the necessity for a new government. There was no blind rush to get out of the federation and go alone. On the contrary it was the obvious desire of most of the towns to reorganize Central America on a lasting basis. The period of fear of neighbors and foreigners had not yet passed, and even Costa Rica clung to a notion of a Central American republic.

In April, 1838, the Costa Rican Assembly decreed that after thirteen years it was apparent that the Central Americans had never "consolidated" themselves. All of the states suffered from repeated convulsions that could be eliminated only by the prompt action of the federal government. Since 1832 there was a general clamor for reform in the basic charter, and nothing had been done.

11. Chatfield to Palmerston, February 5, 1838, F. O. 15/20, MARI Microfilm, Tulane University.

Therefore, the Costa Ricans made a last appeal for a change, calling upon the federal congress to convoke a constitutional convention and asking the states for their cooperation.

Nicaragua took a long step further. Also in April, the Nicaraguans called an assembly which reported that the evils found in Nicaragua, as elsewhere in the republic, were directly caused by the constitution. Because of the long delay in reforming this document, the state of Nicaragua declared itself "free, sovereign and independent" subject only to restrictions that might be agreed upon in a new federal pact.

In the actions just mentioned both Costa Rica and Nicaragua asserted that there was no federal government; the congress, the senate, the court had all ceased to operate. All that was left, they declared, was a president and some of his obedient troops fighting a hopeless war. This was an accurate description. For weeks at a time Morazán was absent in the field and completely out of touch with the secretary of the government who remained in the federal district carved out of San Salvador. Official newspapers ceased printing, the mails were entirely disrupted, and Indian runners carrying messages to Morazán failed to return. Since the creation of a new republic could be accomplished only by the action of the states, the congress on May 31 took cognizance of the conditions and decreed that the states were free to establish any form of government that they wished, provided only that they preserve a "republican, popular, represenative and divided powers form of government." Before adjourning, the legislators made plans for an electoral law to be used in choosing delegates the next year to reform the constitution.

The year of 1838 may be marked as the period of

effective dissolution of the Central American Federation. The symbol, Morazán, was waging frustrating war with Carrera, defeating him in open combat but never destroying him. In the most important city of Guatemala, fear of the Indian mobs disappeared after the bribing of Carrera, and Morazán found that the state officials paid him little heed as long as they did not need his army. The chief of state in Costa Rica was overthrown, and the *jefe,* Braulio Carrillo, informed the Nicaraguan government of his intention to secede completely from the republic. Relations of these two states with the federal regime had practically ceased to exist, and Morazán ignored them even when they seized the federal customs for their own use.

Honduras, torn by meaningless city warfare, announced its separation from the federation and early in 1839 made a treaty of alliance with Nicaragua for their mutual protection. They had little to fear from the outside, but Carrera viewed the alliance as aimed against Morazán and proclaimed his intention of protecting all individual states from the menace of the latter. Only the state of El Salvador persisted in its allegiance to the federation, but even here the towns were not unanimous in their loyalty, and Morazán faced occasional revolts.

His second term of office expired on February 1, 1839, and there was no movement to bother with a new election. He assumed the title of *jefe* of El Salvador, and to a great extent his troops and finances henceforth were Salvadorean even though he might refer to them as federal. Throughout much of 1839 and early 1840 Morazán fought off invasion from the Honduran-Nicaraguan league, encouraged by Carrera. Successful at home, the federal troops then invaded both of the states, won quick victories, and turned on their chief tormentor in Guatemala.

The Indian chieftain had become increasingly intimate with the old ruling groups of Guatemala, Conservatives and Liberals alike. In April of 1839 he once more occupied Guatemala City and installed his own man as *jefe* of the state. A few days later he published a decree separating Guatemala from the federation, an official act to match the reality of many months' standing. Even Morazán now had to face the fact that the union was no more. Foreign nations found it expedient to deal with the individual states (Morazán yet protested this), and the experience of the United States special agent is especially revealing of the chaotic conditions.

John Lloyd Stephens, writer and amateur diplomat with a consuming interest in archaeology, was sent by President Martin Van Buren to negotiate a renewal of the treaty between the United States and Central America. This arrangement had been in force since 1826 and seemed favorable to both parties. Special Agent Stephens was supposed to locate the Central American government and if satisfied that it could continue to carry out its obligations, he should endeavor to get the document extended. This was never accomplished. Although much more interested in seeking ruins than in pursuing diplomacy, Stephens did an honest job of trying to make contact with a Central American government.[12]

Stephens wrote of the restoration of the church position under Carrera, but added that the only bond between that *jefe* and the church was their hatred of Morazán. He met both of the great leaders and was impressed by the sincerity of each. Morazán warned him that the day would come when Central America would need protection from Carrera, but Stephens acknowledged that a true estimate

12. John L. Stephens, *Incidents of Travel in Central America, Chiapas and Yucatán*, 2 volumes (New York, 1841).

of conditions was impossible. About only one thing was he sure; he concluded, along with Chatfield, that there was no Central American government. There remained only a handful of officials, and they were soon to go. Morazán made a last desperate attempt to save his position. He struck at the center of his enemies and on March 18, 1840, captured Guatemala City once more with his Salvadorean troops. About four o'clock of the next morning, Carrera, with the city now supporting *him,* was able to retake the central plaza. Morazán's resistance was at an end when he saw that none of his old Guatemalan followers would come to his assistance. The populace, in fact, largely stayed away from the battle, but those who watched jeered every effort of Morazán. He and his survivors fled from the bloody engagement, going by way of Antigua to El Salvador. Even here it was apparent that he could count on small support.

Briefly the general contemplated another campaign against Carrera then concluded accurately that there were too many groups against him now. Passing quickly through El Salvador, he bought a schooner at the little town of Acajutla. He sailed from there on the fifth of April, stopping long enough at La Libertad to take on board additional chief lieutenants. Then into exile they went, some forty or fifty men including the vice president of the federation and the chief of state of El Salvador. Landing at Puntarenas in Costa Rica, Morazán found asylum for a few of his assistants but not for himself. For a few months he lived in Panama, until in 1841 he was invited to Peru to serve as general in the army of that land in its war against Chile and Colombia. Said Stephens, "I verily believe they have driven from their shores the best man in Central America."

With the departure of Morazán the story of the first federation comes to a close. For a few months the name was still used on occasional documents printed in San Salvador. The Morazanistas and Federalistas were defeated, quiet and everywhere out of power. Carrera was able to establish his puppets in El Salvador and he reabsorbed Los Altos into the state of Guatemala. A new era, one of reaction, was beginning, yet in times of strictest dictatorships or complete decentralization of the states, the dream of federation never died. The amazing tenacity of the Morazán ideal will be shown in the following chapters.

There is a brief anticlimax in the life of Morazán that must be mentioned. In April of 1842 he invaded Costa Rica from South America with plans to use that little republic as a springboard for the re-creation of the confederation. President Braulio Carrillo was unfriendly to Morazán and at the moment was rapidly losing public support in spite of the material gain his regime had brought. As a consequence Morazán was able to arrange a traitorous agreement with Colonel Vicente Villaseñor and much of the army. Carrillo was driven into exile, and Morazán had himself elected president of Costa Rica.[13] But Morazán lost friends when the Costa Ricans discovered that his real intention was to launch an attack on all of Central America and that his immediate program was to invade Nicaragua with Costa Rican men and money. The Conservatives came out of hiding, and a counterrevolt was begun. There was but one battle—in San José—and Morazán was defeated, captured, and put to death.

This action of the Costa Ricans has been roundly con-

13. The activities of Morazán in Peru and Costa Rica are samples of a major reason for Latin American turmoil. There is humanity in accepting fugitives in exile, but the privilege is regularly abused by politicians meddling in the affairs of the host nation.

demned by many writers who use this as evidence that Costa Rica was the chief enemy of the federation. This is not true. While it was probably a tactical error and a great wrong to shoot Morazán, his death came from his interfering in Costa Rican affairs. Costa Rica's role in the federation was one of well-considered inactivity, not murder. For a man whose whole career had been one of warfare, this end must be considered logical and perhaps, in the long run, useful, for it added martyrdom to an idealistic cause.

It is not the purpose here to evaluate Morazán. But to understand the remaining attempts at uniting the five republics, one must take a last look at the Federal Republic in an effort to find the reasons for Central America's breaking apart.

A most important factor in the dismemberment was the lack of training in public affairs, or it might be called a lack of effective leadership. This weakness existed in all of the early Latin American republics, but Central America in colonial times was poor and underpopulated relative to other colonies and attracted few administrators of worth. It furthermore lacked the stabilizing effect of a large business class. After independence officials could have been found who had served under the Spanish and who, continuing in office, might have made the transition to republicanism less troubled. But the public mistrusted these men; the "oligarchy," as it was called, seemed the enemy of the new regime and found itself removed from the pettiest of offices. The federal and state governments in the first years regularly were in the hands of the inexperienced and the theorist. Too wide a gap existed between the latter and the ignorant many. The reforms inaugurated were those sponsored by Central America's few intellectuals and were concepts of society and government as advanced as any to be found in Europe or the United States. They could not find acceptance in a land where traditional leaders, the clergy, and general illiteracy were so tightly combined.

The religious question in itself was almost sufficient to destroy the federation. Enmity toward Morazán unquestionably increased with the introduction of his well-meant reforms of the church, but he was ill-advised to rush them, while the manner of deporting the clericals could not but harm his cause.[14] The church and state relation in Latin America has nowhere been an uncomplicated one and often it has produced most violent consequences. The fortunate nations have settled the problem by gradual means over a century of time (and some have taken that long without settling it). Morazán was trying to achieve a solution during one term of office.

One must not ignore the existence of another religious controversy that began before Morazán entered the national scene. A rivalry was present within the framework of the church itself. Before independence the province of El Salvador, and in particular its leading priest, Delgado, sought a bishopric for that area. It is not just coincidence that he and his province were among the strongest opponents of Guatemala when the confederation was formed. To a lesser degree the same situation obtained in Costa Rica which felt that it should have a bishop residing permanently in that province to avoid entanglements with Nicaragua. Reform and rivalry in the church were thus the twin agents that underwrote Morazán's fall.

The Guatemalan statesman-historian Lorenzo Montúfar blamed the "impossible" constitution of 1824 for the

14. Guatemalan Indians were told that the severe earthquakes of 1830 were caused by divine displeasure over the expulsion of the clergy. Washington *Daily National Intelligencer*, July 23, 1830.

breakup of Central America. He said that the document was so bad that it would have brought about the disorganization of Switzerland or the United States. As we have seen, it is easy to find fault with many of the provisions of this document: it was poorly balanced, it failed to provide authority to important branches of the government, it was unable to solve the perplexing problem of equitable representation that Guatemala's population posed. Needless to say, however, few constitutions are perfect, and for practical political reasons a better enactment might have been impossible.

Would a centralized type of government have been more effective? While in exile Morazán reached that conclusion, the same idea proposed by his enemies a few years before. Presumably the central form of government would have rendered the ignorance of the electorate less significant. It is also likely that fewer officials would have been needed, thereby reducing some of the effects of political inexperience in the land. Successful federalism is rare in Latin America, and it has never proved itself in Central America in the few times that it has been attempted. Certainly it was not supported by tradition in 1824. Its basis at that time was little else but convenience to the state *juntas*. Colonial government was town government. The extent of municipal authority over rural areas, though never defined by law, was often vast in distance and great in Crown acceptance. The Central America of 1824 was not a nation but a league of towns, suspicious of each other and linked only by common concern for protection. A substantial majority of the delegates to the constituent assembly favored a centralized government, many even preferred a monarchy. Pressure from the provincial towns dictated otherwise when the centralists realized the strength of the centrifugal pull of the towns. And so the framers compromised.

Other theories abound. Stephens wrote that he felt the failure came from Morazán's treatment of the church and the financial chaos of his administration. Chatfield questioned the ability of the "Spanish-Indian races" to govern themselves. Salvador Mendieta, a famed Central American writer, primarily blamed a few powerful families in Guatemala, and Chester Lloyd Jones in *Guatemala: Past and Present* concluded, "The plain fact is that no government of any popular basis could have succeeded under the existing conditions."[15] Many Central Americans blamed foreign intervention, specifically British, and since this charge is an important one and so often repeated, a separate chapter will be devoted to its consideration.

Did the Central American Federation achieve anything? In 1838 one of the leaders in congress spoke upon this matter. He said that some ports had been opened and others improved. The government had feebly tried to broaden industry and to expand commerce, but he had to conclude that the existence of the nation was a constant miracle. There were not six schools in all of the republic; there was no system of governmental administration; Central America had no army and no merchant fleet; the justices were untrained and unpaid. Lack of roads, bridges, and internal security caused a decline in local commerce and agriculture. The independence of the republic was recognized by only two significant nations, and consequently commercial treaties were almost nonexistent.

Bloodshed and political instability were demonstrated

15. Chester Lloyd Jones, *Guatemala: Past and Present* (Minneapolis, 1940). p. 41, note.

in the statistics compiled by another Central American historian:[16]

1824-1842

	Number of Battles	Number Killed	Number of Men Wielding Executive Power
Guatemala	51	2291	18
El Salvador	40	2546	23
Honduras	27	682	20
Nicaragua	17	1203	18
Costa Rica	5	144	11
Los Altos (In existence less than two years)	3	222	7

Since the fatalities ranged roughly from thirty to seventy per battle, it is apparent that many encounters were mere skirmishes. Nevertheless their frequency must have brought constant turmoil to the citizens of these states, and it is reflected in an office expectancy rate of less than one year for chief executives. (The state constitutions usually provided four-year terms.) An appalling picture of civil strife is presented by the unadorned figures, and Marure admitted that he erred on the conservative side when he was in doubt concerning their accuracy.

Most of the party's achievements were wiped out before Morazán left office. A few lasted until the reaction which followed under Carrera. The federative idea acquired a poor reputation at home and abroad. The heritage of the generation to come was militarism and little respect for order. National weakness was evident and soon was to tempt the freebooters of other lands. Democratic processes, so optimistically launched, had little chance before

16. Alejandro Marure, *Efemérides de los hechos notables acaecidos en la república de Centro América* (Guatemala, 1895), pp. 141 and 154.

they failed. Majority rule was replaced by force. The practice emerged for defeated politicians to go into exile in one of the neighboring states, there to plan a new coup and turn national disorder into international confusion.

Perhaps something had been learned. Though inexperienced and ill-educated, the people now knew what a ballot was. They knew that they had the right to choose their own officials, even if might often prevented the exercise of that right. No longer were affairs dictated from the other side of the Atlantic. Terrible mistakes had been made, but sometimes the wishes of the majority prevailed, and sometimes the majority was right. It was an intoxicating experience. From 1842 the Central Americans carried a dream to the many conference tables that were arranged. In the next century what might not be accomplished?

Chapter V

Great Britain and the
Federation

THE destruction of the Central American Federation
was a tragedy. This is piously believed by most Central Americans, and the expression appears so often in print as to become hackneyed. Implicit in the tragedy is the effect of fragmentation into five tiny republics. Were the five merged into one, is the belief, the international reputation would be far greater, the nation stronger, and the liklihood of foreign aggression, intervention, or meddling eliminated. While other nations—the United States, France, Belgium, the Netherlands, and even Russia, had some interest in Central America, the only serious threat was Great Britain. The period of its supremacy in Central America was roughly the first half of the nineteenth century. The British tenure thus bracketed the period of the federation and provided an ideal scapegoat—the foreigner —for the failure of that government.

Such has been the verdict of Central American historians, and it served the purpose of our North American diplomats, expansionists, and Anglophobes to perpetuate the decision. To ascertain the validity of the charge is the purpose of this chapter.[1]

1. It is not my intention to describe even briefly most of the

British interest in Central America was concentrated in three distinct areas, in order of importance: Belice on the Caribbean coast and bordering on the Guatemalan district of Petén; Mosquitia, facing the Caribbean with Nicaragua and Honduras to its back and stretching from the Río San Juan on the south to fifteen or sixteen degrees north; and the Bay Islands, chiefly Ruatán, commanding the channels linking the two other regions and at the same time dominating the water approach to Guatemala. Retention of all three as colonies admittedly could threaten Central American sovereignty if that were British policy.

The first promoters of English activity in Belice were buccaneers and privateers who sailed the Caribbean in the seventeenth century seeking Spanish loot. When Jamaica fell into British hands in 1655, the range and activities of these men expanded to the mainland. As mineral prizes became scarcer, they learned the value of the logwood that the Spanish shipped home, and by the 1660's English logwood cutters were settling along the Belice River. It was not a region that appealed to colonists, but the profits were good, and wood abounded, so expansion gradually occurred. Spain, claiming all of Central America by right of conquest, learned but slowly of the cutters' establishments and acted even more slowly to curb them. In the 1730's they attacked and temporarily drove out the British, but the latter soon returned. Despite irregular Spanish opposition, cutting continued and excellent markets were found for the superb mahogany removed. The status of interloper was never accepted by the English

---

British activities in Central America. My sole concern is with those which had any effect on the Federal Republic. The diplomatic aspect is traced in Mary W. Williams, *Anglo-American Isthmian Diplomacy* (Washington, 1916). Miss Williams, using no Central American sources, found the British guilty of deliberately destroying the federation.

Crown, and in 1763, the Seven Years' War brought to its citizens the right to continue the trade by means of a stipulation in the Treaty of Paris. The only concession to Spain was the elimination of British forts—presumably in the entire Spanish Caribbean.

Spain, on the other hand, never recognized the rights of the cutters and continued intermittent efforts to drive them out. An attack on them in 1779 succeeded, and the captives were taken to Havana, but the British forced their releases within a year by threatening Honduras with invasion.

The status of the woodcutting settlements was raised again at the close of the war for independence in the United States, and the Treaty of Versailles of 1783 set the first boundaries for Belice. Between the Belice and Hondo rivers the British could cut and harvest and even put up buildings, but beyond those rivers trespassing was expressly forbidden. The measure failed to restrain the adventurous merchants, and three years later it was determined to extend the limits to include more nearly those forests being worked. The new southern and southwestern boundary was the Río Sibún, giving the British a somewhat larger working space as well as a precedent for future expansion. Spain, nevertheless, claimed absolute sovereignty over all of Belice.

War between the two powers gave Spain one last chance to rid herself of the nuisance in 1798. The attack was badly managed and no Spaniards were able to land. Accepting the new conditions the English merchants spread out rapidly, and by the time Central America acquired its freedom the Belice establishment was enormously enlarged. The new limit on the south was the Sarstún River, dangerously close to the highway to Guatemala City.

The early encroachments of Great Britain on the Mosquito coast parallel those of Belice just described. It was a popular hiding and raiding location for buccaneers and from the mid-seventeenth century relied upon Jamaica for trade as the tiny English villages grew to aid commerce. The chief difference between it and Belice lay in the natives of Mosquitia. The aborigines, the Mosquito Indians, were never conquered by the Spanish, and their tribe, mixed with whites and escaped Negro slaves from the islands, maintained an armed truce with the Central Americans. In the interests of trade the English Crown made solemn treaties with the Mosquitos and recognized their chief as a king. Meanwhile, the British extended some administration from Jamaica and built small towns at Bluefields and Gracias á Dios.

The Mosquitos were unpredictable allies. Clinging to the coastline normally, they occasionally dropped down on Central American villages, stealing slaves, ruining crops, or pillaging. Again, they would engage as middlemen between the two European peoples to carry on a commerce that was officially proscribed by both of the powers. During the many wars of the eighteenth century England increased its grip by adding a fort at Black River, rewarding Mosquito kings, and using the Indians to stir trouble among Spanish colonials. Administration was conducted by a resident superintendent. As in Belice the treaty of 1763 forced the vacating of the fort, but the settlers stayed on. Then the treaty of 1786 provided that all of the English must leave Mosquitia. In general these terms were obeyed although a few settlers remained behind. Officially the protectorate was at an end. The Mosquitos, however, had no love for the Spanish and in 1796 destroyed the only remaining Spanish village in their land. Furthermore, the link with England was kept strong by the Belice merchants who took over the task of giving presents and holding ceremonials for Mosquito chieftains.

The last area of interest to the British in Central America, and never of great importance to them, was in the Bay Islands. These, also, were first utilized by privateers and only occasionally had settlers. There seem to have been long periods when they were deserted completely. In the middle eighteenth century both Great Britain and Spain attempted and failed to create permanent colonies. Briefly the British used one of them as a penal colony, but by 1797 the few residents remaining were under Spanish jurisdiction and remained so until the Central American nation was created.

The British, then, had come into the Caribbean late and had been forced to take the leavings. Spanish claims to two of these regions probably were better in the eyes of international law than those of Great Britain, but the latter's long occupancy of Belice strengthened her title to it substantially.[2] By the time that the Central Americans received their independence in 1821 the British threat was reduced to the single settlement of Belice, small but well integrated, with a history of expansion tendencies.

As the Latin American wars for independence drew to a close in the 1820's, Great Britain above all nations was in a position to spread its influence over the new republics. Her merchants had smuggled goods through Spain's mercantilist curtain to eager Spanish colonials. British ideas of constitutional government were studied and copied by Spanish American lawmakers. Individual Englishmen participated in the rebellions on the side

2. I have arbitrarily set the endless conflict between Guatemala and Britain over Belice beyond the scope of this work. In 1960 the government of Guatemala was still threatening invasion, while the press poured out its volumes of "proof" that Belice was Guatemalan. It is probably a matter of little more than prestige to either nation.

of the Americans. Above all, Great Britain was going to be Latin America's new, great market. For one hundred years Britain had fought—and failed—to force its way into Spain's lucrative trade with the Indies. Now suddenly the doors were opened. Both parties, English and American alike, would benefit. Good, cheap manufactured articles would be exchanged for unlimited quantities of silver, cotton, sugar, indigo. The future was full of promise.

Not so apparent to the Creoles was the huge advantage accruing to the English people in this trade. Virtually all of the commerce would be carried in English bottoms, insured by English bonders, and financed by English capital. A potent monopoly might be created. The Latin Americans could hope that the United States or some other nation might create a healthy competition, but in general, the British dominated the Latin American commercial scene throughout the nineteenth century.

Among the most willing partners to the new exploitation were the republics making up the Federal Republic of Central America. It needed capital, and it needed trade with an industrial nation that could use its agricultural exports. Great Britain did more than fulfill these requirements, for the strategic location of the Belice settlement[3] had forced habits of trade upon the Central Americans that could not be avoided. The only adequate deep-water port facilities of Central America's Caribbean coast were at Belice in the hands of the British. European goods were thus shipped to that point and transferred to shallower craft for Central American ports.[4]

3. It did not become a colony until 1862.
4. An inconsequential number of ships touched at Pacific ports. Guatemala's search for a port is analyzed by William J. Griffith in "El Puerto de Santo Tomás," *Anales de la Sociedad de Geografía e Historia de Guatemala* (forthcoming issue.)

Other English firms sent agents to Central America who brought their goods to Guatemala City and opened branches of their businesses. For greater protection and easier operations several of the men acquired Central American partners or became citizens of Guatemala. In the first years of the Federal Republic they appear to have been the most substantial businessmen in Central America. In this frontier-like environment they often served as bankers and agents for British investment houses. The citizens of no other power played more than the smallest role in these operations.

Given such economic order, it was only logical that the Central American officials turned to the British when they sought financial aid. Between independence in 1821 and the inauguration of Arce as first president, fewer than four years passed. In that time monetary chaos had become rampant. Indian tribute was eliminated, and the Constituent Assembly did away with the old state monopolies on such items as playing cards. Although well-meant, these reforms nevertheless drastically cut state income. Other sources produced less wealth as the disorders of the early years increased. Perhaps the heaviest blow fell when the Mexican government appropriated from the Central American treasury some half a million pesos for its army in Central America. In the name of economic freedom, independence was almost lost. The Constituent Assembly reluctantly decided in 1824 that to balance the budget and tighten receipts a substantial foreign loan would be essential. The administration had many offers—all initially from English firms.

Only mild protests were made by Central Americans. Guatemalan papers reassured the public that all nations had to borrow. The federation needed the funds to suppress tobacco smuggling and to make effective the customs collections. Only then, it was felt, could the nation get on a paying basis. The government was keenly aware of similar development among other young sister republics and hoped to get the same "favorable terms." Officials reported to the press that the government of Chile had just borrowed from the English house of Huller, and Colombia from Charles Herring. Neighboring Mexico "obtained"[5] two loans, each totaling £3,200,000. One at 5 per cent was from B. A. Goldschmidt and Co. The other, at 6 per cent, was from Barclay, Herring, and Richardson. This last house had an agent, John Bailey, residing in Guatemala, and the federation commenced negotiations with him. Bailey represented Barclay's[6] and dealt with the Guatemalan mercantile house of Aycinena as the agent for Central America. The terms agreed upon provided that the British firm would sell bonds on the London exchange and lend to the federation an actual $5,000,-000 but with a nominal value of $7,142,047. The loan was to be repaid in twenty years at 6 per cent interest. Over $100,000 of this was advanced to Central America's government while Barclay's were attempting to raise the money by public sale.

Meanwhile, the federation sought the diplomatic recognition of the major powers, principally Britain's. To this end Marcial Zebadúa was appointed as Central American Envoy Extraordinary and Minister Plenipotentiary to

5. How much of this loan reached the Mexican treasury is unknown. One can judge that, on the basis of the procedures in Central America, the sum was very small relatively. Pesos and dollars had the same value at this time; the pound ranged from about $4.40 to $5.00.

6. Not to be confused with Barclay, Bevan and Co., the present-day Barclay's Bank. I am indebted to the Intelligence Department of Barclay's Bank for this and other information incidental to the demise of the original investment firm. There apparently is not even any family relationship between the two concerns.

Great Britain, arriving in London in April, 1826, and presenting his credentials to Foreign Minister George Canning about a month later. Zebadúa's primary mission was to secure recognition and a commercial treaty (matters, incidentally, which were to drag on for years), but he was also under instructions to consult with Barclay's for the purpose of hastening the balance of the loan.

Negotiations shifted now to London with Zebadúa patiently pursuing various members of the lending agency while the months passed by. Canning was in no hurry. The sudden rise of nearly a score of new republics in the Western Hemisphere was a matter to be considered with great care, and premature recognition and trade agreements might prove harmful to a foreign policy facing the Holy Alliance. Besides, Britain had all of the benefits without the responsibilities. She conducted most of the non-Latin American trade of Central America; she held options on contracts for a canal through the isthmus; and the various loan prospects meant excellent profits for the bond-buying public. Only the United States might break into the neat picture, and it was moving very slowly in Central America.[7]

The burden of goading the Foreign Office into action fell heavily on Zebadúa, and his position became increasingly uncomfortable. He lacked funds for even his own subsistence and so was authorized to obtain advances from Barclay's for living expenses. As the months wore on it must have become apparent to him that the British investors were sobering up from the happy days just passed, for Barclay's warned him that the funds for his legation were exhausted. Adding to this cost was the money uti-

7. The curious hopelessness of the early attempts to keep agents in Central America is entertainingly told by Joseph B. Lockey in "Diplomatic Futility," *Hispanic American Historical Review*, X (August, 1930), 265-94.

lized in Guatemala by Bailey, commissions, dividends, and the upkeep of a central legation in Panama which nearly dissipated the first issue of bonds.

This slowness was only the beginning of Central America's financial troubles. Canning dragged out the discussions regarding a trade treaty when he realized that Britain was in an ideal position to get a very favorable settlement of the Belice boundary by mild blackmail. Central America's need for commerce brought much more cooperation than ever Spain would have extended to Britain. Trade between Central America and Great Britain continued for years without an agreement or diplomatic recognition, but such circumstances were unsettling to Central American business as well as to the administration. The young nation was left in a probationary state that could not but contribute to its instability and its lack of acceptance in the diplomatic world.[8]

A double tragedy then struck Central America in 1826; in that year the bitter civil war began which is described in Chapter III, exhausting the treasury and exaggerating the conditions that made investors wary. Suddenly, on September 14, Barclay, Herring, and Richardson failed. Under the loose banking laws of the times, the firm closed its doors with no advance notice to the public. To Zebadúa they sent a brief note explaining only that since the company was dissolved as of that day, they assumed that Zebadúa would want to name a new agency to which Barclay's could turn over the loan negotiations and some unsold bonds. Zebadúa did, and within a month

8. Britain's recognition was delayed until 1849 and then was given to one republic at a time. Most of the information concerning the Zebadúa mission is in the "Correspondence of the Minister of Central America in London," B10/3/1, 170, Archivo Nacional of Guatemala. The Chatfield-Palmerston correspondence confirms the amount of money involved in the loans.

reached tentative accord with Reid, Irving and Co. and asked his government in Guatemala City to endorse his choice. Subsequently the policy was approved, but in the meantime, he was able to complete details of the new contract.

The bankruptcy of Barclay, Herring and Richardson unfortunately did not bring an end to Central American obligations to that corporation. It remained an issue that was never solved in the lifetime of the Central American Federation. While only a fraction of the $5,000,000 stipulated was ever lent, the Central Americans were nevertheless saddled with substantial payments. Including money advanced to Zebadúa as well as the mission in Panama, the total sum paid by Barclay's was $350,000 and deducted from this were the commissions collected by Bailey and Aycinena, amounting to $21,684. Because of the ruinous discount, Central America owed Barclay's $816,500 plus interest at 6 per cent. To guaranty the debt, Arce's government had pledged all of the revenue from the customs. It is possible that the receipt of the entire loan might have saved the federation as has been alleged, but the discussion is bootless. European investors had been burned by 1826, and the anarchy breaking out in Central America was precisely what was making further investments more difficult. The war reduced Central American commerce upon which the loan was predicated. Interest payments became increasingly difficult to meet.

Given these conditions it is surprising that Zebadúa was able to learn of another investment agency as quickly as he did. But Reid, Irving and Co. behaved cautiously. They declined to give assurance as to when the loan would be accomplished because of "public opinion at the time of the negotiations" and were more than a little vague as to whether they might be able to raise the $5,000,000 desired. They, too, insisted upon some item of the national income as a collateral in order to build public confidence in Central American credit. On November 24, 1826, Zebadúa and Reid, Irving and Co. settled upon the terms of the loan. In general they were the same as the Barclay loan but, in addition, interest still due to the latter would be paid by an advance from Reid, Irving. They were willing to help support Zebadúa's existence while he was without pay—for the moment. Meanwhile, Reid, Irving seem to have sent an investigator to Guatemala. This agent, whose name, curiously, was Charles Herring, Jr. reported on the dismal state of Central American finance. The nation was resorting to forced loans to fight San Salvador. Government officials with whom he dealt freely acknowledged the Central American bills but saw no possible way to pay them. In 1828 the federation's credit came to an end. Zebadúa could get no more advances on his salary and began making personal loans so that his nation might maintain a representative in London. The account grew so desperate that when the legation secretary became ill, Zebadúa lacked the money to send him back to Guatemala as the British doctor urged. Coupled with his complete inability to make progress on the question of recognition, Zebadúa considered his mission fruitless and asked that he be recalled.

At this depressing moment in Central America's life, Morazán achieved his significant military victories, and the federation was temporarily saved. Instantly with the news, a reaction took place in the London money markets. A committee was created by holders of the old Barclay, Herring bonds, and they petitioned the Central American government to resume paying interest now that the wars appeared to be over. For the first three years the service had been kept up, but Central America had defaulted now on three successive semi-annual payments. Thus began a controversy that was never settled to anyone's satisfaction and that was of overwhelming importance in the relations of Central America with Great Britain.

Instead of a $5,000,000 loan that might have given the nation significant stability, the Central American government received a scant $300,000, failed soon even to pay the interest on that sum, and found its chief source of income mortgaged for the payment. The federation and the states individually were to find that demands of British bondholders came first, and for twenty years the threat of intervention was never far away. Even when British conduct was perfectly honorable, and it often was, this danger always existed in the minds of the people, and there began to emerge pro- and anti-British factions who thought that they could put the problem to personal use.

While British-Central American relations were strained by the difficult creditor-debtor position, they were also irritated in Central America by the treatment that government gave to British nationals. In 1827 and 1828 the federation tried and succeeded to slight degree in levying forced loans upon all businesses including those owned all or in part by foreigners. A few such individuals were also required to bear arms. Since most foreigners, especially the successful businessmen, were British, His Majesty's government sharply protested these acts. When Morazán came into office, he deplored the policy and gave assurance that it would not happen again. It was to happen again, many times, and in the late 1830's became another source of rancor.

A new problem then arose. Acting upon his own initiative the English superintendent of Belice captured Ruatán, largest of the Bay Islands, in January of 1830 and in so doing drove off some twenty French families that had been settled there by the Central American government. The pretext for the act was that slaves belonging to residents of Belice were escaping to the Bay Islands as well as to Central America proper and were not being returned by the federation to their British masters. Such an excuse meant nothing to the Central Americans, for they were not only happy to see the British lose valuable property, they seemed sincerely to approve their constitutional provision that all men were free in the republic. Central America provided an asylum conveniently located, and while the number of slaves escaping is unknown, it was large enough to provoke numerous Belice objections that their economy was being ruined.

The Central American government failed to see any just connection between the fugitives and the seizure of Ruatán. They protested the occupation and were pleased to observe the British withdrawal within a matter of weeks. Coincidental with the British decision, it should be noted, was the widespread rumor that Spain was launching a gigantic fleet to prepare the reconquest of the Caribbean. Furthermore, the colonial office was fully aware that its claim upon Ruatán was unsubstantial. Little justification or reason existed for making an issue at that time of title to an unimportant island.

Gradually British policy toward Central America was emerging, but it is clear from discussions within the government that this attitude was shaped by events as they occurred and was not part of any long-range policy. It was not the subject of Parliamentary debate, nor is it easy to find significant differences in attitudes of the major political parties. First of all, Britain's major interest in Central America was commercial.[9] To a lesser extent, but growing in the 1840's, it was also strategic. The desire for expansion was scarcely a motive. Territory might be acquired in the isthmus, but largely through accident and the overeagerness of lesser officials abroad. Colonies were not worth the loss of friendship and trade with the young republic. Ruatán was a case in point, and there were to be others, including Ruatán again. Put in other terms, Great Britain was supreme among foreign nations in Central America and intended to retain that position. Nothing was to be gained by aggressive tactics, and many statesmen seriously doubted that possession of colonies was a paying proposition. Britain would not easily or willingly give up its commercial role nor its stake in Belice, but this does not mean that it opposed the Central American Federation as so often has been charged.[10] British behavior was determined in an *ad hoc* manner by problems as they arose. There were instances which touched upon the existence of the federation, but they reveal no malice toward that government. For example, while Britain refused to give

9. This is amply demonstrated by Robert A. Naylor in his unpublished Ph.D. dissertation, "British Commercial Relations with Central America, 1821-1851" (Tulane University, 1958). The trade was not vast, but it was growing and, in certain selected items such as mahogany, indigo, and coffee, was very important to Great Britain.

10. Among the authorities on Central America accusing the British of deliberately seeking the federation's destruction are: Julius Froebel, *Seven Years' Travel in Central America* (London, 1859), p. 193; Ephriam G. Squier, *Nicaragua, its people, scenery, monuments and the proposed interoceanic canal* (New York, 1852), II, 413; Mary W. Williams, Ruhl J. Bartlett, and Russell E. Miller, *The People and Politics of Latin America* (Boston, 1955), pp. 425-6; Williams, *Anglo-American Diplomacy*, pp. 33 and 38; note by Lorenzo Montúfar (a leading Central American historian), enclosed with official dispatches from Henry C. Hall to Frederick T. Frelinghuysen, March 27, 1883, *Foreign Relations of the United States*, 1883, p. 48. See also, Charles L. Stansifer, "The Central American Career of E. George Squier" (Ph.D. dissertation, Tulane University, 1959).

diplomatic recognition to the federation, the importance of this failure can be easily overestimated. It did not indicate a desire to destroy the nation but was a reasonable judgment on its stability. The decision was within Britain's rights and was designed to get the best territorial bargain from Central America. Obviously many officials knew the difference, but it is apparent that the Central American people did not realize that the various consuls serving Britain were not diplomats. Even such an authority as Bancroft wrote that diplomatic relations with Great Britain were opened in 1825.[11] Certainly Frederick Chatfield took upon himself many quasi-diplomatic functions. On the other hand the United States recognized Central America in 1826, and the step was of only the slightest importance to Central America. In the federation era, in sum, Britain had no trade treaty and gave no recognition, while the United States had a treaty and gave recognition. Yet its commerce and importance were trifling in comparison with His Majesty's efforts.

Secondly, the Barclay, Herring and Reid, Irving loans must be considered in relation to English policy. These, of course, were lent by private individuals, not the government, nor did the government give any assurance to the investors that it might intervene to protect them. But the loans were contracted by the federation, not the individual states, and the British government expected the federation to make the repayment. Following Morazán's successes in 1829 and 1830 British bondholders and government alike congratulated him on restoring the federation. When the federation again fell behind in its payments, Chatfield later took the same attitude as the bondholders —that a strong single nation would be more likely to pay its bills than would five separate states, small and

11. Bancroft, *History*, III, 81.

quarreling among themselves. It was also far easier to present his demands for interest to one official than to travel the length of Central America seeking five. Chatfield, in fact, spent almost all of his eighteen Central American years in Guatemala City. Only when the rupture of the federation was an established fact did Chatfield ask the separate states for their shares of the debt payments. In so far as the Barclay, Herring loan was concerned, the British attitude toward the federation was quite clear; dissolution would make repayment less likely and would create for the agents in the field a far greater nuisance when negotiating.

There exists adequate other evidence that, contrary to frequent charges, Great Britain preferred to see the federation operate as a unit. It had congratulated Morazán when he saved the republic and in 1842, after the separation of the states, it had hoped that the federal government would be re-established. Slowness of communication and foreign office interest in more important areas of the world dictated that to a great extent policy toward Central America would be determined by the daily activities of the agents there. In the 1830's and 1840's Lords Palmerston and Aberdeen reviewed these actions and occasionally overruled their representatives, but on no occasion did they order steps designed to split the federation, and no hint was given that the British interests would best be served by substituting five nations for one in Central America. There was, in fact, very little interest in the form of government that Central Americans preferred.

The key question that must be studied is whether Frederick Chatfield opposed the Central American government.[12] Many people living then as well as writers in the

12. Chatfield's opinions and own accounts of his actions are to be found in his long correspondence with the British Foreign Office;

twentieth century accused him of that mischief. Chatfield's position in Central America was unique. He served Great Britain as consul and chargé in Central America between 1834 and 1852, an extremely long and significant period. He would have been important merely as Britain's agent, but during many of those years other nations, such as the United States and France, were unrepresented or served by very weak individuals. This fact, coupled with the five or six months needed to receive a reply from his superiors in London, made Chatfield the most important foreigner in Central America for almost two decades. It must be assumed that his work was more than satisfactory to his superiors, although occasionally he was cautioned against overzealousness. Some restrictions were put upon him by the foreign office—especially he was to avoid committing his nation in the matter of boundaries and the peculiar status of Britain in Belice and the Mosquito coast. But in most matters his government relied upon him to determine the facts himself and to conduct daily affairs with circumspection. There is no evidence that he was ever told to oppose the Central American Federation or in any wise to favor its split.

Chatfield began his Central American career in 1834 determined to arrange a commercial treaty with the young nation and possessed with obvious good will toward the people he was meeting for the first time. The nation had undergone its three-year civil war in the 1820's and, while recovery had been brought about, the wounds were severe.

---

this has been microfilmed and is on file in the MARI Library at Tulane University. The judgements made of him by others can be found in several travelers' accounts such as those of E. G. Squier and John L. Stephens, American diplomatic correspondence of Central American officials and various Central American newspapers of the Chatfield era. Practically all of these sources are unfavorable to Chatfield. He was a man about whom few people could be neutral.

Critics of Chatfield and Great Britain regularly overlooked the fact that Central America's Federation came close to destruction five or six years before Chatfield's appointment to Central America and at a time when there was no official British representation in the entire land. Chatfield made some effort to prepare himself on Britain's relations with Central America, and he probably had some notion of what a federal system entailed, but he was clearly disappointed to discover that Central America was politically weaker and more backward than he had imagined. He commented that he would normally not recommend negotiations with "a government so little defined" as the Central American Federation but would proceed because prospects of improvement were so distant. He observed that each state maintained a separate army, and there was much indifference to sending representatives to the federal congress. He thought it likely that Morazán would attempt to convert the nation into a centralized state, the better to keep the peoples together. Within six months after his arrival in Central America he concluded that the "wretched, temporizing system of government" would fail unless its leaders brought about immediate reforms.

Unfortunately for his reputation among Central Americans, Chatfield was most outspoken with condemnations of this sort, and it was not illogical for the natives to conclude that he hoped that the federation would fail. Chatfield used similar invective against his own countrymen, however, and frequently discussed the activities of Englishmen in Belice with the same critical tone. In some regards Chatfield was a caricature of the Englishman in the tropics. A Protestant, he loathed the "Romish Church" and looked upon the priesthood as the source of evil as well as of attacks on him. The lack of progress, the willingness to put up with bad government and confusion, he attributed to the priests, "many of them coloured," who said that affairs could not be helped. The priests, he said, taught the people that suffering was necessary and patience was the path to heaven. The clergy, he felt, could end the strife whenever it issued the orders. His repeated assertions that only the Anglo-Saxon could bring progress to Central America certainly was not calculated to endear him to his hosts.

In addition, he was inconsistent. To Chatfield, Mariano Gálvez, *jefe* of Guatemala, was one of the two capable men in the republic in 1834; by the next year Gálvez was a "shrewd, pettifogging and corrupt lawyer." Chatfield engaged in personal tirades on individuals, and much of his abuse was obligingly published by Central American newspapers which helped to advertise his character. He criticized officials freely and was most condescending in the advice that he offered them.

The indiscriminateness of his attacks had one virtue, however. Chatfield and any one party or faction in Central America could not long remain linked. Quite properly he did not attach himself to either of the two major Central American parties, but he held strong and varying opinions of their relative merits from the British point of view. Initially he favored the Liberals whom he considered more enlightened. They generally looked upon the foreigner with less hostility and, in fact, Liberal administrations gave many concessions to Europeans to encourage trade and immigration. Much of their early legislation was frankly anticlerical, and this seemed most fitting to Chatfield. In short, to Chatfield and to most visitors to Central America, the Liberals represented progress and the Conservatives reaction.

Gradually this idealistic attitude changed. He saw the ineffectiveness of the Liberals, their internal quarrels, and their inability to control the "dark, mulatto classes" as a threat to the stability so badly needed for commerce. For Chatfield, with all of his faults, never lost sight of his primary mission in Central America—the encouragement of British trade. Carrera, whom he had earlier feared as a savage, soon appeared to be a leader who could preserve order. It was also apparent to Chatfield that the "white, decent folk" of Guatemala would probably reduce Carrera's excesses. Chatfield had little choice:

I freely confess that I have no predilection for any party or persons in this country; I am not a partisan of the expresident Morasán [sic] or of his friends the existing government, first because I perceive that Morazán has no administrative ability, and secondly because I can feel no respect for Persons who sacrifice the publick interests and resources to their own individual emolument—with regard to the servile party [Conservatives], although I may lean toward them as being persons of property and reputable conduct, nevertheless on publick grounds I cannot very cordially welcome the prospect of their return to power, from a suspicion that no permanent good will accrue from the govt. of a Party embued with the old Spanish prejudices, & subject to the tyrannical influence of the Romish Priesthood; however, between the two evils of only a semblance of govt. without power or principle, as has long been submitted to here, and a substantial one based on obsolete principles, perhaps the latter is best, at any rate it may be the means of leading to the establishment of such outward forms of respectability & decency, as any future rulers will find it difficult to dispense with.[13]

With such shift of opinion one can have sympathy, but putting it into practice in the 1840's was to damn

13. Chatfield to Palmerston, May 13, 1839, F. O. 15/22, MARI Microfilm, Tulane University.

Frederick Chatfield to the Central Americans ever after. Since most of the historians of Central America, native and foreign, bore liberal tendencies, Chatfield got what might be called a bad press. Furthermore, his desire after 1839 to support respectability and to criticize Morazán made it appear that he had actively plotted the overthrow of the Liberals and the federal type of government with which they were identified in the public eye. The facts simply do not support these allegations. As Chatfield's letter to Palmerston amply indicates, as late as May of 1839 he had taken no firm stand for the Conservatives and was unconvinced that the party would do much for Central America. Yet, as we have seen in Chapter IV, the Central American Federation had collapsed the year before. On no occasion did he attack the federation or suggest to local people that another form of government would be better for them. He confined remarks of the latter nature to his dispatches home, and the substance was not revealed in Central America. His unfortunate criticism of government officials was well known, but he refrained from commenting publicly on the federation as an institution. In fact, based upon his activities and his writings, it is impossible to be sure what he personally felt would be the best government for Central America and her foreign commerce. At this time Chatfield had never set foot in Nicaragua and Costa Rica, the first two states to secede from the union. He was close to unknown in both provinces and he could not have had the slightest influence. There is, in short, no way to establish that the failure of the first Central American attempt at confederation was in any sense the work of Frederick Chatfield.

Not so clear-cut is the role played by Chatfield in the remaining years of his Central American career. From the breakup of the federation in 1838-39 until he left Central America in 1852, Chatfield became a man of tremendous importance on the isthmus. Given his abrasive character and the overwhelming part played by British commerce, there was no way that he could avoid publicity. Gradually, as we have seen, he began to look upon the Conservatives as the "better" people of Central America, in other words, the ones with whom he could make agreements that might be consummated. He had consistently failed to conclude the trade agreement which was the chief purpose for his being in Central America, and he felt that the Liberal officials were to blame for not bringing about the stability that a treaty required.

In order the better to fulfill his obligations to his government, Chatfield began wooing the Conservatives by the early 1840's, especially in Guatemala. It is of the greatest significance to realize that such a policy did not automatically mean that he opposed any future confederation. This is the mistake that is made by Lorenzo Montúfar, the eminent Central American historian, Ephraim Squier, the American diplomat, and lesser writers. They assumed that, since Morazán favored the old federation and he was a Liberal, it necessarily followed that his Conservative enemies opposed the federation. There is very little truth in this. The Conservatives attacked Morazán and his government. Yet when they grew in power, the former frequently discussed the creation of a new federal republic and actually signed agreements to this end. Not politically ignorant, the Conservatives of Central America could see quite as clearly as the Liberals that, when the power distribution among the five states was favorable, a federation became ideal for the party in office. For example, in April of 1842 Guatemala's Conservative government rejected the Pact of Chinandega,[14] a reorganization of the Federal Republic, but in October of the same year Guatemala's Conservative minister, Manuel Francisco Pavón, helped negotiate an agreement with all of the other states except Costa Rica. The Treaty came into existence to combat an expected invasion by the exiled Morazán. When it was learned that he was dead, the treaty expired also. Its intended functions were simple, but it did plan to have a single representation for foreign affairs. Chatfield encouraged, rather than opposed, such a step and told the government of Guatemala that "so soon as the states of Central America have consolidated a general authority to conduct their relations with Foreign governments, Her Majesty's government will be prepared to enter into negotiations for the conclusion of a General Treaty of Amity, Navagation and Commerce."[15]

Again, in 1845, Guatemala joined with El Salvador in inviting the other states to a conference to consider a new federation. This association also failed, but the fault lay more with El Salvador than with any other single state. One must conclude that in the Conservative era of the 1840's Guatemala still had taken no stand against a future federation. Thus, if Chatfield were conspiring with the Conservatives against such cooperation, he was failing badly.

Other evidence exists in Chatfield's favor. In 1844 he and the foreign office agreed that the British trade with Central America would be enhanced by dealing with but one nation instead of five. In fact, the separation that took place in 1839 was illegal in Chatfield's mind. He felt that the states were all bound by the Constitution of 1824 and

14. See Chapter VI for terms of this agreement.
15. Chatfield to Principal Secretary of Guatemala, Nov. 18, 1844, B99/1/4, 8762, Archivo Nacional, of Guatemala.

that there could be only one nation in Central America until the states met in a general assembly and repealed that constitution. For many years he refused to consider a trade treaty with any one of the states, but he continued to insist that Britain must negotiate only with the Central American Republic.

The lack of harmony between this policy and his policy of demanding interest payments from the states as individuals did not bother him in the least. He was insisting that the federation technically existed, but for want of anyone to deal with he was bypassing it to collect the debts. He regularly did what he thought was best for Great Britain, and he considered Central American unity to be to Britain's advantage.

Quite aside from the confederation issue, Chatfield was often accused by Central Americans of meddling in local affairs. On that charge he was unquestionably guilty. He knew all of the Central American merchants, politicians, and military leaders of his time—and his "time" included a whole generation. He gave unsolicited advice freely; he told officials how to cope with cholera and how to bury Protestants; he advised Central American governments on methods of collecting taxes and negotiating land grants with foreign corporations. He openly discouraged their attempts to build up commerce through Pacific ports and implied that he knew more about methods of harvesting cochineal than did local farmers. He proposed state budgets to pay off foreign (British) debts and improperly used his office as a place of asylum. He made many enemies, including briefly Morazán. More embittered was one Colonel Juan Galindo, an Irish-Central American engaged in a score of activities of a promotional nature that invariably seemed fraudulent to Chatfield.[16] He had gone to considerable trouble to nullify Galindo's efforts to become Central America's diplomatic representative in Great Britain, and the two remained rancorous rivals until Galindo's death in civil war.

This sort of machination made Chatfield's reputation worse as the years passed, but he let himself be pushed beyond reasonableness by a new factor.

The surprising success of the United States in the Mexican War and the discovery of gold in California brought a sudden halt to the weak and vacillating isthmian policy of Britain's only rival. Involved in our own internal expansion we had ignored opportunities in Central America and had afforded the British little competition for commercial or political leadership. From 1847 western expansion in the United States became an international matter, and many people residing in Central America began to reflect upon what might be the impact of another great nation on those shores. Among these men was Frederick Chatfield.

Chatfield looked upon the United States as more than just a threat to the English position. He assumed that it planned to acquire protectorates in Central America— accomplished more easily, he said, because of the prolonged disunion. Reluctantly giving up hope of getting one commercial treaty for all of Central America, he quickly negotiated separate trade agreements with Guatemala and Costa Rica when they proclaimed themselves sovereign nations in 1847 and 1848.

These definitive independence movements opened a Pandora's box of international mischief for Central Amer-

16. Several phases of Galindo's colorful and almost unknown career are traced by William J. Griffith in "Juan Galindo, Central American Chauvinist," *Hispanic American Historical Review,* XL (February, 1960), 25-52.

ica. Nicaragua, Honduras, and Costa Rica gave momentary consideration to accepting a protectorate from the United States. Then, encouraged by a renowned meddler, Ecuador's General Juan José Flores, the Costa Rican government which was harboring him made serious efforts to acquire British protection in the fashion advocated by Chatfield. President Carrera of Guatemala toyed with the same scheme, lending ammunition to the charges that Britain sought the dismemberment of Central America. But, it must be remembered that Central America was already dissolved. Only after the five states failed completely to unite did Chatfield seek to extend hegemony over any of the individual states. Even this failed when Palmerston declined to act upon the requests.

As these affairs were viewed by newly arrived American agents—Joseph Livingston at León and Elijah Hise at Guatemala in 1848 and Ephraim G. Squier replacing the latter in 1849—they indicated the logical and incorrect assumption that Britain sought the perpetual separation of the five states. Since the United States State Department concluded that such was British policy, it therefore ordered the diplomats to make every effort to restore the federation. This instruction strengthened the notion that the British and Chatfield must have destroyed the republic.

Obviously the British sought to oppose the progress of the United States on the isthmus, and Chatfield was given such orders. But what Palmerston and Chatfield were attacking was not the Central American Federation; they were striking out at the new threat to British commercial domination. They long had favored the existence of the single republic as being good for trade. Now with the United States acquiring many friends by supporting the popular federal idea, England could defend herself best by aiding those separatist states where Chatfield's influence was the strongest. Hence, though he failed to get protectorates over Guatemala and Costa Rica, Chatfield did get their final approval of the trade agreements.

A correlative issue that can be only mentioned here was the new struggle for interoceanic communication. The United States and Great Britain had engaged in perhaps their most important nineteenth-century diplomatic clash, one that could easily have led to war. Central American writers can be excused for believing that the issue of federation was of significance to the two great nations. The truth, of course, is that they fought each other in a power contest in which even Latin America's commerce dwindled in importance. The prize was nothing less than the world's most important highway.[17] Central America was unfortunately the battleground, and its rights and interests were frequently trampled in the last years of the 1840's.

Britain sought to dominate the Central American waterways by concessions in the Bay of Fonseca, by extending their influence on the Mosquito Indians, and by claiming that the protectorate reached to the Río San Juan, the northern boundary of Costa Rica, which was the likely entrance point for a Caribbean-Pacific canal. Squier's measures included treaty negotiations with Nicaragua, Honduras, and El Salvador that would give the United States exclusive canal or rail rights, but these settlements were not submitted to the United States Senate. For months Chatfield and Squier pulled the strings of their respective puppets and exhibited astonishing initiative against one another.

Neither man was to win in the battle for Central American advantage. Their importance declined as their governments more clearly saw what was at stake, and the

17. See Miss Williams' *Anglo-American Diplomacy*.

Clayton-Bulwer Treaty was signed in 1850. While that document did not end Anglo-American rivalry in Central America, it signaled the close of an era and, specifically, the decline of British influence.

In the late 1840's, then, the question of a federation continued unabated, made more complicated by foreign activities, but not altered in basic structure. Great Britain and its representative, Frederick Chatfield, were guilty of intervention in the affairs of Central America. Chatfield too often trespassed upon the rights of nations, occasionally violating his instructions from home. But he cannot be fairly accused of conspiring to destroy the Central American Federation, nor can one say that British policy favored the existence of five separate states. The most reasonable charge that can be made is that Britain opposed the threat of United States ascendancy on the isthmus between 1848 and 1850 by tightening relations with Costa Rica and Guatemala. In this indirect, but nevertheless real, sense, Britain fought the re-creation of a federation.

With no British factor in evidence at all, the Central Americans before and since failed to unify the five states. England was but a convenient scapegoat for Central Americans who personalized the issue by blowing up out of all proportion the figure of Frederick Chatfield. A lonely, unpopular man, whose whole life was given to his work, Chatfield fought constantly for Britain's best interests which could not often coincide with those of Central America. As the only tangible representation of Her Majesty's government, he was the ideal object of the Central American public's spleen.[18] It was always good politics to label an

18. "All publick evils have an end—The pestilence of the small pox has passed away—The colera passes away—bloody revolutions, tyranny, and barbarism, a la Malespín, a Carrillo, pass away; Carrera will soon pass away; but there is an evil—horrible and interminable; there is a curse ever alive which corrodes like a gangrene the heart of Central

opponent as an ally of Chatfield, and one could never lose votes by attacking the consul in speech and press. He asked and gave no quarter; he hired spies and read other people's mail; he was officious and probably an insufferable bore, but he did not destroy the Central American Republic.

America, and that is   Chatfield, and he is the eternal agent of England . . . . "Chatfield to Palmerston, quoting from *El Progreso* of San Salvador, May 9, 1850, F. O. 15/64, MARI Microfilm, Tulane University.

Chapter VI

The Minor Prophets

A PHENOMENON was born in 1842 in the town of Chinandega, Nicaragua. It has lived a long life, made up of alternate years of lassitude and brisk activity, usually verbal, sometimes military. It is old and tired now, but it is not yet dead. This phenomenon is the peculiar motivation which causes Central American statesmen to drop whatever they are doing and get together for a new proposal to confederate their governments. It is made more strange by the fact that often the conferences are arranged in the midst of the ruins of the last great failure. Such was the case of the Chinandega agreements.

As early as 1839 when the rupture of the first Federal Republic of Central America became apparent, feelers were put out by several of the governments to ascertain the extent of interest for a new federation. For two years the states exchanged notes concerning the important subject of the selection of a site for the talks. Chinandega, San Vicente, Santa Ana, Tegucigalpa, and Comayagua were the most frequently mentioned locations, but no more than two states could agree upon one town, and none was acceptable to all five. Finally, paying heed to the Nicaraguan warning that disaster would occur if no decision were reached, Honduras, El Salvador, and Nicaragua sent delegates on March 17, 1842, to Chinandega for the purpose of forming a new federal union. Guatemala and Costa Rica were invited also, but their respective *jefes,* Rafael Carrera and Braulio Carrillo, declined to take part. Soon a provisional government was announced for a league of the three central states. Temporarily there was a council made up of one delegate from each state chosen by his assembly. Antonio José Cañas was selected by a "majority of the states" to be the Supreme Delegate. Guatemala, Costa Rica, and Los Altos (a region briefly separated from Guatemala) could become members by their free adherence to the bases of the pact.

The Chinandega agreement was intended to create a new federal republic. The states were free and sovereign in every matter which was not expressly reserved to the supreme authorities, and no state could interfere in the affairs of another. Each state was to recognize the legal and judicial acts of the others and mutually to protect the political and civil rights of citizens. True to Latin American tradition criminals were to be extradited upon request unless the offenses were of a political nature. Individual states could not make alliances against one another nor treaties with foreign powers.

The pact of union had popular representation. Legislative power lay in a bicameral congress: the deputies were elected on a basis of one for each 50,000 persons while three senators were chosen by each state assembly. This congress was to meet every two years.

The president of the republic was to be elected for a four-year term by electoral *juntas* whose composition was not described. There was no vice president. In case of a vacancy in the presidential office the combined houses of congress would choose a successor by lot from among the names of three men polling the greatest number of votes in a preliminary ballot. If congress were not in session, the senior senator would act as president for the balance of the unexpired term. The justices of the supreme court were three in number and elected by the two houses of congress. Almost the sole source of national income was to be the customs duties collected at the ports.

Such was the outline for the new confederation. It amounted to little. Guatemala would have nothing to do with it and encouraged Honduras' *jefe* Francisco Ferrera to shun it also. Costa Rica would accept the plan only with a large number of reservations.

Pressures from outside made a reorganization imperative. The British were plotting on the Mosquito coast, the Mexicans were conspiring in Soconusco, and Morazán was scheming in Costa Rica, all strong motivations for a confederation. A new attempt was therefore made, and on July 27, 1842, the three middle states again organized a government. It was called the Confederación Centroamericana, and its constitution encompassed many of the changes desired by Costa Ricans and Guatemalans. Nevertheless, the pact was ratified by only the central three states.

Executive power rested in a council, one member elected by the assembly of each state, which was headed by a supreme delegate with a one-year term. The legislative power resided in a loose gathering of representatives who acted more in the capacity of emissaries than legislators. Not significantly stronger than under the first Chinandega Pact, Central America, in the pithy words of Salvador Mendieta, was united by saliva.[1] The states retained

---

1. Salvador Mendieta, *La Nacionalidad y el Partido Unionista Centroamericana* (San José, 1905), p. 46.

their sovereignty, and the confederation was too weak to enforce its rule.

While this fiction of a government continued until 1845, another similar agreement was concluded later in 1842. On October 7 a compact was signed at Guatemala City by all of the states except Costa Rica. Not a true government, it was called a treaty of union and amounted to a defensive alliance compelled by foreign factors. Great Britain was making claims relative to seizures of goods and money belonging to her subjects who had refused to contribute to forced loans levied especially upon them during recent wars. Furthermore, although Morazán had been killed in September, the news had not yet reached Guatemala, and the alliance expected to have to oppose his forces shortly. Little attention was paid to the agreement when his death became known.

The treaty of alliance was signed by Francisco Pavón for Guatemala, Pedro Nolasco Arriaga for Honduras, and Joaquín Durán representing both El Salvador and Nicaragua. The states agreed to make common cause in case of attack, and they would not send armed forces across each other's borders without permission of the state concerned. The importance of extraditing deserters was stressed. Governments achieving power by revolution would not be recognized—an idea to be frequently echoed in Central American history. In foreign affairs the states agreed to act as one. There were no provisions for internal administration at all. A very simple confederation, it was an *ad hoc* organization at best. Especially revealing is the fear already existing that the states would be consumed by the meddling in each other's affairs. Unfortunately, such early realization has not reduced the extent of this tragedy in the past century.

Meanwhile, the Confederación Centroamericana continued to function and accomplished one thing in the two years of its life. In March, 1844, at San Vicente in El Salvador, Fruto Chamorro of Nicaragua was chosen the Supreme Delegate. In April he and the delegates from Honduras and El Salvador were informed that a band of Guatemalan insurgents led by the exiled former president, Manuel José Arce, had invaded El Salvador to overthrow the regime of Francisco Malespín. The latter asked for help from the *confederación* to repulse Arce. Chamorro succeeded in getting Nicaraguan troops to join against Arce, but they had to fight Hondurans who objected to Nicaraguans crossing the border to get to El Salvador. Comic opera intrigues unfolded in rapid succession, and wars between El Salvador and Guatemala, Nicaragua and Honduras, Nicaragua and Guatemala, and El Salvador and Honduras briefly ensued. The *confederación* finally proved able to subdue Arce, but only because it was in the interest of enough members to do so. It was clear that the *confederación* had no power to enforce its orders. When his term expired in 1845, Chamorro announced that his title no longer existed, and the *confederación* died with his position.[2]

The ashes of Chinandega were not yet cold when a new proposal for unity was made. Former Supreme Delegate Chamorro had specific plans which he recommended for discussion. Surprisingly the people of Central America were not discouraged by the failure of the Chinandega Pact; in the newspapers and correspondence of the times there was more enthusiasm than in 1842 for an agreement. The many little wars, scarcely more than skirmishes, had

2. Most of my discussion of the confederacion comes from Costa Rican newspapers of the era which advised the public of the dangers of entangling in such alliances.

pressed home the dangers of disunity. Nicaragua was frightened by the extension of British claims in Mosquitia and angered by correspondence from Chatfield. Nicaraguan officials sent out queries to the United States to learn what protection, if any, might be afforded by that nation.

Until about this time the United States had been viewed in rather favorable light by Central America, but in the year 1845 the first criticism was voiced when some of the Central American press compared the United States' behavior toward Mexico with that of Mexico toward Central America. Nevertheless, no Central American state had yet been injured by activities of the United States, and that power seemed to be the best buffer against the British, but the United States government would make no commitment. The next best alternative was to strengthen the union internally. In this atmosphere Chamorro made his proposals.

His plan called for the customary three departments, executive, legislative, and judicial. Each state should have ten representatives in the congress for five year terms and would nominate its candidate for chief executive. The provisional capital was to be located in Sonsonate, El Salvador, until a permanent site could be made ready. The nucleus of a federal army was to be a two hundred man contribution from each state. The existing courts would take on the responsibilities of the federal judiciary. All powers not specifically delegated to the federal government were retained by the states. However, Chamorro's plan, as submitted to the newspapers, was very vague in detailing just which powers were enumerated for the federal government.

As in the past much time was wasted discussing the selection of a town in which to meet. Before the end of

1845 the town of Sonsonate was agreed upon by all of the states as the headquarters for the conference. There was much enthusiasm and prediction of success when it appeared that all five states would send delegates. Many people felt that the Sonsonate conference was the last chance. Twenty-five years had passed since independence, and different laws, interests, and customs already were developing. The difficult problems of trade and commerce and the increasing number of exiles demanded solutions on a broad, federal basis that might bring wider acceptance in the family of nations.

By assuming their debts most of the states of Latin America had received diplomatic recognition from all of the major powers. Central America remained the "pitiful exception." Foreign Ministers Aberdeen, Guizot, and Martínez de la Rosa of Great Britain, France, and Spain respectively, all voiced the same requirement that Central America must have a general authority to represent the states in international matters. Such external pressure made the urgency of confederation all the more apparent.

Urgency was not enough. Brief attempts were made to hold discussions in May, June, and July of 1846. No Nicaraguan delegate appeared at any time, and on no occasion did representatives from more than three states meet at the same session.

The immediate reason for failure was the recurring religious issue. The Malespín government in El Salvador had been favorable to the Church, and under the influence of Bishop Jorge Viteri, many of the liberal religious reforms were discarded. In January, 1846, a new and less conservative president, Eugenio Aguilar, replaced Malespín. Bishop Viteri began making charges that Aguilar planned his overthrow and exile in the manner that Morazán disposed of Archbishop Casáus. Color was added to the claims by the coincidental information that Casáus had died in exile and was being returned to Guatemala for burial. On July 11, Viteri sent a unique threat to Aguilar to the effect that as apostolic delegate he held the right to unite El Salvador with Guatemala. He had thus far not done so to avoid the inevitable bloodshed, but unless Aguilar proved more friendly to the Church, the bishop would carry out his warning.

When Aguilar tried to see Viteri about the admonition, crowds formed about the bishop's home, and the women, who were in the majority, cried that they wanted no government except that of the bishop. Revolt broke out the next day; *barrio* fought against *barrio* and neighbor against neighbor, but most of the government and the army supported the president. Attempting to help Viteri, Malespín entered the war, but his forces were defeated, and Malespín killed. Viteri was exiled to Nicaragua and soon became bishop for that area.

The significance of this revolt for our story is that the trouble took place in El Salvador in July of 1846 at the very time that the Sonsonate conference was being held. President Aguilar declared a state of seige on July 13. By reason of this declaration the delegates found their freedom of movement impaired, and they complained to the government. Aguilar's tactless reply was that he had forgotten about the existence of the conference and had therefore neglected to exempt the Sonsonate district from the provisions of the declaration. The Costa Rican and Guatemalan delegates were united in considering the oversight a deliberate affront and a premeditated blow to destroy the meetings.[3] It was on this note that the talks

3. Rafael Escalante (Costa Rican delegate at Sonsonate), to Ministerio de Relaciones Exteriores de Costa Rica, July 25, 1846, unnumbered manuscript, Sección Gobernación, ANCR.

ceased, and Honduras' representatives suggested moving to a more peaceful town.

The pessimism one might expect from the Sonsonate failure is not very evident in the two discussions that immediately followed. First, a plan of Costa Rica, Nicaragua, and Honduras to place themselves as protectorates of the United States was tabled because those countries decided that union among themselves might be achieved earlier. Then, plans were made to hold a conference with the goal of another full scale federation.

This, the sixth formal attempt, took place in Nacaome, Honduras, in 1847. As usual the states represented were Nicaragua, El Salvador, and Honduras, and as usual one of the reasons for the agreement was the fear of the British whose zealous consul general, Chatfield, had just proclaimed that the Mosquito kingdom extended at least to the Río San Juan and probably well beyond it. The British Crown, furthermore, reminded the Central Americans that the Mosquitos were under its protection.

The three states agreed to a pact on October 7, which called for a constituent assembly and provisionally established a federal form of government. Especially invited to attend, Guatemala declined. Carrera had just decreed the creation of the independent Guatemalan republic on the grounds that it could thus better defend itself against the United States' plan to acquire the entire isthmus.[4] This decree was ratified and made official by congress on September 15, 1848. Costa Rica almost simultaneously accomplished the same ends but hedged in its most recent constitution (1847, art. 24) by alleging that it was ready to join in a new covenant whenever the other states agreed. Although evidently following the procedures with consid-

4. *Niles' Weekly Register,* May 29, 1847.

erable interest, the Costa Rican government failed to be represented at the Nacaome meetings.[5]

By March of 1848, El Salvador, Honduras, and Nicaragua had produced a compact and ratified it. In the end Costa Rica considered the project but declined to adhere. The Ticos feared the expense. There would be too many people in government, extra courts, and executives. They wanted no inteference in local matters and especially opposed the military draft. This Costa Rican reluctance, Salvadorean intrigue in another attempt to create an independent Los Altos out of Guatemala, and numerous reservations to the ratifications made the Pact of Nacaome worthless from the start.

Central American diplomatic correspondence and newspapers indicate that the period from 1848 until about 1852 was filled with conversations among the states regarding a new federation. While actual results were negligible, the discussions tumbled one upon another so rapidly that it is indeed difficult to ascertain which talks were preludes to any particular agreement. The activities give an appearance of a great deal of confusion at the time and make bewildering reading today. The reader must keep in mind that this era is the climax and high point of British interest in Central America, discussed in Chapter Five, and marks the beginning of active interest on the part of the United States. A writer on Central America, Wallace A. Thompson, once reported, "The question of Central American union has never stood on its own merits; there have always

5. Ever willing to economize, Central American governments have often received reports of conferences through diplomatic channels or the delegates of other nations. Occasionally private citizens have been enlisted for this work if they happened to be residing temporarily near the seat of discussions. Plans still exist for combining Central American embassies in the most distant lands.

been too many entangling factors."[6] This judgement is especially pertinent to the mid-nineteenth century. Pushed and pulled by the two English-speaking powers, the Central Americans could scarcely cooperate objectively. The re-establishment of their ideal was often confused with military alliances for defense, while opportunism and expediency reigned.

In the often-ruined city of León, Nicaragua, the old business of discussing confederation was resumed again in 1849. Once again, the participants were Nicaragua, Honduras, and El Salvador. On November 6 they signed an agreement to preserve their "order, stability and internal peace" by establishing a common representation in foreign matters and planning a federation for some time in the future.

This new government actually came into existence January 9, 1851, bearing the name "National Representation of Central America" with its capital occasionally at Chinandega but sessions of the government meeting more often at León, just a few miles away. The National Representation was composed of two delegates from each state, elected for four-year terms and instructed to vote as individuals rather than by states. True to form, Guatemala and Costa Rica declined to accept the option of joining. José Francisco Barrundia was elected the first president of the young confederation. The three states united their diplomatic staffs but failed to obtain recognition from the United States and Great Britain. Secretary of State Daniel Webster gave authority to the American Chargé to Nicaragua, J. Bozeman Kerr, to recognize the National Representation if he thought the action justified, but Kerr's investigations convinced him that the government lacked popular

6. Wallace A. Thompson, *Rainbow Countries of Central America* (New York, 1926), p. 270.

support and was unable to restore peaceful conditions. He labeled it an "irresponsible junto of six men of low cunning." He doubted that the convention of 1849 could be regarded as an actual government and said that its "imbecility" was sufficiently marked to make him wary.

As for the British, Chatfield refused to consider the National Representation as the spokesman for Central America and sharply rejected recognition in the bitterest kind of language.

The new government, created to give unified foreign policy to the three states, became mired in local Nicaraguan affairs, specifically the struggle of León versus Granada. Recognition might have lent some atmosphere of prestige, but it could not have saved a cabal from the unmixed apathy of the citizens that Kerr described in his reports home. It is significant to note that Kerr, in the best observation post for an impartial witness, considered the organization just as dishonest and futile as did Chatfield. This latter had especial reason to dislike the representation when it shortly denounced the English interests in Mosquitia and refused to recognize the pretensions of the Indians to a monarchy.

In October, 1852, President Trinidad Cabañas of Honduras summoned a meeting of the representation at Tegucigalpa. The members drew up a constitution and submitted it to the people of the three states. This new document changed the name of the government to the "Republic of Central America" and altered in some particulars the nature of the loose alliance that had been in existence. One interesting and unusual addition was to give power to the "Republic" to use force to bring about peace *within* any of the member states. The legislatures of Nicaragua and El Salvador promptly declared their states independent because the organic statute had been referred to the people directly and not to the legislatures.

The infant republic's existence was quickly snuffed out in a war between Honduras and Guatemala and the resumption of civil strife in Nicaragua. Guatemala in the meanwhile re-elected Carrera as its president, and in 1856 the Guatemalan congress named him president for life. This affirmation of his power made it possible for Carrera to spread his influence beyond the borders. He installed a henchman, Santos Guardiola (known to Central American writers as "the Butcher"), as president of Honduras and brought about a Carrera style of stability there. While Guardiola and Carrera remained in office, they opposed all confederation movements at home, and so much of the vigor disappeared for several years.

Considering the amount of foreign activity in Central America in the middle of the nineteenth century, it is perhaps not surprising that the next of the minor prophets of federation was an American, William Walker. The stage was set for him by the discovery of gold in California and the resulting profits to be found in transporting passengers across the Central American isthmus. In 1849 Cornelius Vanderbilt secured a contract from Nicaragua which granted to him the right to transport passengers through that state. His newly organized Accessory Transit Company was soon thriving from the profitable carrying of thousands of "Californians" each month to the Pacific shore. The usual route of the "49ers" was from New York or New Orleans to San Juan del Norte, then by river vessel up the shallow San Juan to Lake Nicaragua and across the lake to La Virgen. The weary travelers then rode in carriages on a macadam road to the Pacific port of San Juan del Sur. The trip, though difficult, was considered far superior to the alternatives, and the discomforts were largely confined to the 150-mile link through Nicaragua.

Many of the travelers were mere freebooters, who in crossing that strife-torn land thought they saw opportunity. The vision was encouraged by local *jefes* who eagerly hired the Americans, famed for their better rifles and shooting eyes.

Walker was introduced to Nicaragua by one of such men, Byron Cole, who, acting as agent for two Nicaraguan Liberal leaders, Francisco Castellón and Máximo Jérez, sought willing filibusters in the United States. Unsuccessful in law, medicine, and journalism, Walker had tasted excitement in trying to set up republics in Sonora and Lower California, narrowly escaping with his life. Cole convinced his principles that the "grey eyed man of destiny" was just the leader whom they needed, and in 1855 he and some three hundred men were brought to Nicaragua to drive out President José María Estrada and the Conservatives who were clustered about Granada. The pay was to be gold, glory, and land.[7]

Thus began what Central Americans call the National War. Walker was quickly in control of southern Nicaragua. He captured Granada and forced a compromise on the enemy troops under General Ponciano Corral. According to the terms, a moderate, Patricio Rivas, was named president; Corral, secretary of war; and Walker, commander in chief of the army. Walker found himself unable to hold these disparate forces together. Corral sought help from Guardiola and Honduran conservatives, but his treason was discovered, and he was put to death by Walker. The Liberal allies also became worried about the man they had invited to help them and contemplated their own means of getting rid of him.

7. Still the basic study of Walker is William O. Scroggs, *Filibusters and Financiers* (New York, 1916).

Help came to Walker from anti-Vanderbilt factions in the transit company who needed his aid in getting control of the stock. They gave him money and added men to his phalanx while he in turn was to cancel Vanderbilt's concession as soon as he held sufficient control of the Nicaraguan government. If the conspirators wanted legal basis, some could be found in the fact that Vanderbilt was to have paid Nicaragua a share of the profits each year but regularly reported that there were none to divide.

By mid-1856 a combination including Vanderbilt, an allied army of Costa Ricans, Guatemalans, Salvadoreans, Hondurans, and some dissident Nicaraguans all opposed Walker. It was a rare moment in Central American history. Almost all factions were united, united in this instance to drive the Yankee invader from the land.

Some groups in the United States, uncertain perhaps of Walker's motives, urged the recognition of his government. It was rumored that Great Britain was supporting Costa Rica and supplying it with arms to fight Nicaragua and at the same time to occupy more of the disputed territory between the two states. The anti-British aspect added to the glory that hung around Walker, and his exploits aroused great enthusiasm among many Americans. Somehow it was assumed that Walker was aiding the Liberals and therefore, the cause of democracy. In the southern part of the United States many thought that Walker was adding land to the American domain, and his repeal of anti-slavery legislation, though the result of some complicated reasoning on Walker's part, was viewed quite simply in the South as an effort to increase the potential slave territory of the United States.

From late in 1856 the greatest burden of the resistance fell upon Costa Rica, for Walker stayed close to the border in attempting to protect his supply lines, namely the Accessory Transit Company road. Forces on both sides in this struggle were crippled by desertion and cholera. Costa Rica's President Juan Rafael Mora decreed the closing of the San Juan to cut Walker's strength, and the British fleet helped enforce the rule. This pressure gradually reduced Walker's army to a handful, and in May of 1857, he surrendered to the captain of a United States sloop of war at San Juan del Sur and was returned to the United States.

He made two other attempts to install himself in Central America that are pertinent to this study. He returned to Nicaragua in the same year but was promptly arrested by the American navy (incidentally trespassing upon Nicaraguan sovereignty) for violation of existing American neutrality laws. The chief result of this episode was a storm in the United States Congress between the opponents and supporters of Walker.[8]

Walker lived to make one last try to establish his nation. He planned to attack Nicaragua through Honduras and finance himself by means of the customs house funds at Trujillo. Here, he failed badly. Trapped in the coastal swamps of Honduras, he was wounded and decided to surrender to the commander of a British ship in Honduran waters. This time he was unable to avoid Central American justice, for the British turned him over to the Honduran authorities whose court-martial promptly resulted in conviction and death by firing squad.

8. James D. Richardson, ed., *A Compilation of the Messages and Papers of the Presidents* (Washington, 1897), V, 466. President Buchanan said that the proper procedure would have been to capture Walker on the high seas. He added that North Americans could and should "civilize" Central America and that perhaps it should be the task of the United States government in order to forestall the sanguinary Walker breed.

Walker's career has a dual connotation to the idea of Central American confederation. In the first place, it showed that in cases of extreme and imminent danger the Central American states could work together, though cooperation might cease and internal strife resume when the threat had passed. Secondly, Walker's efforts constituted another attempt to unite Central America. He had no intention of adding Central America to the United States; what he pursued was a personal empire according to the testimony of many of his friends and followers. Scroggs reaches the conclusion that Walker sought a federated state of Central America, based upon his own military force and over which he would be the dictator.

He failed for many reasons, but the chief one was that he had made an enemy of Cornelius Vanderbilt. The united Central American states might have brought about his defeat, but it was only assured by the power and planning of the Commodore. Thus, this unique venture in Central American federation was attempted by the foreigner and destroyed by the foreigner. Walker's was the only attempt of a person from outside the isthmus to bring about a single government by the use of force.

Some of the fear of Walker remained strong enough to affect Central American attitudes in the latter part of the 1850's. In that period both Nicaragua and Costa Rica were favored by moderate and progressive presidents, respectively Tomás Martínez and Juan Rafael Mora. In 1858 they bloodlessly negotiated what should have been the definitive settlement of their baneful boundary dispute. Resolved to take advantage of the good feelings engendered as well as the Yankeephobia that arose from the filibusters' activities, the men suggested uniting their two nations and inviting the other three to join in a common pact. American diplomats viewed the plan as aimed at the United States. In an effort to sway the disinclined Carrera, Martínez made the radical proposal of using Guatemala City as the center for the constitutional discussions. Mora agreed that he would attend in person and asked his congress for authority to treat on matters of uniform weights, monetary systems, tariffs, postal services, troop contributions, and representation abroad. It was one of those rare instances in Central American affairs in which Costa Rica played a leading part in federalism.

When Martínez failed to get favorable response from the other states to convene in Guatemala, Mora suggested San Salvador as the site, with the stipulation that all five of the presidents be delegates. By this means it was thought possible that a federal navy of twelve ships might be created quickly to be used in opposition to any renewed filibustering. Meanwhile, before any meetings were held other than those of Mora and Martínez, the former sought and received election as Costa Rica's president for a third term. It was one too many for his domestic opponents who organized a barracks revolt, overthrew him, and shortly thereafter put him to death in a counter uprising. With the passing of the leading figure went the Costa Rican–Nicaraguan bid for a confederation.[9]

The climax of confederation futility was reached shortly thereafter, getting under way in 1862. It was sparked by another novelty in such affairs when two conflicting camps arose, each professing to be in favor of and holding discussions for, separate confederations. President Gerardo Barrios of El Salvador took the initial step of reaching an

9. Apparently Felix Belly, a French promotor of canal schemes, was one sponsor of the negotiations and urged the Central Americans to get a territorial guarantee from France, England, and Sardinia as protection against the United States. Manning, ed., *Diplomatic Correspondence, Inter-American*, IV, 112, *et passim*.

agreement on the matter with Honduras. This was not difficult to achieve for the Honduran president was one of Barrios' creations, Victoriano Castellanos. In Nicaragua they had a third ally, Máximo Jérez, opponent of his president, Martínez, but a member of the cabinet and also a Unionist.

The Barrios-Castellanos-Jérez plan was to conquer Guatemala and overthrow the Nicaraguan regime while laying the foundation for a confederation with Barrios at the head. Jérez' role was to undermine the Nicaraguan government. Defensively allied against the triumvirate were Carrera and Martínez.

At this impossible moment the Foreign Minister of Costa Rica, Francisco María Iglesias, came northward under secret instructions to sound out each of the other four governments on its attitude toward union. Iglesias carried with him his own plans which were similar to those of the late President Mora. He interviewed some important individuals with regard to his project but made little headway. At La Unión in El Salvador he discussed confederation with General Jérez, who claimed also to be a Unionist, but warned Iglesias that he was wasting his time. It was Jérez' belief that the people of Central America did not understand a federal form of government and had no interest in it. They might learn, and such a government might be formed, but only by force. On this discouraging note the two men parted company, Jérez going to see President Barrios to obtain his "force," and Iglesias resuming his journey toward Guatemala and the most important opinion of all, that of the dictator Carrera.

Twenty years in office had made the former swineherd prosperous and cautious. He gave Iglesias a grand reception and treated him in a most friendly fashion. But he said that there was no unity in his cabinet concerning Guatemala's policy on confederation, and therefore he could not act. Obviously this was a new Carrera, anxious to avoid war. Dejected, Iglesias returned to Costa Rica and found little solace there. His mission a failure, the administration found it advisable to disclaim him. Much of the cabinet and the congress turned against Iglesias, and the president publicly regarded the journey as a personal junket unconnected with the government.[10] In April, 1863, Iglesias resigned from the cabinet.

Meanwhile, Jérez failed to get Nicaragua to agree to confer with El Salvador and Honduras in regard to confederation. President Barrios gave him command of some Salvadorean troops and instructions to invade his own country. When this was attempted, the Nicaraguans remained loyal to their president and quickly routed Jérez. Barrios was no more successful at home. His machinations goaded Carrera into action, striking both at El Salvador and its ally, Honduras. Though at first failing, the Guatemalan chieftain triumphed in the end, as he usually did, and drove Barrios out of El Salvador. The war ended in October, 1863, with Conservatives, friendly to Carrera, ruling all of the republics except Costa Rica. That nation, which had participated but slightly in the struggle, granted asylum to Barrios and suffered the penalty of severed diplomatic relations from the other four.

Gerardo Barrios has been viewed by some Central Americans as a prophet of confederation, who like Morazán was destroyed by evil, conservative forces. It is hard to reconcile this with his activities. He interfered in the internal affairs of Honduras and Nicaragua, brought about a war in four of the five nations, and did nothing of a

10. Francisco María Iglesias, *Pro Patria* (San José, 1900), pp. 34-55.

peaceful or constructive nature to achieve the Central American dream. He was just another ambitious *caudillo,* and he suffered the fate of the unsuccessful ones. His death by execution, though made possible in a repugnant breach of a government's promise, brought him much undeserved praise and a measure of martyrdom.

A final word must be said about Rafael Carrera. He had, late in his political life, achieved one of his greatest aims, the consolidation of friendly, conservative regimes in each of his three neighbors. In Nicaragua it was to last for thirty years; in Honduras and El Salvador the parties were driven out of office in consequence of the Liberal upheavals in Guatemala in the 1870's. During this era there was a measure of peace and stability not prevalent before. Perhaps the Conservatives were more forceful in suppressing opposition; perhaps the Liberals were a more peaceful minority group; perhaps everyone was tired of the years of turbulence. Suffice it to say that Carrera brought order in his own land and aided its flowering in the others. This is not meant to be an apology for the man. His vicious villainies are too well documented. But that side of him has been often enough printed to the exclusion of the other.

Carrera was frequently charged with being the demon who destroyed all opportunity for confederation in the nineteenth century. It is true that he often fought—and defeated—the men who led such attempts, but it is less true that he opposed the abstract ideal of confederation. The simple substance is that he opposed the men who stood in the way of Carrera. If many of them were Unionists, it was often because that was a handy pseudonym for a military alliance against him. He had enemies among separatists, the clergy, and Conservatives as well as Unionists.

He was not the evil genius of disunion but a despotic symbol; the whipping boy of separatism.

No less than eight times in twenty-one years (1842-63) formal meetings were held to discuss the reconstruction of the Central American Republic.[11] Not one was successful. Almost exclusively these efforts were led by Liberal administrations in the three middle states of Nicaragua, Honduras, and El Salvador, so much alike and so intertwined in each other's affairs. Observing the consistently negative results, many Central American statesmen concluded that a different answer would be forthcoming if Guatemala should assume its logical position of leadership. Carrera, as the life-time ruler of the most powerful state, had done nothing for Central Americanism. This, perhaps, was his greatest crime. It remained for the next generation of Guatemalans to bring forth the apostle of union.

11. The total can be made greater if one accounts for each change in location or any extensive passage of time. Where at all possible, I have combined attempts that had continuity of action or leadership. Another construction could easily be made of some of the conferences.

Chapter VII

The Age of Justo Rufino Barrios

WITH the death of Rafael Carrera in 1865 there passed from the Guatemalan scene a thirty-year regime of clericalism, self-perpetuation, and tyranny. He had hand-picked his successor so his influence remained for another six years, as the new president, Vicente Cerna, changed few political policies and remained closely tied to the church. But Cerna lacked Carrera's energies and talents. Furthermore, the opposition had been suppressed so long that the government failed to show the needed vigor when the Liberals arose in rovolt. There were sporadic outbreaks in Guatemala in the late 1860's, and in 1869 a Liberal party candidate for president made a creditable showing. Cerna managed to obtain his re-election and continued to rule until two new leaders came to the fore. One was a deputy in the assembly, Miguel García Granados; the other was a soldier, Justo Rufino Barrios. They were soon to emerge as the leaders of a new generation of Guatemalans.

Justo Rufino Barrios was brought up in San Marcos province in the independent atmosphere of western Guatemala's uplands, known as Los Altos. He inherited from his father an *hacienda* which sprawled across the border of Soconusco province of Mexico and which provided him with a comfortable income. His biographer would have us believe that Barrios became a rebel because he was exiled for falling in love with the daughter of a local official who opposed his suit.[1] A less romantic reason was that Barrios' father was one of those Liberals who had spent time in exile for opposition to the Carrera administration. Los Altos, it should be recalled, was once briefly an independent state and, being far from the capital, was a frequent center of intrigue. Thus young Barrios grew up in an area where Liberal chiefs recruited and trained their forces.[2] His attachment to the Liberal view was a foregone conclusion.

Gaining experience in small local campaigns, Barrios soon acquired recognition from García Granados as one of the leaders of the Liberal party in its military assault upon the Cerna administration. The chance they sought came in 1871. Liberals in El Salvador, aided by Honduras, overthrew the administration that had been responsible for the death of Gerardo Barrios.[3] Taking this as a reliable cue that the conservatives in Guatemala were also weakening, Barrios and García Granados pressed their campaign against President Cerna, captured Antigua, and drove Cerna out of office and into exile.

On June 3, 1871, the Guatemalan Liberal party agreed upon the Act of Patzicia by which García Granados was named provisional president of Guatemala and plans were

1. Victor Miguel Díaz, *Barrios ante la posteridad* (Guatemala, 1935), p. 25.

2. Some of the reasons for regional discontent were revealed in the earliest decrees issued by Liberals when they reached office. The Los Altos town of Champerico was permitted to become a port of entry, and the monopolies on tobacco and liquor were weakened to the extent of permitting their importation from Chiapas. The Indian opposition to these old monopolies was a prime source of revolt. *The Overland Monthly*, XIV (February, 1875), 162.

3. Gerardo Barrios and Justo Barrios were apparently unrelated.

made for the calling of a constituent assembly. In the following year, Barrios, who was the more powerful man of the two, won the regular presidential election, and a new legend was in the making.

The triumph of the Liberal party and its leaders, Barrios and García Granados, encouraged the other Central American republics in the belief that Guatemala might now participate with them in a new pact of confederation. The first move was made by Honduras, where a portion of the press began urging a complete merger with El Salvador. Other Hondurans wanted a diet which could serve as arbitrator of regional disputes. The new role of the United States was made apparent by the suggestion of Central Americans that Charles N. Riotte, Minister to Nicaragua, serve as presiding officer of the sessions, whenever they might begin. As it turned out, Riotte could not perform the functions requested of him because the meetings were held in El Salvador, but Secretary of State Hamilton Fish gave permission to Riotte to serve and lend his support to the movement in any way possible, because "such was American policy."

The meetings were then held without Riotte in La Unión, El Salvador. Present were delegates from the host state, Honduras, Guatemala, and Costa Rica, but the last instructed its agent to agree only to restricted preliminary steps. No one represented Nicaragua, apparently for two reasons. The Costa Rican boundary question had arisen again, and Nicaragua feared her neighbor's administration which on this rare occasion was in military hands. Probably the domestic situation was more serious. Seventy-three Jesuits, just banned from Guatemala in one of Barrios' first reforms, had settled in León. Public opinion on accepting the Jesuits was strong on both sides of the question, and the government saw the wisdom of moving slowly in foreign affairs until it could be sure of unity at home.

A convention was signed on February 17, 1872, but El Salvador's President Santiago González announced his disappointment in the results. He thought that the delegates had spent too much time with impracticalities and noted that the agreements went into unnecessary detail. He deplored the absence of Nicaragua and feared that an outbreak of the old Jesuit controversy might jeopardize even the small beginning that had been made. He also delineated for the first time a growing stumbling block in confederation movements—namely, the question of foreign debts. The La Unión agreement called for an equal sharing of the burden of these responsibilities but offered no suggestion for their equalization. They ranged in amount from practically nothing in Costa Rica and El Salvador to about $25,000,000 owed by Honduras to Great Britain.

President González had found sound reasons for failure to achieve a confederation, but he overlooked one very practical problem. At the very moment that the emissaries convened at La Unión, Honduras was preparing for an expected invasion by the combined forces of Guatemala and El Salvador. It was just another of the pointless Central American skirmishes. Honduras severed diplomatic relations with the other two on March 25, 1872, and they replied with the anticipated assault. The war lasted only a matter of a few weeks and resulted in the overthrow of the Honduran administration. A government more satisfactory to Barrios was ordered into existence.

It was precisely the sort of activity that has made so much of Central American politics meaningless. González owed his office, in part at least, to the regime which he helped to destroy in Honduras a year later. Then, while the three states—Honduras, El Salvador, and Guatemala —assembled to discuss unification, they secretly planned to attack each other. Needless to say, nothing came of this attempt at confederation.

These events made it increasingly clear that a new strong man had completed his apprenticeship. Guatemala's President Barrios felt secure at home and, well entrenched there, began to assert his influence more and more in the isthmus. Until his death in 1885 he was the dominant figure in Central American affairs. His support of any project was necessary for its success; his hostility foredoomed failure. His control over El Salvador gave him the right to levy troops in Santa Ana during the Honduran war, and El Salvador followed his precept in banishing the Jesuits.

This action aroused the ire of the Guatemalan archbishop, and Barrios found it expedient to exile him as well. The clergy were forbidden to attack the government or to incite the people in sermons. A series of liberal decrees —some under the García Granados government but supported by Barrios, but most put into effect after 1873 when Barrios was inaugurated—attacked the very basis of the position of the church in Guatemala. Tithes were abolished. All religious communities were outlawed and their property was given to the schools. Convents, monasteries, even churches and orphanages were confiscated. Clerical clothing could not be worn in public. Education now became not only secular but free and obligatory. The marriage laws were changed to require a civil ceremony to precede any religious service. Cemeteries were taken from church control also and put under the municipalities. Clericals were not permitted to hold office. In short, the complete separation of church and state was accomplished.[4]

4. Holleran, *Church and State,* pp. 159-96. An outstanding anti-

Barrios was now ready to undertake the program so dear to the hearts of Central America's liberal politicians. He distributed a circular to the other four states proposing a conference in 1876 to be held at Guatemala City for the purpose of planning a federal union. On the suggested agenda were fourteen items, most of which had been debated so many times before. Barrios said that he sought a pacific means of managing international affairs—a single state organized for purposes of common defense and foreign policy. He suggested that diplomatic staffs be combined as a first step. Then, the states could work toward the establishment of one fleet, one system of roads, and other forms of communication. Crowning all of his projects was the creation of one school system, one law, and one citizenship for all of the five people.

The conference was held in Guatemala City in 1876 just as Barrios asked. After brief discussions the delegates went to their homes to "think over" the terms. There was little to be considered. As in 1872 Guatemala was preparing to go to war, this time against El Salvador. While seeking friendly cooperation from the states, Barrios concluded that he could not get it from the incumbent officials next door. So his forces invaded El Salvador, in the usual manner of aiding the party out of power, and succeeded in installing a more cooperative president, while Guatemalan troops were still present. The new chief executive, Rafael Zaldívar, reportedly promised Barrios that he would relinquish the position to the Guatemalan chieftain whenever he was ready to proclaim a union.

It was a decade for intermeddling, and the republics took strange steps to promote the old confederation idea. In January of 1876 President Tomás Guardia of Costa

---

clerical supporting Barrios in the Guatemalan Assembly was Lorenzo Montúfar, Central America's best known historian.

Rica made the unusual, if useless, suggestion that the only way to settle the constant boundary question was for Nicaragua to unite with Costa Rica to form a single state. President Pedro Chamorro replied that Nicaraguan relations with the other three Central American states were good and such a merger might be construed as a threat to them. He reminded the Costa Rican government of a similar situation that had arisen in 1863 when Gerardo Barrios first sought a union of El Salvador and Honduras, and war had broken out because the other states "misunderstood" his motives.[5] He therefore rejected Guardia's overtures.

Costa Rica then petitioned Salvadorean help to change the chief executive of Nicaragua to one "more friendly to Barrios" (of Guatemala). Barrios, on the other hand, was asking Costa Rica to expel three Jesuits from Guatemala who had just found asylum among the Ticos. Permitting the priests to reside in Costa Rica strained the ties between the two countries, concluded Barrios, and stood in the way of federation. President Guardia's attitude was that the Costa Rican tradition of religious toleration was highly cherished, and if Barrios were sincere in his aims, the presence of a few Jesuits would not act to prevent union of the two states or of all five. In the light of such minor irritations no progress toward peaceful unity was made.

Then, in 1880, Barrios was re-elected president of Guatemala by a huge majority. Assuming that he had a mandate, he resolved to renew his confederation efforts. It was necessary first to settle some unfinished business on the northern frontier. During the first presidential term of Mexico's Porfirio Díaz, a number of armed incursions took place along the Mexican-Guatemalan boundary in the Soconusco area, a region in dispute since the days of Cen-

5. *La Gaceta de Nicaragua* (Managua), March 11, 1876.

tral American independence. Both parties appear to have been guilty of violating the other's territory, but Barrios, whose home was in the disputed region, complained that the Mexicans moved the line farther south every year. Through his Minister to the United States, Lorenzo Montúfar, he, in 1882, requested the good offices of the United States to determine to whom Soconusco (as well as the rest of Chiapas province) belonged. Mexico remained adamant and would discuss only the question of the precise physical location of the boundary line. Barrios journeyed to Washington personally and, contrary to the efforts and wishes of his agent, Montúfar, reached a settlement with Mexico which ended Guatemala's claims on both Chiapas and Soconusco. It must be concluded that Barrios risked the anger of the public and a cabinet split because he was playing for higher stakes. His goal was peace with Mexico at any cost to free his hands for the conquest of Central America.

He began with diplomatic measures. In December of 1882 he announced his desire to retire and to watch the nation flourish under the measures that he had inaugurated. He protested that ill health and the burdens of office prompted the step. He gracefully accepted the assembly's refusal to accept his resignation and listened carefully to the suggestion that the creation of a confederation might relieve him of some of his duties so that he could continue in office. Barrios remained at his post.

In January he sent emissaries to the other four states to seek their support for his plan and to determine their attitudes. The labyrinth of Central American affairs is evident in that one of the agents was the foreign minister of El Salvador. While these men were on their way south,

Barrios published a letter to the Liberals of the entire isthmus to ease their minds concerning his ambitions.

In this fifteen page circular he declared that he had long felt that a union would solve the many problems that faced Central America. So far he had been too absorbed in the internal affairs of Guatemala to give any attention to the broader question, but by 1882 Guatemala had achieved such peace and prosperity that he could now take the time to perfect a plan for union. He already had reached a working agreement with President Zaldívar of El Salvador, and they were presently making a detailed arrangement for a convention. He went on to say that he would refuse the presidency of Central America if it were offered to him and vigorously denied any intention of using force on any recalcitrant state. He wrote of the weaknesses of his people, saying that they lacked respect for law and order, that they did not deliberate peacefully, that they conspired and attacked. Because of these faults he had done less for Guatemala than he had wanted. Nevertheless, he hoped that union would give all groups more representation in government, more liberty, and more guarantees for the people.

Barrios' pamphlet included his protestations of friendship for all of the Central American states, as well as his reiteration of his pledge to keep all of his operations in the open. He denied the allegation that he might intervene in the affairs of the other countries.[6]

The document was honorable and forthright. Unfortunately for Central America and the memory of Barrios, he had other arrangements.

The governments of Nicaragua and Costa Rica received the commissioners after both Honduras and El Salvador had accepted Barrios' proposals for a conference.

6. Justo Rufino Barrios, *Carta* (Guatemala, 1883).

The first two nations had scarcely announced their intentions to do the same, when, as so often happened, the people of Costa Rica determined to be heard. The press became filled with articles of opposition to the suggested meetings. Many citizens questioned the constitutionality of Costa Rica's joining a confederacy, while others deplored the dangers of being absorbed by the mixed races in the other, more heavily populated states. The legislature then refused to sanction the sending of representatives. Faced with so much opposition President Próspero Fernández decided to avoid trouble, and on May 26, 1883, he announced that he would defer action until the people regarded the discussions more favorably.

On hearing this declaration, the government of Nicaragua asked Barrios if he thought that any practical results would accrue from the convocation of the remaining four states. Barrios' negative reply was sufficient to deter Nicaragua, and no conference was held.

Was this a result that Barrios had anticipated? He had long been strengthening his military forces. It was said by foreign witnesses that he had made preparations for three or four years that assumed the failure of his diplomacy. By his own admission he had stored 50,000 new Remington rifles. Monetary resources had been accumulated. To modernize his army he had sent officers to schools in France, Germany, and the United States. One of his sons was then attending West Point. In his army were many men from Spain, France, Germany, and the United States—professionals, not just adventurers. The ranks were made up of men between the ages of eighteen and fifty under a program of compulsory military training.[7] He was ready for a bold stroke.

7. San Francisco *Evening Bulletin*, March 25, 1885.

With an eye for the dramatic, Barrios startled the Guatemalans with a piece of showmanship. On February 28, 1885, "Boccaccio" was being played at the Teatro Nacional in Guatemala City. An officer interrupted the performance, mounted the stage, and read to the delighted audience a proclamation written by the president. Witnesses do not record whether the entire six pages were read or not, but it is unlikely, for the opening words were received with tremendous enthusiasm.[8]

The simple details would have been stirring enough, even if they were not accompanied by ominous troop concentrations in the streets. The paper began with a lengthy argument for Barrios' assuming supreme military command of all of Central America, but doing this as the tool of the people. The greatest cause in the hearts of all Central Americans was that of union; it would make them one country, one people; no longer would there be wars and bloodshed. It was a time for peace and prosperity, and everyone had appealed to him as the only person who could lead Central America along the path of progress. If it meant sacrifice, he was ready. He would shed blood only if necessary, but the time had come and the step must be taken. Doubtless there were enemies, but they would be subdued. Germany and Italy had united by force of arms, and Central America could follow their steps.

The officer continued to read the argument. Barrios had stored vast quantities of ammunition, and he admitted the purchase of the Remingtons. He especially appealed to the officers and soldiers to remain loyal to the cause and their commander, assuring them that he would march

8. William E. Curtis, *The Capitals of Spanish America* (New York, 1888), pp. 104-5.

into battle at their head, if it were necessary to resort to force.

Then, impressively, the officer read to the excited audience Barrios' confident coup. As supreme military commander of Central America he called into existence a Central American union. He asked each state to send fifteen delegates, popularly elected, to meet in Guatemala City on May 1 to draw up a form of government and to arrange for the election of a president and the establishment of a capital city. Anyone who opposed these steps would be considered a traitor to the republic. No treaties, negotiations, loans, or territorial adjustments made by any Central American state after that date would be recognized.

Barrios had even planned a banner for the republic. On a field of three horizontal stripes, two blue, the center one white, there was a coat of arms made up of a column on which perched a *quetzal* (Guatemala's national bird). Its motto read "Libertad y Unión, 15 Sept. 1821-28 Feb. 1885," the date of independence and the date of the assumption of military command by President Barrios. The flag was reminiscent of the old cry of "Dios, Unión y Libertad" of sixty years before, but Barrios had withdrawn *Dios*.

The same message was telegraphed to the other four states, and Barrios awaited the replies while his troops poured into the city. On March 5 the Guatemalan Assembly unanimously approved the program of the president. Honduras accepted the plan on March 7. Nicaragua opposed the scheme, began calling up troops, and took steps to form an alliance with other reluctant states. Costa Rica's president announced that his people would resist to the last man. But it was his puppet in El Salvador who surprised and disappointed Barrios. Zaldívar not only telegraphed to Costa Rica's government asking for advice, but he told Barrios that he would call congress into session and consider the implications of the proclamation. The supreme commander became enraged and warned Zaldívar that he could not tolerate any delay.

To the reader today it appears that the one man was as guilty of duplicity as the other, but Zaldívar had a unique advantage. The only Central American cable that connected with the outside world had its terminal in La Libertad, El Salvador. When Barrios attempted to inform Europe and North America of his good and honorable intentions, as well as his promises to resign when the union was consummated, his former friend had the messages garbled so that a distorted version reached the world.

In any case Barrios would have received little foreign support. His old enemy, Porfirio Díaz, was back as president of Mexico and only too willing to prevent the rise of Guatemalan prestige and power. Díaz promptly offered to help Nicaragua and Costa Rica, and he sent troops into Chiapas to mobilize along the border. The policy of the United States was clear and specific. Secretary of State Thomas F. Bayard announced that his country favored a voluntary combination of the states but that "the United States would not countenance the use of force by one to coerce the others."[9] To protect American citizens and their property from the expected war, five warships were sent to the Caribbean coast of Central America, and three others were held in readiness at New Orleans.

Whether they were to intervene and land troops, if needed, is not so clear. Secretary of State Bayard was reported to have "smiled" in answer to a newspaperman's question as to the purpose of the fleet movements. Aside from protecting property of Americans, there was also

9. Bayard to Henry C. Hall, March 10, 1885, *Foreign Relations of the United States, 1885*, p. 81.

legitimate need of the fleet to help remove a number of destitute laborers from Guatemala's east coast. The workers had drifted down from the United States in search of fortune and had found nothing but bad luck. There were several hundred of them; they were troublesome to Guatemala and likely to become more so with war commencing. For this reason an American consul had asked for a ship to send the men home at almost the same moment that a show of force in the Caribbean might frighten Barrios into peace.

That general had some 15,000 men poised to attack El Salvador, but he apparently preferred to let the enemy take the initiative—and the blame. Meanwhile, United States Minister to Guatemala, Henry C. Hall, worked hard to avert war. He talked with many of the leaders in both states in trying to promote peace. He visited San Salvador and reported to Washington that the public there was incensed with Barrios. He, furthermore, observed that the Liberal leader was losing support at home. He suggested that if the State Department could get Díaz to discontinue his threats, Barrios, with little loss of honor, might feel that he could back down.

But it was getting late. José Durán was sent by Costa Rica to Nicaragua and El Salvador in a successful effort to create a defensive alliance among the three. It went into effect March 22, under the leadership of Zaldívar, and was to last until the overthrow of Barrios.[10] The Costa Rican and Nicaraguan forces were to be used primarily to neutralize Honduras where a number of Guatemalan detachments were located, while El Salvador under Zaldívar could concentrate complete attention on Barrios.

Ultimately Barrios must have concluded that time was against him, and he precipitated the war by invading El

10. Costa Rica, Secretario de Estado, *Informes del Secretario de Estado al Congreso Constitucional*, 1885 (San José, 1885).

Salvador. The first battle, on March 31, 1885, at El Coco, El Salvador, was a victory for Barrios, but two days later the Supreme Military Commander of Central America was stopped at the little town of Chalchuapa, and in an assault upon its defenses Barrios was killed. Few Central American campaigns ceased more suddenly. The Guatemalan troops broke and fled almost instantly, and the war was over. The diplomatic corps quickly arranged for an armistice which was accepted and respected. The Assembly of Guatemala immediately revoked Barrios' ambitious decrees of February 28. His dream was finished.

There was a ludicrous anticlimax. Scarcely a week after the armistice, President Zaldívar called for a renewed union attempt at Santa Tecla, El Salvador, to meet on May 15, at which time he would resign his position, presumably to show his good will toward the other states. Weak and impoverished Honduras, as was its custom, agreed to the proposal. Costa Rica's president said that he lacked authority to send delegates to Santa Tecla, and Guatemala's government felt that it was too soon after the last debacle to try again. Nicaragua declined with contempt, saying that its troops were not even home yet from the last "opportunity" of this sort and adding that its relations with Guatemala would remain strained until some settlement was made as a result of the late war. The meeting was not held.

The reader might well be puzzled over the collapse of Barrios' presumably highly trained army. It seems likely that these troops succumbed to some of Zaldívar's "cable propaganda" which was designed to lead them to expect prompt foreign intervention. Barrios' sudden death in combat was a major attack on the Guatemalan morale, and it furthermore appears that most of the "trained troops" were reluctant conscripts who were only too eager to accept defeat as a reason for going home.

The good works of Justo Rufino Barrios should not be lost in the noise of his attempt to confederate Central America by force. He introduced railways, telegraphs, highways, schools, and hospitals in an astonishingly brief period of time. He brought modernization and progress to remote regions of his land. He eliminated the secular control of the church over the state. His title of Reformer was well earned, and he moved Guatemala years ahead of its neighbors. Yet he was a dictator. He brooked no opposition, and he was cruel. He may have wanted to extend to all of Central America the progress which he had brought to Guatemala, but it was to be by the use of force, and this would have meant that the evils, too, would have been exported. It has been said that his real purpose was to acquire Nicaragua before a canal treaty could be concluded so that he might gain the expected revenues. This theory would help to account for his apparent haste, since such a treaty was then pending in the Senate of the United States. It helps to explain Barrios' actions, but it does not justify them. He was a man on horseback, and he lived and perished by the sword. It was well that his account could be balanced that day at Chalchuapa and not after he had put all of the isthmus to flames.

As if Barrios had never lived, the Central American statesmen resumed their convening proclivities. Honduras, El Salvador, and Guatemala agreed upon an exploratory treaty for union discussions on September 12, 1885. Incomplete and unsatisfactory to most of the leaders of the states, it at least indicated a quick revival of optimism.[11]

11. The successes were too minor to be mentioned here. El Salvador, *Anuario diplomático del Salvodar* (San Salvador, 1885), pp. 52-59.

Barrios' Liberal party continued in office after his death, and a virtually unbroken string of Liberals served as president until the 1940's. Hence it is not surprising that Guatemala played a much more positive role in confederation movements than it had in the Carrera era preceding. Frequently, in fact, Guatemala began to take the initiative in peaceful steps in the manner that its size, population, and influence might suggest.

So it was in 1887. Costa Rica and Nicaragua interposed objections to the treaty of 1885, and in an attempt to satisfy them, Guatemala's new president, Manuel Lisandro Barrillas, invited all of the governments to accredit delegates to Guatemala with their own proposals. The response was complete, and on January 20, 1887, the men assembled in that city.

The chief significance of the resulting treaty was that it was the first occasion since 1839 on which all five states actually signed a pact dedicated to union. There were in attendance the four Central American ministers to Guatemala as well as Fernando Cruz, foreign minister of the host state. When the assembly adjourned on February 16, thirty-two articles had been agreed upon. Seven were of concern to our story. The adoption of arbitration was obligatory in the event that other peaceful means failed to settle disputes arising between states. A list of acceptable arbitrators was appended to this provision, the list including most of the major powers of the world. There was to be no interference in each other's internal affairs. Because the states considered themselves "disintegrated members of a single political body," all citizens would have the same rights no matter in which republic they might be residing. Beginning on September 15, 1890 (September 15 was always a magic date for Unionists), reciprocal free trade would go into effect among the five states. The only exceptions were to be those products taxed in domestic trade. It was agreed that two months hence there would be another conference to attempt to unify their legal codes. Article 27 required that the states "labor practically and pacifically" for a union, and it was decided that a conference should be held in San Salvador in 1890 for that purpose. The treaty was ratified unconditionally by Guatemala, Honduras, and Costa Rica. El Salvador accepted it with some reservations, while the Conservative government in Nicaragua took no action.

After such a smooth beginning it was decided to hasten the San Salvador congress, so a delegate from each of the five states met in that city on October 15, 1889. Later moving to Managua, Nicaragua, they completed and signed their work on November 7. They declared that they had recreated the Republic of Central America; there was no change in domestic affairs, and the states remained autonomous. For foreign matters the states were to be united under a supreme executive who would be one of the five presidents, selected by lot and holding this office for one year only. He would be aided by a body of five other men —one being named by each president for a one year term also. A majority of this group was required to confirm all acts of the supreme executive. He was chief mediator among the five states, but he had no recourse to the use of force. The capital was to rotate so that it would always be in the country headed by the man then acting as supreme executive. This pact was looked upon as provisional —perhaps for as much as ten years—with the purpose of accomplishing complete integration of the states into a single government during that period. It was to go into effect on September 15, 1890.[12]

12. Tercer Congreso Centro-Americano, *Pacto de unión provisional* (Managua, 1889).

The greatest wisdom in this document was that it, more than any of its predecessors, recognized the necessity for the gradual application of the principles that the framers all professed to believe in.

El Salvador had ratified this agreement, and Costa Rica's congress was debating it, when in June, 1890, President Francisco Menéndez of El Salvador died suddenly under unusual circumstances which were kept secret from the public. Then, instead of the vice president, a military dictatorship under General Carlos Ezeta assumed control of the nation. The Menéndez government was considered popular and enlightened, and its overthrow brought sharp repercussions throughout Central America.

The Costa Rican congress stopped its hearings on confederation on the grounds that the times were not "propitious."[13] Guatemala would not recognize the legitimacy of the Ezeta government, and both states mobilized troops. A brief and inconclusive war was fought, and in the end the story was the same as usual. There were no lasting results.

Another ineffectual attempt to confederate was made in San Salvador, this time in 1892. The tentative government agreed upon was called the Diet of Central America and included all but Costa Rica. It seems never to have functioned and passed out of existence in 1893 because of Honduran claims that Nicaragua was permitting exiles to plan a revolt within the latter's boundaries.

With these almost continuous attempts being made it would seem logical that one of them should succeed, if only for a few years. Some of the states finally did achieve a measure of concerted action, and though its duration

13. Ezequiel Gutiérrez, President of Congress, to government of Costa Rica, ANCR, No. 3708.

was brief, the new confederacy had the distinction of being recognized abroad. This story began in Nicaragua.

Between 1863 and 1893 Nicaragua was regularly governed by administrations that were predominantly Conservative, and as a consequence, the state had played a very minor part in Unionist proceedings. In 1893 the Conversatives quarrelled among themselves over the matter of dividing the patronage between Granada and León. One result was that the party was sufficiently weakened to be overthrown. A young Liberal, José Santos Zelaya, emerged as president and perhaps the most important man in Central America. There is a striking resemblance between his administration which followed and that of Barrios in Guatemala. They were both dictators for about fifteen years; they brought material progress and liberal reforms; they were ruthless and left chaos behind them; and what is of chief significance to the confederation story, they constantly meddled in the affairs of the other states in the name of Central American union.

Zelaya soon began a campaign which resulted in a Central American republic even though it was not his immediate goal at the time. Determined to put an end to the British protectorate over the Mosquito preserve, he used a war with Honduras as a pretext for occupying the more important points and seizing the powerless Mosquito government for Nicaragua. The amorphous region, so long claimed by Great Britain, was managed locally by a combination of British and American commercial interests and the British consul. In the course of his military maneuvers Zelaya declared martial law and expelled the consul. There resulted much discussion and heated diplomatic negotiation, with Americans, English, and Nicaraguans threatening the use of force. In time, Nicaraguan suzerainty was recognized over the Mosquito territory, as it is today. However, the British government demanded $15,000 indemnity for the action against the consul and enforced its demands by the occupation of the port of Corinto. The United States intervened, payment was promised within fifteen days, and the British withdrew.[14] They left behind a large measure of ill will and a determination among many Central Americans that they should strengthen themselves to prevent such actions in the future by tying again the old knots of brotherhood.

To this end, President Policarpo Bonilla of Honduras, Zelaya's close friend and an ardent Unionist, sent out invitations in 1895 for a conference of the chief executives to be held at Amapala. The president of Guatemala declined to attend, as did Costa Rica's, so only Bonilla, Zelaya, and El Salvador's Rafael Antonio Gutiérrez were present.[15] By June 20 they had achieved harmony and had signed the Pact of Amapala. This treaty was ratified quickly by each state and was sent to Guatemala and Costa Rica which were urged to adhere also.

The three executives settled upon seventeen articles which created a very loose type of confederation. It was to be called the República Mayor, or Greater Republic of Central America, but with the voluntary accession of the two reluctant states, the name would be changed to the República de Centro América. The flag and coat of arms of the old republic were used. The three states did not renounce their independence and autonomy in internal matters, and their constitutions remained in force so long as they were not contradictory to the pact.

14. Laudelino Moreno, *Historia de las relaciones interestatuales de Centroamérica* (Madrid, 1928), p. 129. Moreno says 15,000 pesos; the United States consul reported the amount as 15,000 *pounds. Consular Reports,* 1895, LXIX, 387.

15. Aro Sanso, *Policarpo Bonilla* (Mexico, 1936), p. 307.

For the administration of the *república,* a diet composed of one member and an alternate was named by the legislature of each state for three-year periods. Decisions would be made by a majority of the diet, and one member would be selected annually for negotiations with other powers. The government would reside each year in a different city to be selected by lot from among the existing state capitals. The *república* was primarily charged with the conduct of foreign affairs, but provisionally any treaties made would be ratified by the individual states until a general assembly was created.

This assembly would come into existence within three years and would be composed of twenty members from each state chosen by their respective legislatures. The diet held its first meeting on schedule, September 15, 1896, the seventy-fifth anniversary of independence. By lot the members determined that in the future they would meet in San Salvador, Managua, and Tegucigalpa in that order. The diet then drew up its own internal rules, one of which called for the abolition of the various foreign offices, an act consummated in surprisingly quick fashion. Costa Rica almost immediately recognized the new government. José Dolores Rodríguez was named Envoy Extraordinary and Minister Plenipotentiary to the United States, and on December 24, 1896, was received by President Grover Cleveland.

For the first time in over fifty years a single individual was accepted as the foreign representative of a group of the Central American states. Cleveland modified his recognition, however, by reminding Rodríguez that the action in no wise affected the existing responsibilities of the separate states. It should be noted in passing that the president made no changes in diplomatic assignments because of the new government. His successor, William McKinley, decided that the three states constituted an association, not a federation possessing central powers of administration and government. For that reason McKinley also made no changes in designations but left one minister accredited to Nicaragua, El Salvador, and Costa Rica and another to Honduras and Guatemala.[16]

In some matters, at least, the Greater Republic of Central America was able to function as a unit. Only one diplomat, Rodríguez, represented the three peoples in Washington, and he acted for Nicaragua's interests in carrying out the terms of a Cleveland award concerning the omnipresent Costa Rican boundary controversy. Interestingly, the Costa Rican government dealt with Rodríguez but insisted that he was the agent of Nicaragua, not the Greater Republic.

The boundary discussions and an alliance between Costa Rica and Guatemala prompted by fear of the Greater Republic, brought increasing agitation to include those two states in the diet. Costa Rica's foreign minister, in what was by now a typical delaying tactic, declared that his government wanted to join but thought that it should wait awhile rather than deluge the new federation with additional problems. He said that the three states would have enough complications for some time without adding Costa Rica's.

Nevertheless, a Costa Rican delegate was sent to a meeting in Guatemala City in 1897 to discuss proposals for adding the two reluctant states to the larger republic. A pact was completed to which Guatemala immediately adhered. As a special inducement to Costa Rica, the presidency was offered to her chief executive, Rafael Iglesias. The Tico government then announced that it would not

16. Richardson, ed., *Messages and Papers of the Presidents*, X, 178-79.

stand in the way of complete Central American union, and Iglesias directed his delegate to accept for Costa Rica, subject to a referendum.[17]

The question of complete Central American federation was now put squarely before the citizens of Costa Rica. As so often before the Tico press jumped enthusiastically into the fray. Solidly they agreed that this was but another attack on the nation's sovereignty. They accepted the fact that union was desirable and perhaps inevitable, but they felt that conditions in all five countries were so bad that, as one said, they could not possibly combine into one "good" power. The facts were that both Nicaragua and Honduras were harassed with civil strife, Costa Rica was caught up in a number of municipal scandals, and Guatemala, besides being insolvent, was under a dictatorship which just at that time had suppressed the newspapers. The consensus of the Costa Rican press was that joining the other four states would make Costa Rica worse off and that President Iglesias had succumbed to the flattery of the other chief executives.

The opinion of the Costa Rican press coincided with that of the congress, and when that body convened, it decisively refused to ratify the action taken in Guatemala by the president's representative. A similar decision was reached in Guatemala's congress.

The three states of the Greater Republic had been linked only on a provisional basis, and it was now believed to be the time to strengthen the republic by a permanent constitution. For this purpose a constituent assembly met at Managua in June of 1898, and on August 27 it completed its labors. The name of the young republic was changed to Los Estados Unidos de Centro América. Although full machinery of government—a federal legisla-

17. *La Prensa Libre* (San José), June 20, 1897.

ture, executive, and judiciary—was provided, the individual states continued loath to give up their individual authority. El Salvador exhibited much distrust of the close relationship between the other two presidents, Zelaya and Bonilla. The feeling was accentuated when, according to law, the capital was moved to Managua. President Gutiérrez also had cause for concern at home. Some of the public was cool toward the federal idea and a candidate for the presidency, General Tomás Regalado, announced his intention to destroy the new Estados Unidos. His claim was that since the constitution was not submitted to the people or their directly elected delegates, it lacked public sanction and was illegal.[18]

Meanwhile, the permanent constitution went into effect as of November 1, 1898, and a federal executive council sat at Amapala for the election of a president and a federal congress. A few days later General Regalado, who by now had control of most of the Salvadorean army, raised his banner in a barracks revolt. Succeeding quickly, he took over the government and announced its separation from the confederacy as of November 13. The executive council attempted to act according to the constitution and called upon the troops to suppress the revolt. This placed the issue directly in the hands of the various commanding officers. In El Salvador most of them remained loyal to Regalado, while in the other two states no vigor was apparent in carrying out the orders of the council.

With this exhibition of impotence the leaders of the United States of Central America decided that its existence had ended, and on November 30 notification was sent to the individual states of the dissolution "because of grave

18. William Merry to John Hay, December 10, 1898, *Foreign Relations of the United States, 1898,* p. 173.

events in El Salvador."[19] Thereupon Nicaragua and Honduras reassumed their full sovereignty.

Why had this ambitious effort toward confederation failed after so much enthusiasm for success? The machinery was adequate. The states were protected by law, and in theory no citizens' rights were endangered. The federal authorities had certain specific powers, and these included the concentration of military authority exclusively in its hands. A separate federal district was being organized. In short the constitution of 1898 endeavored to correct the shortcomings of the charter of 1824.

What went wrong? It was easy to blame Regalado. As Herrarte wrote, "In reality, Regalado's despicable treason covered with ridicule and shame the noble ideal of Central American union."[20] But there will always be Regalados seeking opportunities. Some writers feel that the absence of Guatemala and Costa Rica was not a serious problem and that they would have soon joined a successful union. In my opinion there can be no successful union *without* those two states. Their absence and, in particular, the public debate concerning joining which took place in Costa Rica indicated all too clearly that a huge segment of the population was very cool toward federation.

Another theory for the failure which was just beginning to be postulated was that all of the federations attempted had no impact on the people, that they were mere bureacratic changes which did not weaken localism one whit. Suggestions for overcoming this weakness were soon made. This is the story of Salvador Mendieta, who will be treated more thoroughly in Chapter IX.

19. Joaquín Sansón, Secretary of Federal Executive Council, to President of Costa Rica, November 30, 1898, Ministerio de Relaciones Extranjeros de Costa Rica, 1899.
20. Herrarte, *La Unión*, p. 236.

Opportunism, apathy, fear of loss of liberty, localism—the reader can take his choice. Another Central American attempt at confederation had failed.

Another thirty years of Central American history had elapsed. Another generation had spent its energies in futile and pathetic talks, meetings, conferences, and conventions. Localism still had its way. Wars continued unabated, but they were rarely of significance. Boundaries were not changed by them; indemnities were not paid; the struggles settled few issues; and only rarely were they dignified by being concluded with treaties. It was apparent that Central American confederation, whatever its other attributes, would not of itself assure peace. The social, political, and economic problems which fostered the continual strife were not solved by drawing up constitutions. A feeling was growing that peace must come first, before federation could have any serious meaning. It was toward this end that the next two decades were to be devoted.

Chapter VIII

The United States and
Federation through Peace

FROM the beginning of the twentieth century two new
trends became evident in Central American confederation movements. They were both of signal importance
and rather quickly the two complemented each other. The
first of these was the clear-cut entrance of the United
States into the internal affairs of the five nations, and the
second of the trends was the increasing emphasis upon
peace machinery as a prerequisite to confederation. Within
a very few years after 1900 the United States arrogated
the peace treaty program, aided Central America in achieving a temporary measure of cooperation, and then summarily destroyed the entire machinery by refusing to respect the obligations that the treaties imposed.

The United States, occupied for more than a hundred years by territorial and then industrial expansion,
gave Central America but scant thought throughout most
of the nineteenth century. Only on the occasion of some
unusual circumstances did North America pay her Central American neighbors much attention. In 1825 the
United States extended diplomatic recognition to the federal republic, the first non-Latin American state to take

that step. In the next year a treaty of commerce and friendship between the two nations was negotiated. Central Americans generally looked upon the United States as a sympathetic friend. El Salvador's futile attempt to annex itself to the United States was recounted in Chapter III, as was the interest of the Central Americans in having the United States represented at the Panama Congress. The similarities in political structure, probably deliberately made by the Central Americans, were recognized by North American government officials as a form of sincere flattery and reason for a sort of vested interest in the younger state. In 1825, fearful of Spain, Central America's cabinet minister, Marcial Zebadúa, made reference to the new Monroe Doctrine in a speech to the federal congress. Said Zebadúa, "This policy, (Monroe's), lets the Executive Power hope that we shall find in the descendents of Washington the most decided cooperation in case our independence is menaced by the European powers."[1]

That the United States was genuinely interested in Central America, yet at the same time had no intention of meddling, is evident in the elaborate instructions of Andrew Jackson's secretary of state, Edward Livingston, to our chargé d'affaires in 1831. This man, William Jeffers, never reached Central America, but the State Department for several years continued to use the same directive to subsequent emissaries. The gist of the order was that the two federations had much in common; they both struggled for the cause of republicanism everywhere, while their economies should easily be complementary. Jeffers and his successors were advised to stay out of domestic affairs and show nothing but understanding toward the Central American problems. They were not to assume any superiority for the United States, nor were they to seek any especial

1. Chamorro, *Historia*, p. 137.

advantages. Temporarily the Central American union had been broken, but at the time that he wrote, Livingston believed that conditions were better. It was the duty of the chargé to reiterate the necessity of union and the advantages of the federative type of government.[2]

Little advantage was taken of this early feeling of sympathy and friendship. Certainly the United States did not abuse its position in the 1820's and 1830's. Relations can be described as minor, perhaps trivial, for many years. Some disenchantment with Central America emerged when John Lloyd Stephens reported to Washington his complete failure to find a Central American government in 1839.[3]

Active interest on the part of the United States began about 1848, partly from the discovery of California gold and partly from a sudden fear that British influence was going too far on the isthmus. It is also not pure coincidence that the interest became substantial during the administration of President James K. Polk, a period of unbridled manifest destiny for the American people. Much of this activity was merely designed to thwart Britain's machinations which were sketched in Chapter V and need not be repeated here.

When Great Britain occupied San Juan del Norte in Nicaragua during February of 1848, President Polk and Secretary of State James Buchanan agreed that it was the duty of the United States to reunite the five Central American nations for defense against the English.[4] Buchanan, in fact, said later that only Polk's determination to resist European colonization prevented the parcelling up of all of Central America.

2. Edward Livingston to William Jeffers, July 20, 1831, Manning, ed., *Diplomatic Correspondence, Inter-American*, III, 3.
3. See Chapter IV.
4. John Bassett Moore, ed., *The Works of James Buchanan* (Philadelphia, 1909), VIII, 377.

To implement this resolve, Polk sent a new chargé to Guatemala, Elijah Hise, with secret instructions to do all in his power to develop the political stability of the states by encouraging a strong federation. The alternative, he was told, was revolution and ruin, inviting European encroachments and jeopardizing the "American system." He was instructed to learn and report all that he could concerning the advances of the British and the nature of the Mosquito Indians' "kingdom."

As so often happened in the early diplomatic history of the United States, accident and illness contravened. It took Hise six months to reach Guatemala, and during this period British influence increased. When he arrived, Hise saw the significance of obtaining transit agreements and, left largely on his own by slow communications, succeeded in negotiating a treaty with Nicaragua in June, 1849. This protocol granted to the United States or its citizens the perpetual right of way across Nicaragua and permitted the fortification of the route, while the United States pledged itself to protect Nicaraguan territory. The treaty was never ratified. Before the document or any other correspondence from Hise reached Washington, a change in administration took place, and the new president, Zachary Taylor, recalled Hise and sent in his stead Ephraim G. Squier.

The United States now had as its representative a man formed from the same matrix as Frederick Chatfield. Belligerent, tactless, and self-reliant, both were unafraid of man or consequence, and they ran at each other head-on. Each considered the other as nothing less than the enemy to be frustrated and repulsed by any means. For example, Squier *bought* on his own initiative the strategically important island of Tigre from Honduras for the United States; a week later Chatfield captured it from the Hondurans still there, by means of a cannon mounted on a small boat.[5] Neither man's methods were calculated to settle the troubled Central American waters. Each came close to establishing protectorates over one or more Central American state. Although personally not liked in Costa Rica, Chatfield was able to disperse considerable British influence over that state, as to a lesser degree he had succeeded doing in Guatemala. Lacking Chatfield's tenure, Squier worked diligently to place the other states in the American sphere of influence. He was especially successful in Honduras and Nicaragua in promoting anti-British feeling.

The culmination of the contention was the Clayton-Bulwer Treaty of 1850, which, while by no means settling American and British rivalry in Central America, ended the danger of war and ultimately brought about the decline of Britain's importance in the area.

Growing American interest is evident in the Walker episode of the 1850's, described in Chapter VI. These activities bore no official sanction from the United States and, while annoying and probably frightening to the Central Americans, should not be looked upon as elements in the new Central American policy of the United States.

This policy became more apparent under the direction of Secretary of State Hamilton Fish. No longer concerned with the intrigues of Great Britain, the State Department was free to design a program of bilateral benefit for the first time. Fish considered some form of Central American union to be highly desirable and openly urged it throughout his term of office. To implement the proposal, former Confederate general George Williamson was appointed Minister to Central America in 1873 just as it was be-

5. *Executive Documents of the Senate of the United States,* 31st Cong. 2nd sess., no. 43, p. 6. Both acts were disavowed by the respective governments.

coming apparent that the Convention of La Unión had failed. Fish felt that the United States could be more helpful in promoting confederation if one man, rather than five, represented United States' interests.

Fish told Williamson that he had reason to believe that certain European powers were more or less instrumental in bringing about the dissolution of the Central American confederation in 1839 for purposes of their own. He realized that these actions were probably less important than certain natural forces that pulled upon the states. It was to be United States' policy to encourage the Central Americans' progress; a federal government, properly framed and administered, would surely increase the prosperity and the happiness of the five states. He therefore directed Williamson to make it his chief duty to bring about a reunion as carefully and discreetly as he could.[6]

Following his instructions Williamson spent considerable time and energy in seeking out opinions and encouraging united action by the small republics. He reached the conclusion that everyone wanted a Central American confederation except the office-holders. These people, he said invariably called such a movement "desirable, but impractical because of jealousies, absence of communications and the difference in debt structure." He felt that the three northernmost states might be able to ally but that Costa Rican interests tended toward isolation or incorporation with Colombia.[7] He also observed that settlement of the Nicaraguan–Costa Rican boundary dispute was a requirement for constructive action.

6. Fish to Williamson, June 17, 1873, *Records of the Department of State, Diplomatic Instructions, American States,* Vol. 17, National Archives of the United States.

7. Williamson to Fish, September 14, 1873, *Foreign Relations of the United States, 1874,* p. 96. Was there deliberate irony in sending a former Confederate general to help unify the Central American states?

Williamson discussed the issue of confederation with each president, even taking the long trip to Puntarenas for a brief visit with Costa Rica's Tomás Guardia. Williamson put his hopes in a conference to be attended by all five of the presidents, and in this respect he had made a correct analysis. Unless a Central American president was in favor of an agreement, it would not be approved. Too readily had these men found occasion to repudiate the actions of their representatives. Williamson's scheme of using the chief executives as the delegates would smoke them out and force them to take public stands on the issue.

He received acceptances from all of the presidents except Nicaragua's Vicente Quadra, who claimed that the constitution of his state prohibited him from going beyond its borders. This rather weak excuse destroyed the prospect of a meeting, and as time went by, Williamson's enthusiasm was worn down. After six months of fruitless talks he summarized for Secretary Fish his new attitude toward the Central American problem. He wrote in effect:

1. The memory of bloody struggles in the past made friendships and alliances difficult in the present.

2. The old federal debt which had been apportioned among the states had been met in various ways that encouraged disunion. Some had repudiated their obligations with the resultant harm to their credit. Others had paid off at rates which created very heavy tax burdens.

3. The extent of local prejudices was "unimaginable."

4. Each state considered itself superior to all of the others.

5. There was much less homogeneity in race among the people than generally believed.

6. He expected to find identity of interests—all of the

states were agricultural, for instance—but he failed to find such feeling.

7. No important leader since Cabañas had made federation an issue. (Williamson was on weak ground here.)

8. The absence of roads prevented cooperation. The only people that Central Americans ever saw from a neighboring state were peddlers and soldiers. It was quicker and easier to travel from New York to Constantinople and return than from Guatemala City to San José, Costa Rica, by land. Communications between governments was made more difficult by the fact that all of the capitals were in the interior; only San Salvador and Guatemala City were connected by telegraph, and that line had just been completed when Williamson wrote.

9. Costa Rica's traditional policy was one of isolation, and it was unlikely to join with any of the other countries.

Williamson went on to say that the foreign danger had lessened for Central America. He had no information that any outside power had recently tried to oppose a union, although while the French were in Mexico they were rumored to have encouraged Carrera to resist it.[8] Most foreigners seemed to anticipate the ultimate acquisition of all of Central America by the United States. Disillusioned and discouraged, Williamson concluded that he could foresee no union for many years to come and perhaps never.[9]

This judgement is a serious indictment of the confederation movement. The North American diplomat (and one must remember that he was a former Confederate) went to Central America not only with instructions to encourage cooperation but with the firm belief that it would

8. Gerardo Barrios had held similar views. Gerardo Barrios, *Manifiesto de Gerardo Barrios* (New York, 1864), pp. 33, 42.

9. Williamson to Fish, June 24, 1874, *Foreign Relations of the United States, 1874,* pp. 172-74.

be good for the five peoples. His preliminary survey of opinion led him to believe that the vast majority of Central Americans wanted to unite. Yet, even with the prestige of the United States behind him, and not faced by any unusual Central American crisis, General Williamson failed completely and inferred that similar promoters would obtain the same result. The reasons that he offered for the lack of success were enlightening, for most of the reasons continue to be applicable today. Material improvements are made, but attitudes and memories endure.

Finally, Williamson was correct when he observed that there was no foreign opposition to the confederation. Chatfield had been gone for twenty years. Britain's hegemony had been on the decline since the Clayton-Bulwer Treaty. The United States was obviously gaining in significance but as yet was not supremely important in Central America. If it had influence at all, it was on the side of Central Americanism at this date.

Thus far United States activity in Central American affairs was little more than the expression of sympathy. In the same light one can view the diplomatic recognition extended by President Cleveland to the Greater Republic of Central America in 1896. Real participation, or intervention as the Latin Americans came to call it, arrived with the twentieth century as United States' canal interests crystallized and its investments magnified.

The confederation attempt that brought the United States fully onto the stage was characteristically introduced by a Liberal dictator, Nicaragua's ambitious José Santos Zelaya. In the year 1902 Zelaya suggested that the other presidents join him at the port of Corinto to take up measures for the settlement of their international disputes. Manuel Estrada Cabrera, president of Guatemala and

Zelaya's chief rival for domination of Central America, re-fused to come. Nevertheless the other four chief executives met and agreed upon a treaty which was basic to the next twenty years of their states' relations. The pact was signed to "erase the resentments of past differences." The second article proclaimed the principle of obligatory arbitration, the contracting parties agreeing to submit their difficulties to a Central American tribunal made up of one arbitrator and a substitute from each state for one-year terms. These men might be re-elected. They could not serve as members of the tribunal in cases to which their own nations were a party. In the event of an evenly split decision one of the substitutes would be called upon to cast the determin-ing vote. The court could not act upon boundary disputes. These must be placed before "foreign arbitrators of Amer-ican nationality." This was a wise move, for it cleared the tribunal's docket of time-consuming and long-standing issues. Petitioned by the others, Guatemala's government announced that it agreed in principle with the treaty but never signed it.

The Tribunal of Central American Arbitration was to commence its sessions on September 15, 1902, but the members did not convene until October 2, in the city of San José, Costa Rica. The jurists nominated to these im-portant posts were Octavio Béeche of Costa Rica, and first president of the court, Salvador Gallegos of El Salvador, José Leonard of Honduras, and Julián Irías of Nicaragua.[10]

The tribunal failed to achieve any distinction for want of business, but it was a beginning and was used as the basis of more important negotiations.

The next year a similar but less ambitious pact was

10. Costa Rica, Ministerio de Relaciones Extranjeras, *Informes del Secretario de Estado al Congreso Constitucional, 1903* (San José, 1903).

signed at San Salvador. This agreement obtained Guatemala's endorsement but lost Costa Rica's. The Corinto Pact was reapproved, compulsory arbitration was sustained, and nonintervention in each other's domestic affairs was demanded. Little was accomplished that had not already been achieved.

An equally unnecessary confirmation was made in 1904, again at Corinto. The governments of the four northern states agreed upon four more articles assuring each other of their friendly intentions, and they promised to provide military support for one another whenever peace was endangered.

But still there was no peace. President Manuel Bonilla had acquired his Honduran office by revolution, and Zelaya interfered in that state at will. There were believed to be exiles in several states busily preparing for the overthrow of Estrada Cabrera. By 1904 President Theodore Roosevelt became concerned with the unrest in the entire Caribbean area, considering it as endangering American interests in general and the canal works in particular. He expressed himself in his annual message that December in a caveat that was to become known as the Roosevelt Corollary to the Monroe Doctrine. It was to the effect that chronic wrong-doing might in time require intervention by some civilized nation, and in the Western Hemisphere, because of the Monroe Doctrine, the United States might find itself forced into that role.

By March of 1906 the corollary was put to test. Armed *emigrados* converged upon Guatemala from each of the four neighboring states. Their purpose was the overthrow of Estrada Cabrera and his replacement with Manuel Lisandro Barillas, the former president. Guatemalan troops were successful in repulsing the invaders, and, blaming Honduras and El Salvador in particular for permitting the attacks, Estrada Cabrera mounted an offense against them. The United States Minister to Guatemala made several efforts to mediate the dispute but without success. As Guatemala was not a signatory, the Corinto Pact was inoperative and untested.

By July the skirmishes had ripened into war. Salvadorean casualties reached the thousands, and the commanding general, former President Tomás Regalado, was killed. Roosevelt now took personal charge of peace negotiations and telegraphed the governments of Guatemala and El Salvador urging prompt and peaceful settlement. With the Mexican government of Porfirio Díaz concurring, he sent the warship *Marblehead* to Central American waters in order that the United States might present her good offices to conclude the war.

After a great deal of discussion regarding each other's intentions, commissioners for the three belligerents met on July 20, 1906, on board the *Marblehead* off the coast of El Salvador. Also in attendance were the American and Mexican ministers to Central America and observers from Costa Rica and Nicaragua. In the course of that one day a treaty was drawn up and temporary peace was installed.[11] The treaty called for disarmament within eight days and immediate cessation of hostilities. Greater vigilance was required of each state over *emigrados* residing therein. A full treaty of peace, friendship, and commerce was to be negotiated within two months. Most important, the contracting parties promised that in the event of new difficul-

11. It has been suggested that the very rough seas that day had much to do with the haste of the proceedings. The absence of any means of communications with their governments also helped the delegates to make rapid decisions. Philip M. Brown, "American Diplomacy in Central America," *American Political Science Review*, VI (Supp. 1912), 160 n.

ties they would be submitted for arbitration by the presidents of the United States and Mexico.

In compliance with the *Marblehead* talks a Central American conference met in San José, Costa Rica, from September 15 to 25, 1906. All five states were invited, but after some hesitancy Nicaragua backed out. President Zelaya, who had his own plans for uniting Central America, was believed by some to be capable of exercising them if the United States did not interfere. His refusal to participate was a protest against the role the North Americans played in bringing the conference about, as well as a belief in the adequacy of the Corinto Pact which he had initiated.[12]

The San José conference concluded the required treaty of peace, friendship, and commerce, confirmed the Corinto Pact, and re-established the Central American Tribunal of Arbitration which had not yet reviewed a case. Closer to the Unionists ideal were two additional conventions. One fashioned an International Central American Bureau at Guatemala City for the purpose of "preserving and encouraging Central American interests." It was to begin its somewhat nebulous functions on September 15, 1907.

The second convention outlined a Central American Pedagogical Institute in San José. Costa Rica was charged with organizing and financing the school, but the other states were expected to share in the costs. Teachers, laboratory equipment, and scientific materials, as well as the library would be sought in Europe. Nicaragua was invited to participate in this one program even though not signatory of the general treaty. Initially each state could send at least twenty students of each sex to the institute. This was a new scheme that was practical and augured well—

12. Raymond Leslie Buell, "The United States and Central American Stability," *Foreign Policy Reports*, VII (July 8, 1931), 165.

the first of several attempts to achieve confederation by commencing with a single school or school system.

But the Central American curse was still operative. This time the revolt occurred in January, 1907, in Honduras, and President Manuel Bonilla accused the plotters of having the support of Zelaya. Bonilla's army pursued them back into Nicaraguan territory, killing some Nicaraguan citizens in the act. Zelaya demanded indemnification, and the case was brought before the tribunal under the Corinto Pact. That body ordered a disarmament before it would render a decision. Nicaragua refused to accept the premise, the tribunal adjourned, and the war began. Honduras, El Salvador, and Costa Rica declared the pact broken and no longer binding upon them.[13] By March, Zelaya defeated the Honduran army as well as some irregulars from El Salvador who had entered the fray. He then helped the revolutionists banish Bonilla and install a new president. As Zelaya prepared to invade El Salvador a general conflict seemed imminent.

As a final effort to bring about a peaceful settlement of the most troublesome issues, Presidents Roosevelt and Díaz invited the five states to convene their ministers in Washington later in 1907. The regular sessions of the Central American Peace Conference began November 14 in the building of the Bureau of American Republics. The conference was ambitious and unique but a logical outgrowth of the increasingly close ties in the Western Hemisphere. The events of these sessions are well known and need not be repeated in full here, but the thread of federation is never long concealed in the patchwork of Central American affairs, nor was it to be so at Washington. All was harmony at first. Before the men assembled, the

13. Costa Rica, Ministerio de Relaciones Extranjeras, *Informes, 1907.*

presidents of the three central republics met at Amapala and, agreeing to forget past differences, announced that they would convene again after the Washington conference, an act as unnecessary as it was typical of the past.

In Washington the friendliness continued. Aided by the American representatives, William I. Buchanan, and the Mexican Ambassador to the United States, Enrique Creel, the rules of procedure were quickly agreed upon. Luis Anderson, Costa Rica's foreign minister, was selected chairman. Led by El Salvador, the delegates in turn announced that their states no longer held claims against any of the others. A Honduran proposal to grant full amnesty to political fugitives was also accepted with pleasure by all.

Typically the subject of confederation did not long lie neglected. During the second session the Honduran delegation presented a plan to unite the five republics. They repeated the familiar story that it was the dream of every Central American and that it was the only way to end the isthmian wars. The men said that they recognized the many past failures but believed that the new roles of the United States and Mexico would bring about success. They suggested ratifying whatever conventions emerged from the Washington conference and then holding a constituent assembly for the designing of a greater republic.

Tension immediately appeared. Nicaragua alone strongly supported Honduras, and, on being informed of what had transpired, Zelaya volunteered to resign his office if that would hasten the great day.[14] Costa Rica objected that the subject was not on the agenda and, with El Salvador, came out in favor of a Guatemala plan of

14. Sanso, *Policarpo Bonilla*, p. 382. *This* former President Bonilla was a Honduran delegate at Washington, not to be confused with Manuel Bonilla just overthrown by Zelaya.

retaining their friendship on the basis of the San José treaties of the year before.

When the Honduran-Nicaraguan body insisted that the conference should permit the legislatures to act upon the motion as a referendum, the unsurprising reply of the other three states was that while confederation was a noble ideal, the times were not propitious. Rather, they said, the delegates should concentrate on strengthening commerce, communications, and economic interests and on unifying customs and laws. Following this pattern, they urged the support of the Pedagogical Institute and the Central American Bureau. Buchanan and Creel succeeded in getting the most divisive motions tabled and averted a serious schism, though ill-feeling lasted almost until adjournment.[15]

The conference continued until December 20 without further incident. A treaty and six major conventions, as well as a number of lesser ones, were the consummation of the five weeks' labor. In brief, they were as follows: a treaty of peace and amity was agreed upon for a ten-year period; Honduras was neutralized; arbitration of disputes was to be compulsory; important political refugees were not permitted to reside in the department bordering states whose peace they might jeopardize; and recognition would not be granted to governments obtaining office by revolution.

The conventions provided for extradition of individuals charged with crimes, plans for a Central American railroad, annual conferences of the Central American republics for the next five years, and two measures from the San José Treaty—the Central American Bureau at Guatemala and the Pedagogical Institute at San José. Another convention, and the key to the whole peace plan, was for

15. Buchanan's report of the conference is in *Foreign Relations of the United States, 1907*, pp. 665-727.

a Central American Court, "the most remarkable judicial organ in the world."[16] The treaty and all of the conventions were quickly ratified (an unusual achievement in itself) and became the law of Central America before the middle of 1908.

What was the significance of the Washington agreements? A ten-year program was now under way, one that was to constitute the core of Central American relations for that time. It seems clear that the underlying motive, the long range goal in the minds of many of the delegates, was to make the Washington Peace Conference another, more elaborate measure on the way to confederation.[17] President of the conference, Luis Anderson, declared that the republics must have peace or there could be no union. A federation could not maintain peace in Anderson's opinion. While there existed the possibility of aggression by one government against another, Central America could not be one.[18]

Thus, peace and confederation had become intertwined. While the Washington agreements remained in effect, usual efforts at union were at a minimum and channeled into these practical steps. The treaties amounted to a ten-year attempt at confederation, by more complex means than before and not supported any more unanimously than were earlier plans.

Many informed people held out great hope for the future because of what they expected from the Washington conference. This was especially true of those who maintained that the little republics needed the moral suasion of some outside power to enact the venerable dream.

16. World Peace Foundation, *Pamphlet Series,* VII (Boston, 1917) p. 129.
17. *The Outlook,* Jan. 11, 1908, p. 60; *Review of Reviews,* May 1908, pp. 611-13.
18. *La Prensa Libre* (San José), Sept. 21, 1908.

There was reason for this optimism. Instead of a fragile political framework which would be destroyed at the first dispute, there was now the machinery to settle all issues without recourse to arms. The treaty was the pledge that the states would use this machinery; the court was the means to carry out the pledge. The five republics gave it authority to do more than merely discuss questions wherein diplomacy had failed. Perhaps that was sufficient power for a court of arbitration, but this was to be a court of justice, and the jurisdiction assigned to it made it unique in juristical history. It could take cognizance of the claims of a citizen of one country against the government of another where there was a treaty violation or denial of justice. It could determine cases between governments and individuals when submitted by common accord. It might even have jurisdiction in cases involving the major branches of one of the governments if the legislature concerned decided to present the matter. The court determined its own scope and could appoint commissioners to enforce its decisions throughout Central America.

It would seem that the founders expected too much, and there was danger that the court might become overburdened with trivia. Clearly, a great deal was anticipated, but the court was never plagued with minor questions. One of the court's chief architects and spokesmen, Luis Anderson, wrote that the court was intended not as a mere commission of arbitration but as a genuine judicial tribunal—to sift evidence, consider arguments, and pronounce judgments in accordance with principles of international law. Although it grew out of recommendations of some American delegates at the Second Hague Conference, the court had many original ideas and was the first of its kind in history. To Anderson the court was "the national conscience of Central America." It should be added that compulsion would assist the conscience, for the republics bound themselves to submit all controversies, not just those which they were pleased to present.

The court was composed of five judges, one selected by each state's legislature for five-year terms, at an annual salary of $8,000. The court's life was fixed for ten years, and it was determined that it should be placed at Cartago in Costa Rica, a site believed to be farthest from the usual centers of intrigue. For the inauguration Buchanan and Creel made the journey to Costa Rica together as good-will representatives, and during the last stages of the trip, they were accompanied by the newly named judges of the court. They were greeted by the Costa Ricans with popular enthusiasm and many ceremonies, and on May 25, 1908, the Central American Court of Justice was declared to be in existence.

The court was viewed with much interest outside Central America as well. Many statesmen and jurists looked upon it as an important international experiment, and a new step to eliminate the scourge of war. Swept up by the fervor, Andrew Carnegie donated $100,000 for a Central American Peace Palace in Cartago. (The building was nearly completed in 1910 when a violent earthquake made rubble of the structure. Carnegie made another grant of equal size provided that the site be changed, and San José was agreed upon.)

Before the eyes of the Western world, the Central American Court of Justice accepted its first case. In June, Honduran elements had risen in revolt against President Miguel Dávila. Rumors flew and charges were made that in violation of the Washington Treaty, the governments of Guatemala and El Salvador were supporting the rebellion. Honduras' ally, Nicaragua, asked Costa Rica to intervene and call the contending parties before the court. President Cleto González Víquez fulfilled this function in a letter to each of the presidents. All of the states consented to appear in court, bringing about the most unusual circumstance of a non-contesting state bringing belligerents into international trial. González Víquez declared that the world's opinion of Central America depended on preserving and respecting the tribunal.

The court convened and acted promptly. Three days after the complaint was filed, interlocutory decrees were issued against Honduras, Guatemala, and El Salvador requesting that they withdraw their forces from the frontiers, restrict the activities of their exiles, and remove from command certain Salvadorean officers. Meanwhile the states were to submit proof of their charges and defenses. Within five days the decrees had been carried out, and the revolution had subsided. While the court debated, other factors helped to bring about a peaceful solution.

In Washington, Secretary of State Robert Bacon told the Central American ministers that if the states failed to permit the operation of the peace machinery, the United States might be forced to intervene. The Central Americans did not need a State Department warning to become concerned. One writer declared that no matter who caused the revolt, they were all playing with fire. The court at Cartago would not turn out to be the salvation of Central America but the open door to the United States. If the states did not settle their own affairs and quickly, they would be swallowed up as Cuba or Panama had been.[19]

In the years following the Spanish-American War and the Panama Canal grab, Yankeephobia was a strong feeling, of course. The theme of many Central Americans was

19. *Ibid.,* July 9, 1908.

unity or absorption. "Behind the court is the well-fed garrote of Theodore Roosevelt," said another article. Especially in Costa Rica isolationism reared its ready head and announced that the little republic should return to its traditional policy and abstain from the affairs of the northern neighbors. Otherwise the court might prove to be a real menace to Costa Rican independence.[20]

While opinions crystallized in the separate states, Guatemala and El Salvador presented their defense to the court. The gist of it was that by international law the nations could not be held responsible if Honduran rebels outfitted themselves across the border. A familiar precedent recalled was that of the Cuban insurgents who had organized in the United States during the late nineteenth century. On December 19, the court announced its decision. It ruled that El Salvador and Guatemala were not responsible for aiding Honduran revolutionists; governments could not be held liable for acts of factions. Honduras on its part had failed to prove negligence or hostile intent toward Guatemala or El Salvador, held the court, hence no indemnity was to be paid.[21]

To its credit the court had acted promptly and decisively, and the states abided by its verdict. A general war had probably been prevented. To the world it appeared that the court was off to a noble start, but in retrospect two real hazards can be seen. First, in Costa Rica, the home of the court, there was an increasingly large faction which now distrusted and feared the court's presence. The court had been placed in Cartago because the founders felt that Costa Ricans would maintain a more detached attitude toward the institution than would the other peoples of the isthmus. Now some of the strongest protests were

20. *La República* (San José), July 28, 1908.
21. Buell, "United States and Central American Stability," p. 168.

coming from the Ticos. Isolationism looked like the good old days as San José and Cartago filled with foreign lawyers, newspapermen, and diplomats, while Uncle Sam brandished his big stick.[22]

Perhaps more significant a menace was the manner of the court's voting. The decisions of the five judges were made on strict national lines. Costa Rica, the only neutral in the matter, had cast the deciding ballots in favor of the defendants. The other judges had merely voted in accordance with their own nation's interests. What would be the result if no one were neutral? The court was intended to be an independent, international tribunal, not a political sounding board.[23] The true stature of the men would have to be decided by the future. In the meantime, another product of the Washington Peace Conference had begun operation.

This agency was the International Central American Bureau. It now had specific functions assigned to it: to combine efforts toward peaceful reorganization of "Central America, the mother country;" to make public education uniform in nature; to develop and expand commerce; to advance agriculture and industry; to make uniform the legal codes, customs systems, exchange rates, and higher standards of health and sanitation. This office, also, began its work with enthusiasm, too much perhaps, for those Central Americans who opposed the logical outcome of such activity. Officials of the bureau began to think of it as a state, with authority over the five republics. It put forth strong Unionist propaganda. It used as its insignia the flag of the old Federal Republic of Morazán's day,

22. Objection was also growing to Costa Rica's share in furnishing the complimentary building.

23. Dana G. Munro, *The Five Republics of Central America* (New York, 1918), p. 219.

and it sought diplomatic immunity and duty exemptions for its staff.

Before these numerous functions could be put into operation ratification by the states was essential. A furore arose when the proposals were received in Costa Rica and El Salvador. Many citizens of the former state, long opposed to confederation in any form, looked upon the bureau as a means of introducing Central American union through the back door. In El Salvador, where public feeling is always more sympathetic to confederation, fear of the movement was engendered by the fact that the bureau was located in Guatemala City, time-honored enemy to Salvadoreans. The demands of the two republics were met in 1910, and the office was emasculated and returned to the vague pursuits outlined for it in 1906 in San José. The bureau then settled down to scheduling the annual Central American conference and publishing the very useful magazine, *Centro América*. This arrangement continued until September 15, 1923, when the bureau died in the midst "of the greatest indifference."[24]

Central America's most ardent unionist, Salvador Mendieta, greatly lamented the bureau's change in policy and declared that the office merely "vegetated in the city of Guatemala for fifteen years, serving as the docile instrument of government, especially to that of Estrada Cabrera, spending prodigious sums, without removing a single obstacle, without erecting a single basis for national reconstruction."[25]

At Washington the Central American republics had agreed to hold annual conferences of a general nature, and these duly met each year from 1909 through 1914 in the various capitals. A great many conventions were approved,

24. Moreno, *Historia,* p. 246.
25. Buell, "United States and Central American Stability," p. 167 n.

but the results can be seen in two actions that were taken. At Managua in 1912 the delegates felt that it was wise to sign a convention to encourage the prompt ratification of conventions. Then, in 1914 it was decided at Tegucigalpa to initiate no more agreements until something was done about the numerous compacts from earlier conferences that still remained unratified.

As for the Pedagogical Institute, it was often a topic of discussion at the conferences. Plans were made for a building in 1910 and again in 1913, but in outlining its purposes the statesmen foundered on the rock of confederation, and the institute never functioned.

The Central American Court of Justice had been constituted for a ten-year period during which it considered ten cases. The first, in 1908, has already been mentioned. Of the others, five were cases brought by individuals and are of no interest to this study. In each instance the plaintiff's case was ruled inadmissable.

Revolutions in Nicaragua occasioned two more hearings. These suits also proved of little avail. The first revolt, actively abetted by the United States, overthrew Zelaya. Neither his designated successor, José Madriz, nor the insurgent leader, Juan José Estrada, indicated interest in letting the court settle the quarrel. Estrada was even quoted as saying that "such mediation would be a grave offense to the American government." Secretary of State Philander Knox did nothing to urge the contenders to utilize the services of the court. That body was further weakened by the replacement of the Nicaraguan jurist when the administration changed following the successful revolt.

The court's second failure at mediation occurred in 1912 when revolt flared against the strong American influence exerted upon new President Adolfo Díaz, who had been a follower of Estrada and Madriz. This time the insurgents were willing to accept a ruling of the court, but Díaz was not and found his salvation in requesting and getting a detachment of marines from the United States.

In these two instances the precedent was set that a nation or faction could disregard the court with impunity if it had the support of the United States. While it is true that the court's jurisdiction over internal political matters was very questionable, it would seem that the Central Americans wanted it to have broad powers, and the limits of its scope had not been marked. It was indeed unfortunate for Central American unity that this great experiment in international relations should occur at a time when the United States reflected its most imperial mood. History is not made of "might have beens," and the court would have had a plethora of internal differences at any rate, but from 1910 it was operating in an unsympathetic climate. It was the first time that the United States deliberately countenanced Central American disunity.

During the entire previous history of independent Central America, United States' policy, when there was one, favored any action which would help cement the states together. Now unusual American interests in Nicaragua were putting an end to that practice and destroying the influence of the court which might have led to confederacy. These interests assumed that another canal would soon be started, this time through Nicaragua, and that it would result in large profits.

The consummation was the famous Bryan-Chamorro Treaty between the United States and Nicaragua, which resulted in the final two cases brought before the Central American court and which in their turn meant the end of the court.

Negotiations for this treaty were begun with the Nicaraguan government of Adolfo Díaz in 1912 immediately after his office had been preserved for him by the marines. It was signed August 5, 1912, and finally ratified in 1916. The terms granted to the United States perpetual proprietary rights to build a canal through Nicaragua, the right to establish a naval base on the Gulf of Fonseca, and renewable leases for the Corn Islands. In return Nicaragua received three million dollars to be spent under joint supervision for welfare and reduction of the public debt. Most of this money remained in the United States in the hands of a few financial interests.[26]

Central American protests were reinforced by voices from other lands in the hemisphere in spite of the stipulation of the United States Senate that nothing in the convention was intended to affect the existing rights of any of the states. In March and August, 1916, Costa Rica and El Salvador, respectively, presented their formal complaints to the Court of Justice.

Costa Rica alleged that the treaty was in violation of agreements made in 1858 and 1888 which granted to them free navigation of the lower San Juan and the right to be consulted before Nicaragua made any concession for the construction of a canal.

Inasmuch as they shared the Gulf of Fonseca with Nicaragua, both El Salvador and Honduras were greatly displeased with the provisions concerning that body of water. They declared that none of the three had the right to alienate any of the shore without the consent of the others. Furthermore, a United States' base would be a threat to their sovereignty and a target in the event of a major war. According to El Salvador's government such installation

26. Thomas A. Bailey, "Interest in a Nicaraguan Canal, 1903-31," *Hispanic American Historical Review*, XVI (February 1936), 2-28.

would prevent the prospect of any other confederation of Central America by turning Nicaragua into a protectorate.

When Secretary of State William Jennings Bryan proposed similar arrangements for the other nations of Central America, their ministers in Washington expressed a complete lack of interest. They said that he totally misunderstood the situation, and what they wanted was not benefits but Central American unity. They objected strongly that any state should subvert its sovereignty in the fashion that Nicaragua followed. They lamented that it was the beginning of the "American invasion."

On September 30, 1916, the court announced that it had jurisdiction over the two cases. It did not rule the Bryan-Chamorro Treaty null and void, for the court disclaimed jurisdiction over the United States, but the jurists held that Nicaragua violated the treaties of 1858 and 1888 with Costa Rica as well as the Washington Treaty of 1907. In March of the next year the court declared that the rights of El Salvador had also been infringed.[27]

Keen observers could now see the end of the court; neither the United States nor Nicaragua paid any attention to the decisions. The latter had no representative at the hearings, and its judge remained absent. Then, giving the necessary year's notice, the Nicaraguan government withdrew from the court, destroying it and the basis of the other Washington pacts as well. On March 12, 1918, the ten-year life of the court was completed. The other countries did not consider it worthwhile to renew the agreement, and so the Central American Court of Justice quietly expired as of that date.

Most writers, and none more than those from the

27. Isaac J. Cox, *Nicaragua and the United States* (Boston, 1927), p. 727.

United States, have condemned United States' policy for the court's destruction. Many felt that the Bryan-Chamorro Treaty should never have been made. It has served no useful purpose except to keep some unknown enterprising power from building a hypothetical canal. As time goes on there is little reason to conclude that a Nicaraguan canal is likely in the predictable future. The sole heritage of the treaty was ill-will.

Granted that there was little political wisdom in the treaty, at least one eminent international lawyer has averred that it was legal, and the court itself refused to pronounce otherwise. El Salvador and Costa Rica were probably entitled to reparations, although they protested that reimbursement was not the issue. The United States erred in more than concluding the treaty, for it refused to abide by the decisions of the Central American court, and it declined to appear before the Permanent Tribunal at The Hague. "We had let justice fail."[28]

The Bryan-Chamorro Treaty should not be charged with full responsibility for the termination of the court. As has been pointed out earlier in the chapter it had already been weakened by the cases concerning Nicaraguan internal affairs. Furthermore, as Roscoe Hill states, it became a political body in 1911 when the new administration in Nicaragua forced a changing of justices.[29] We cannot remove Central American politics from our accusations, but the United States surely administered the *coup de grace* to its ten-year-old child.

28. Manley O. Hudson, "The Central American Court of Justice," *American Journal of International Law,* XXVI (October 1932), 781; *North American Review,* CCVII (1918), 816. The latter article eloquently praises the United States for helping to found the court initially, however.

29. Roscoe R. Hill in A. Curtis Wilgus, ed., *The Caribbean Area* (Washington, 1934), p. 280.

Andrew Carnegie's attractive new peace palace, never used by the court, was completed in 1917, just in time to be given to the government of Costa Rica along with the archives and furnishings of the court. Today the Casa Amarilla serves that republic as the home of the foreign office.

In previous chapters it has been seen that a failure to federate by one means was regularly followed by another attempt of the same type. It was not until the turn of the century that emphasis shifted to concentrating on peace machinery as a prerequisite to union. It was not surprising then, that the denouement of the Washington Peace Treaties brought about other treaties of peace, still complicated by Central America's necessity of living with the agents of United States imperialism. World events of 1917 and immediately thereafter were also conducive to international peace negotiations. The failure of federation in 1917 and the presence of the United States' money and troops only intensified the desire for collective security.

How should the states begin this time?

Chapter IX

The Central American Unionist Party and the Second Washington Conference

THE early twentieth century introduced Central Americans to the novelty of attempting confederation by means of modern peace machinery, just as it also introduced them to the threat of domination by the United States. By 1920 a refreshingly new approach to Central Americanism had reached maturity and presented itself to the popular mind.

A group of Guatemalan students was responsible for this innovation. In 1899, while yet in college, they founded a society called "El Derecho," dedicated to the conviction that the people of Central America were really one, not linked but separated by political forms. The movement grew almost spontaneously from the menace that was apparent in the Spanish-American War, the failure of the República Mayor in 1898, and a serious economic crisis of the period in all of Central America.

Initially the students remained aloof from the existing political parties. They believed that a majority of the citizens in each of the five nations wanted a Central American government, and that it could only be achieved by the people, not the states. Too often in the past, a promising confederation was destroyed because of the ambitions of one of the presidents or his followers. So the students began a program of education—opening reading rooms, making speeches, holding annual student conferences in the five republics. They founded a *revista* in which they could publish articles spreading the gospel. The results were not spectacular but solid. Each of the other four states soon had a similar coterie of students, Costa Rica being the last to be represented by such a group. On July 14, 1904, the young men formed the Partido Unionista, not designed to defeat existing governments so much as to unite peoples, especially young Central Americans who would be closely linked all of their lives. It was hoped that when these men reached maturity they would play significant roles as statesmen and leaders of the union ideal.

The party presented a unique approach. The students (all under 20 in 1899) declared that state boundaries were troublesome, arbitrary, and needless, and should be forgotten. The scheme of linking five states, however wisely, had always failed and would continue to fail, for jealousies must always exist among them. What the Union party sought was not a confederation but a true union with a centralized government. To accomplish this end they advocated that the map of Central America be redrawn with the five states destroyed and replaced by nineteen smaller regions and a federal district. Insofar as possible the new provinces were designed on a practicable basis. Like areas were combined. For example, the district to be called Colón included most of the inhospitable coasts of Honduras and Nicaragua. Thinly populated areas were made comparatively large, such as the fat panhandle of northern Guatemala which was named Las Casas. The larger cities were almost always to be provincial capitals. Cognizance was taken of political considerations. Granada, Managua, and León—old and bitter rivals in Nicaragua— were all made capitals in a neat bit of gerrymandering. Aside from its obvious merits and its equally obvious impossibilities, the plan probably afforded the students many pleasurable hours of discussion and mapmaking. The federal district remained a football in Unionist schemes just as it had always been in the numerous conferences among the states. Tegucigalpa, La Unión, Chinandega, and Choluteca were proposed as headquarters, but in later years the party gave consideration to Guatemala City, a place expressly avoided earlier as a clear source of trouble.[1]

Directed by their dynamic leader, Salvador Mendieta, who had devoted a long lifetime to the cause, the Union party made valuable contribution to the standard of Central American politics. They campaigned for greater freedom of the press and the courts, the right of assembly and of political organization, as well as impartial electoral commissions. To accomplish their ends they abstained from the use of intrigue or armed force. While they crusaded for Central American union, they adopted national reforms as essential goals, too. They regularly favored any measures which pointed toward confederation such as the Washington Treaties discussed in Chapter VIII, even though they were not steps which the party itself might have proposed. The unionists grew in numbers and strength, and they began to reach significant proportions about the time of the collapse of the Central American Court of Justice. This event temporarily dominated the public's atten-

1. Salvador Mendieta, *Exposición presentada á la Asamblea Nacional Constituyente de la República de Centroamérica* (Managua, 1921) and *Alrededor del problema unionista de Centro-América* (Barcelona, 1926).

tion and brought about a renewed effort at confederation that weakened the Union party's movement. The Costa Rican government invited the other four states to send plenipotentiaries to San José to revise the Washington Treaties that were now generally considered null and void. This was no inconsistency on the part of Costa Rica, for there was no mention of confederation in the agenda. A search for collective security was the motive.

As one might expect, one of the other states quickly introduced the subject of confederation before the meetings began. This time it was Honduras that proposed broadening the scope of the sessions to consider what Honduras felt was the "underlying principle of any Central American conference." The other nations agreed with numerous provisos. Guatemala's government felt that such a change in purpose would require time for study and urged a preliminary meeting for Guatemala City early in 1918 to draw up an agenda and to determine dates, places, and other details. Then El Salvador provoked an argument by suggesting that the United States and Mexico should be represented, too, as in 1907.[2] The president of Nicaragua agreed to send a delegate provided that Panama should be invited as a prospective member of the Central American family. He further declared that the sessions might be more tranquil if held in Washington or Panama. These conditions became sore points immediately. The subservience of Nicaragua to the United States was a source of much friction and irritation, and bringing Panama into the agenda could only exaggerate these feelings. Honduras objected that Panama had never been part of the original Federal Republic, which was true, and that it was not a sovereign state because Article 136 of its constitution permitted United States intervention. The Hon-

2. Costa Rica, Ministerio de Relaciones Exteriores, *Informes, 1918.*

durans also felt that while the historical and traditional ties binding the five states together might be weak, they would disappear entirely when other nations were included or even if the meetings were held outside Central America.

The Yankee issue also brought about a cooling of feeling in Costa Rica, for its government was not recognized by the United States because of what Woodrow Wilson considered a violation of "constitutionalism." Federico Tinoco had secured the office of president of Costa Rica by a popularly accepted *coup d'état* that was virtually bloodless.

The question of holding the conference was still unsettled when, late in 1917, a series of earthquakes occurred that brought great destruction to Guatemala City and made another site necessary. The Nicaraguan government extended the hospitality of Managua as an alternative, but since they also had not recognized Tinoco's government, they could not invite Costa Rica. The rebuff stirred up the old jealousies, and no conference took place.

The long shadow of Uncle Sam was not easily removed from Central American affairs in the war and post-war years. Undermining a confederation was not *per se* a goal of the United States, then or at any time. A divide-and-conquer policy was not necessary for the simple reason that the United States could conquer without dividing, if that were the aim. Nevertheless, neither the United States nor Nicaragua had any intention of changing the status of their relationship. Indeed, Emiliano Chamorro, co-author of the famous treaty which was the principle thorn, had in 1917, just become president of Nicaragua. The United States was involved with other troublesome dictators. Estrada Cabrera, with enemies all over Central America, was still the friend of the Yankee and still in the saddle at Guatemala. Tinoco's presence also clouded issues considerably, the more so for being an unrecognized dictator whom the United States clearly opposed. On several occasions the State Department openly suggested that he resign. Nicaragua and Honduras both made overtures toward an invasion of Costa Rica to overthrow Tinoco, but the United States declined to go to that length.[3] In sum, the atmosphere was too tense to permit friendly negotiations in 1917-18 among the Central American peoples.

The United States was apparently in Central America to stay. Any diplomatic action of consequence was taken only in the light of the Yankee's attitude, and many elements were becoming irritated by that necessity. Chamorro and Estrada Cabrera felt secure because of the support that their despotisms could claim in Washington and New York, while, in traditional fashion, insurgents were incited by neighboring governments if relations between the two states were unfriendly. This occurred reciprocally in Costa Rica and Nicaragua. The former had the larger army, and Tinoco prepared an invasion. In a humiliating request, Chamorro called upon the United States for troops to repel the invaders. Although the war did not come about, the harm was done, for it was embarrassing to Central Americans everywhere for one of their number to seek intervention. The move pressed home to them the lowly state to which they had fallen.

Some measure of the antagonism toward the United States could be seen at Versailles. The Honduran delegation was headed by former President Policarpo Bonilla who sought a clarification of the Monroe Doctrine. His interpretation was that "all of the republics of America

3. Robert Lansing to Minister to Honduras, T. Sambola Jones, November 4, 1918, *Foreign Relations of the United States, 1918*, p. 270.

have the right to their independent existence . . . that no other nation can acquire any portion by conquest nor intervene in its government or internal administration . . . ." He also wanted it made clear that the doctrine in no wise prevented the confederation of any of the Latin American states.[4] El Salvador also wanted an exact expression of the Monroe Doctrine. Costa Rica's problem was more than philosophical. President Tinoco, at first genuinely popular, lost more and more in favor as he expanded the army and increased controls over the people. Economic conditions deteriorated badly because of military expenditures and lack of recognition by the United States. The result was a crippling reduction in the budget for schools and communications, items close to the heart of the Costa Ricans. It was a "process of economic strangulation."[5] Then the people were humiliated needlessly by Wilson's refusal to permit their representation at the peace conference of Versailles on the metaphysical grounds that since the Tinoco government was not recognized, it therefore did not exist and, not existing, could not declare war on Germany nor make peace.[6]

Two states remained friendly to each other in this caldron. Apparently in an effort to strengthen his precarious position, President Francisco Bertrand of Honduras suddenly decided upon unification with El Salvador in a new bilateral union. It was a superficial scheme and seems never to have gone beyond the step of acquiring a name— La República de Morazán.[7] Accusing Bertrand of trying to rig the coming elections, the competition in Honduras

4. Sanso, *Bonilla,* p. 522.

5. John Foster Dulles, "Conceptions and Misconceptions Regarding Intervention," *Annals of the American Academy of Political and Social Science,* CXLIV (July, 1929), 102-4.

6. *Senate Documents,* 66th Cong., 1st. sess., no. 77, p. 2.

7. *El Diario* (San José), July 10, 1919.

arose in revolt. The United States Minister to Honduras intervened, Bertrand resigned, and the República de Morazán disappeared.

Meanwhile, the Central American Unionist party was reaching maturity. Members helped the International Bureau, now just a clearing house, agitating for a gala celebration of the centennial of independence which would come September 15, 1921. What better object, they reasoned, than to organize a new confederation to begin that day. So tentative plans were made for preliminary meetings to be held during 1920 that might lead to formal conventions. Considering that the chief obstacle was Central America's oldest dictatorship, the Unionists now turned on Guatemala's Estrada Cabrera. Complying with their pacific promises, they attacked him with propaganda, primarily, and urged him to resign. The United States, although still supporting him, admonished him to cease suppressing civil liberties, and the American Minister announced that serious responsibility would lie with persons who disturbed the peace of the country. Estrada Cabrera made promises of protection to the Union party, but when he failed to keep them, the Guatemalan Assembly met in April of 1920, declared him insane, and forced his resignation. Public opinion, the assembly, and the diplomatic corps had conspired to bring about a relatively peaceful revolution. The guiding hands, however, were those of the Central American Unionist party.

With the dictator's opposition gone, the International Bureau followed the plan of the Unionists, encouraged by the government of El Salvador, and called for an ambitious conference to be held at San José, Costa Rica, in December, 1920.[8] Superficially, the request looked just like a

8. El Salvador, Ministerio de Relaciones Exteriores, *Libro Rosado* (San Salvador, 1921), pp. 4, 134.

dozen previous invitations, but there were significant distinctions that brought a feeling of optimism to the delegates. In the first place, the locale was Costa Rica, and it was considered a minor triumph to get that much interest from the usually reluctant land. Secondly, the date was propitious. On numerous occasions the Central Americans had shown their enthusiasm for anniversaries and especially that of September 15, 1821. Delegates might be expected to be particularly diligent to effect some agreement for the one-hundredth birthday of independence. And then it was a pleasant surprise that Nicaragua was sending delegates. The "arrangement" between that nation and the United States had not changed, and most Central Americans had expected that Nicaragua lacked the freedom to negotiate with her neighbors.

On December 4, 1920, in Andrew Carnegie's temple of justice, the representatives of the five nations assembled and established their internal organization. The Costa Rican Minister of Foreign Affairs, Alejandro Alvarado Quirós, was chosen president of the conference, with Alberto Uclés of Honduras as vice president and Ramón Castillo of Nicaragua, secretary. It was decided to eliminate any provisional or preparatory agreements and instead to create a committee of five to draw a definitive pact of union.

The committee work had scarcely begun when a member from Nicaragua raised the inevitable question of the Bryan-Chamorro Treaty and forced an immediate decision regarding it before any other business could continue. Several compromises were attempted to save the conference. In general these sought to preserve the treaty and at the same time protect the rights of the other states. On December 22, Castillo went home to seek his government's permission to modify his position so that it might more easily conform to the desires of the other states on the matter of riparian rights along the Gulf of Fonseca.

The government of Nicaragua sent back its final instructions to its delegates to the effect that it proposed to adhere strictly to the obligations imposed by the Bryan-Chamorro Treaty, and it further declared that the other states of Central America must consent without any reservation if they desired future diplomatic discussion or arbitration of the treaty. If this concurrence were not forthcoming, Nicaragua would not subscribe to the pact of union. The Nicaraguan government was thus putting the responsibility upon the other four nations for the failure or success of the present federation movement.

This ultimatum was too much for them to accept, and Nicaragua's new president, Diego Chamorro, uncle of the famous Emiliano, recalled his remaining delegates and left the four republics to their own devices. By January 19 of 1921 these states had completed a pact of union without Nicaragua and without specific reference to the troublesome treaty. One article of the covenant provided that Nicaragua might adhere at a later date if it so desired, while another required the faithful compliance by each state to its existing treaty obligations until altered or denounced by action of the new federal government. But these lures failed to tempt the Nicaraguan government to come into the fold.

This latest addition to the list of Central American confederations was called La Federación de Centro América. Within it each state was to preserve its autonomy and independence for internal affairs as long as its actions were not contrary to the federal constitution. This document was to be drafted on the basis of the pact of union just as soon as a national constituent assembly could be called.

In the meanwhile the Provisional Federal Council was ordained with a delegate from each of the four states serving. Their duties were to convoke the assembly, make preliminary arrangements, and promulgate the constitution after its completion. Immediately after ratifying the pact of union (or Pact of San José, as it came to be called), the congress of each state could elect its delegate to the council. The notice of ratification, as well as the name of the delegate, was then sent to the International Central American Bureau, and that organization planned to call the men together as soon as three states had chosen their respective council members. The sessions of the council were scheduled for Tegucigalpa not more than thirty days after ratification of the pact by the third state. The Provisional Federal Council would then call the Constituent Assembly into being, also at Tegucigalpa, whenever deputies were named by a minimum of three states. Needless to say, it was hoped that all of this might be accomplished by September 15 of the same year, 1921.[9]

Ratification came quickly in Honduras, El Salvador, and Guatemala. To help generate public enthusiasm the Central American Unionist party held a convention in Santa Ana, El Salvador, during the debates in the various states. It was reported that 12,000 people turned out to greet the convention delegates. The party called for unreserved ratification of the Pact of San José, stressing the pacific and nonpartisan action of peoples rather than governments. As in the past the party recommended a much more highly centralized union than the one pending, but the members were urged to continue to support any movement which would strengthen relations of the Central Americans.[10]

9. *Ibid.*, pp. 102-13.
10. Jorge Cardona, *Convención Unionista de Santa Ana* (San José, 1921).

Since three states had now ratified the Pact of San José, the Constituent Assembly could be summoned into being. The presence of the fourth state would be energizing, and eyes were focused upon historically isolationist Costa Rica to see what its congress would do.

That body was in no hurry to do anything. Newspaper accounts made it appear that public opinion was sharply divided, and the congressmen wanted the atmosphere cleared before they were forced to vote. As in the past most people seemed to feel that a confederation in the abstract was a desirable thing but that the time of actual consummation was another matter. Always smarting a bit under the charge of being separatists, the Ticos at last found another scapegoat. They began to blame Nicaragua and the restrictions demanded by the state for the initial failure to obtain unanimous agreement on union. But that was beside the point, and the Costa Rican press knew it. The only question that was still to be resolved was whether Costa Rica would ratify or not. While the conference at San José had still been in conclave, a Costa Rican delegate, Alvarado Quirós, the president of the conference, had made a diplomatic error which may have meant little but gave the impression that the conference was of no great significance. When the four states were ready for the formal ceremony of signing the Pact of San José, the envoys found it necessary to delay a few days while Alvarado Quirós took a holiday to visit Puntarenas to watch a dozen hydroplanes arrive from the United States.[11] Granted that the sight was unusual in 1921, placing such a junket ahead of the creation of a new Central American Republic greatly reduced the dignity and solemnity of the diplomats' work.

11. *El Diario* (San José), January 14, 1921.

Not wishing to alienate the people of Nicaragua, but still wishing to shift the blame for disunity to another nation, Costa Rican Unionists adopted the approach that the Nicaraguan government had sold out to "the Jew bankers of New York," who kept Nicaragua in its servile role. Naturally, a watchful eye was kept on the United States as well. The mission of the hydroplanes was questioned only briefly, but when the United States Navy Department shortly thereafter announced the creation of a new squadron of several cruisers to be based at Panama, the Costa Rican press agreed that all of Central America now belonged within the orbit of the United States. The impression was growing that the United States wanted no Central American unity and was using Nicaragua to see that none emerged.[12]

When the debate began in the Costa Rican congress, party lines were quickly destroyed. Several of President Julio Acosta's followers attacked him for supporting the confederation, while many of his oldest opponents applauded his stand. There was some sentiment for calling a plebiscite since the congressmen had not been elected on this issue, but the plan was not consonant with the constitution and not tried.

Confederation was analyzed from many angles. The religious element was briefly introduced; one priest, who was a deputy in congress, maintained that a Catholic could not in all conscience be a Unionist. The sharpest rebuke to this statement came from another priest in the congress who retorted that Catholics were Unionists in the United States, and there was no reason why they should not be the same in Costa Rica. Nothing further came of

12. *La Tribuna* (San José), January 23, 1921; Charles E. Chapman, "The Failure of the Central American Union," *Review of Reviews,* LXVI (December, 1922), 613-17.

this locally, but, on the basis of this split evidence, the Honduran government was later to charge the Costa Rican clergy with destroying the confederation movement.[13]

A better target was the United States, and some of the deputies took the opportunity to vent their time-honored Yankeephobia. They affirmed that Costa Rica was now "surrounded" by the United States and that, therefore, only a spiritual union was possible. A confederation of Central America would have to be achieved by force, as in Italy and Germany, and the only state capable of it was the United States. *That* force, they assured the chamber, was not wanted.

On June 22, the Costa Rican congress finally polled itself, and the advocates of union not only failed to get the necessary two-thirds vote, they were in the minority nineteen to twenty.[14] The subject quickly lapsed into insignificance in the public eye. While the United States had come in for its share of the blame, it had done nothing to prevent or even discourage Costa Rica from joining the confederation. At the most the United States was guilty of diplomatic ineptness in the displays of force while the debates were going on. There can be but one conclusion: in 1921, as on so many occasions before, there simply was not a majority of people in Costa Rica who favored taking the actual steps that would lead to confederation with the rest of Central America.

And so the three northern states were left to salvage what they could. Composing a quorum they could, and did, activate the Federation of Central America. The president of the Provisional Federal Council issued instruc-

13. Victor Sanabria, *Bernardo Augusto Thiel, segundo obispo de Costa Rica* (San José, 1941), p. 234. Archbishop Sanabria said that most of the clergy opposed the confederation of 1921 but that no church policy was established concerning it.

14. *El Diario* (San José), June 22, 1921.

tions that the National Constituent Assembly should convene in Tegucigalpa, Honduras, on July 20, 1921. When
that day arrived great popular demonstrations accompanied
the opening ceremonies of the assembly. Policarpo Bonilla
was chosen its president after the delegates got down to
work. In attendance were several unofficial Nicaraguan
representatives from the Federal League of Nicaragua and,
true to the pledges made at Santa Ana, Salvador Mendieta
and other leading members of the Unionist party. Mendieta was elected one of the secretaries of the Constituent
Assembly.

While this body was drafting a framework of government for the three states, there were disquieting events
occurring. Many Unionists charged that the absence of
both Nicaragua and Costa Rica was due to the efforts of
the Conservative party ruling in the former country. They
assumed that the overthrow of Chamorro in favor of the
Liberals would bring about Nicaragua's immediate adherence to the cause of federation. Costa Rica would have
to follow suit, they concluded. This notion was politically
useful to the insurgents of Nicaragua who exploited its
popular appeal. It was also handy for the government of
Costa Rica, which now officially stated that, if Nicaragua
joined the federation, the Costa Rican congress would
again consider ratification—a meaningless promise, but
good for the record. Chamorro thus became the scapegoat
for two separate elements of Central America, and by August there were armed incursions on both borders of Nicaragua.[15]

Another disturbance was created when the bishop of
San Miguel, El Salvador, asked the assembly to invoke
the name of God in the preamble to the new constitution.
This request was ignored and served to alienate the Cen-

15. Cox, *Nicaragua*, p. 763.

tral American bishops from the federation on the grounds that it did not recognize the rights and customs of the Catholic church. Most of what the clergy had in mind had long been abolished in the states of Central America individually, but this was an excellent opportunity to revive old complaints.

On August 30, the assembly decreed that the flag and coat of arms of the 1823 Republic of Central America should be ordered into existence again, and on September 9, the constitution was promulgated, as the assembly adjourned for the last time. Time did not permit the new government to convene, but September 15 officially marked the birthday of the new constitution, one hundred years to the day after independence. A commission was then sent to Washington to seek recognition for the new nation.[16] During November the states of Honduras, Guatemala, and El Salvador made their plans for the election of a permanent council, the deputies, and the senators.

Before the young federation was strong enough for such a test, it was dealt a crippling blow. On December 5, 1921, President Carlos Herrera of Guatemala was overthrown by a military coup led by three generals, José María Orellana, Jorge Ubico, and José María Larrave. They recalled the old assembly of Estrada Cabrera, forced Herrera to resign, and named Orellana in his place. The new administration then appointed new delegates to the federal government at Tegucigalpa, although Orellana's opponents claimed that he had no intention of turning over any authority to that body. The Provisional Federal Council viewed the new appointments as illegal and announced

16. Mendieta writes that Secretary of State Charles Evans Hughes assured the commissioners that recognition would be granted just as soon as elected officials took office, planned for February, 1922. Mendieta, *Alrededor*, p. 104. I have not seen this promise reported elsewhere; it appears premature.

that the men would not be received. According to the constitution the federal government was empowered to preserve order in the states and suppress revolts. Under this authority the council was called upon to request Honduras and El Salvador to raise troops for the purpose of restoring the legitimate government in Guatemala as well as maintaining the federation. Policarpo Bonilla, however, wise in the ways of Central American politics, advised the council to seek out the attitude of the United States before taking another step.

In view of past policies it was logical to assume that Secretary of State Charles Evans Hughes would support Herrera and refuse to recognize Orellana's government. The circumstances were similar to those of cases such as Tinoco's in Costa Rica in which Wilson had applied his policy of "constitutionalism." Orellana had been a follower of the noisome Estrada Cabrera, and the election of Herrera was frequently cited as Guatemala's only fair and democratic election in fifty or more years.[17] But Hughes cast aside Wilson's device and informed the several Central American states that the United States expected all of them to comply with the principles of the treaties of 1907. This was at best a peculiar stand, for the United States was the force which just a few years before had made those very treaties inoperative. Hughes added that the interference by one Central American state in the internal affairs of another might cause a serious conflict and the United States would view such intervention with the greatest concern. Insofar as Guatemala's relations with the federation were concerned, that statement was the deathblow. Orellana dropped any pretense of supporting the

17. Thomas R. Dawley, Jr., "How the Central American Union Was Born," *Current History*, XV (January, 1922), 625; (no author), "Fall of the Union Seen at Close Range," *Current History*, XVI (May, 1922), 287.

federation, recalled his delegates, and on January 14, 1922, he decreed that Guatemala resume its full autonomy. Based in part on that action as a platform, he ran for the presidency in February and was elected by a preposterous majority. In less than two months' time he secured recognition from the United States to the vexation of much of Central America.

For the second time in less than a decade blame could legitimately be placed on the growing might of the United States for the destruction of a Central American confederation. Herrera had been elected constitutionally and had been overthrown by the use of force. The United States prevented the application of the police power to right this wrong—a police power which Guatemala had freely given to the federation. Central Americans were cynically amused when Hughes asked them to respect the 1907 treaties. Moreover, there were ugly rumors that a Wall Street loan to Orellana was at the root of the United States' actions, and the rather precipitate recognition gave credence to these beliefs.[18] It was an unpopular role that the United States had assumed and one that engendered considerable fear in her neighbors.

This is not to declare, however, that the confederation would otherwise have succeeded. The Central Americans cannot that lightly shrug off their share of the responsibility. If the United States had not warned them to avoid war, and if they had fought as they did so often in the past, the three members would have been split just as surely, and the federation would have collapsed just as completely.

Inasmuch as the United States rendered the federation impotent to do anything concerning the Guatemalan de-

18. Arthur Warner, "Guatemala—our Blow at Pan Americanism," *The Nation,* CXIV (June 21, 1922), 745.

fection, the remaining states felt that there was no recourse left but to resume their autonomy also. El Salvador's decree went into effect February 4, 1922, and that of Honduras on February 7. The latter state also announced the reintegration of the recent federal district of Tegucigalpa back into its dominion.

Once the restraint of hoped-for confederation disappeared, Central America reverted to the old pattern of intrigue. There were conspiracies along the Honduran border against El Salvador's President Jorge Meléndez; *emigrados* in Nicaragua were planning the overthrow of Honduras' Rafael López Gutiérrez; and Liberals in Nicaragua were renewing attempts to rid themselves of Chamorrism. To make his post more secure, Diego Chamorro recommended a meeting of the three presidents concerned plus appropriate United States diplomats to help quiet the convulsion. The President of Honduras suggested that the site be an American ship, so the United States made the cruiser *Tacoma* available for this purpose in the Gulf of Fonseca. The meetings were held on board the *Tacoma* in August, 1922, and the chief topic of discussion was the time-honored problem of exiles and their evil influence on neutrality. It was decided to keep political refugees of any other Central American nation out of military and political offices. Frontiers were to be guarded closely to prevent invasions by exiles. Then, because of the abiding confusion over the status of the 1907 Washington Treaties, the three states resolved that the Treaty of Peace and Amity was still in effect. To this single stipulation the governments of Guatemala and Costa Rica shortly sent their concurrence.[19] Finally, as might be expected, the three pres-

19. Raymond Leslie Buell, "The United States and Central American Revolutions," *Foreign Policy Reports*, VII (July 22, 1931), 189.

idents determined to hold another preliminary conference whose aim would be a "practical union" of their republics.

In accordance with these Tacoma Pacts the governments of Honduras, Nicaragua, and El Salvador each recommended to the United States minister in its own capital that the conference called for might initially meet in Washington. When this word was passed on to Hughes, he and President Harding found the idea acceptable. But from there on the wishes of the Central Americans were completely ignored insofar as this conference was concerned. The word "preliminary" was forgotten, and no further reference was made to drawing up protocols or agenda. On October 21, 1922, the United States formally invited the five Central American nations to send representatives to Washington for a discussion of general Central American affairs.

How much the United States had risen in world importance was made evident by the differences between the Washington Conference of 1907 and this new meeting in 1922. The United States was clearly in charge this time, and the Central Americans were but secondary partners. The invitation itself specified the agenda. "Tribunals of inquiry" were to be considered rather than a revival of the Court of Justice. No mention was made of confederation, which was the chief purpose of the talks in the minds of the Central Americans. Additional topics could be added to the program only by unanimous consent of the delegates. Since this left a veto in the hands of the United States and its puppet, Nicaragua, unwelcome topics such as the Bryan-Chamorro Treaty were easily excluded. Then, in a wicked blow at Latin American prestige, Mexico, the co-sponsor of 1907, was not even invited in 1922.[20] Lastly,

20. Hughes to Roy T. Davis, Minister to Costa Rica, October 21, 1922, *Foreign Relations of the United States, 1922,* II, 430.

instead of a Central American, Hughes, himself, assumed the post of chairman of the sessions.[21]

Four of the Central American states quickly agreed to the summons. Only Costa Rica offered a delay. President Julio Acosta was loathe to send anyone to Washington if the United States planned to take part. He cabled his minister in Washington, Octavio Béeche, to inform Hughes that in the opinion of the Costa Rican government the conference should be attended by Central Americans only. Béeche, however, convinced his chief executive that it would be best to forget his objections for the good of the conference, and along with José Andrés Coronado, Béeche made up the Costa Rican delegation, although both almost immediately resigned.

The representatives assembled in Washington on December 4, 1922. Feelings of Yankeephobia were not reduced among the other states when they discovered that the Nicaraguan group was led by former President Emiliano Chamorro, but the great issue that divided the participants from the very first day was not Chamorrism. It was the old matter of confederation.

In his opening address Alberto Uclés, chief of the Honduran delegation, lamented the lowly state to which Central America had fallen. He had confidence, he said, in the disinterestedness of the United States, but he felt that the most urgent item of all had been left off the agenda and this was the primordial question of returning to the federation. He stressed the fact that the people of Central America did not want to be separated but that their governments kept them apart. Union, he declared, would help to solve the problems of suffrage, alternation of power, and security of life, and it would also bring internal and external peace.

21. Summer Welles was the other United States' participant.

To put the subject on the agenda required a unanimous vote, impossible to attain in this instance. Only El Salvador was enthusiastically behind Uclés' speech, and for six meetings the delegates wrangled over the issue. Generally, Hughes remained neutral, upon occasion moderating the debates but not taking part. Two weeks passed without any other business being discussed. In order to get on with their work, the delegates voted to suspend discussion on confederation until 1926 at which time they would hold separate hearings for that single topic. It was clear that no other proposal would be acceptable to the Washington Conference, but Doctor Uclés had the final word on the thorny proposition. He insisted that nearly everyone in Central America wanted a federation. The Swiss, he said, had overcome greater obstacles of language, race, and religion than the Central Americans had to face. Why, then, was there no confederation? The secret, he explained, was that the men in power did not want that power reduced, while those who wanted to get into authority, wanted to find that force intact. He concluded that the Central American, still crudely feudal, did not have "the patriotism of a Japanese."[22]

With confederation once more set aside the conference finally began its real work. A robust program ensued. By February 7, 1923, one treaty, eleven conventions, two protocols, and a declaration had been signed, and the delegates could adjourn. They had drawn up agreements on everything that the "tropical imagination of the delegates could invent."[23] The details need concern us but briefly. A Treaty of Peace and Amity replaced that of the same name of the 1907 program and made several significant departures from the first document. The recognition of revolution-

22. Mendieta, *Alrededor,* pp. 120-39.
23. Cox, *Nicaragua,* p. 769.

ary governments was made very difficult; the leaders of such movements were ineligible to hold certain of the chief public offices; and proscription applied even to relatives by blood or marriage. The neutrality of Honduras was no longer to be respected, and compulsory arbitration of disputes was abandoned as a guiding principle of international affairs. Perhaps the most radical departure from 1907 was in the organization and functions of the Central American Tribunal created to replace the Court of Justice. It was not permanent but of an *ad hoc* nature, and each of the five Central American states was to name six jurists to a panel. Four of the six could be nationals, but one of the other two must be chosen from a list offered by the United States, while the remaining judge had to come from a slate compiled by any other Latin American nation. The panel of thirty was to be drawn upon when diplomatic measures failed to settle a dispute, and the two states desired to present the case for arbitration. Each state could use one jurist from its own list, but the two litigants would have to agree upon the third man.

The most significant difference between the courts, however, was not so much in makeup as in scope. It will be remembered that the 1907 court seemed almost limitless in its authority, and the tribunal of 1923 was specifically denied the right to rule upon "questions or controversies which affect the sovereign and independent existence of the republics . . . ." Perhaps the new court was more realistic in being less ambitious. Nevertheless, it was evident that political considerations had replaced the idealism of sixteen years before. Both the convention for the establishment of an International Central American Tribunal and the General Treaty of Peace and Amity were to remain in force until January 1, 1934. In these and almost all other cases ratifications were exchanged rapidly—generally by June of 1925.

The Washington Treaty accomplished little or nothing for Central American confederation in the long run. It is true that wars between states were reduced to a minimum in the 1920's, and there was a lessening of interference on the part of exiles. Both of these results could just as well be attributed to frequent United States' interventions which, while often unpopular, probably had the merit of increasing the prospects for peace. Internal disorders and revolutions, however, continued virtually unchecked. Only in El Salvador and Costa Rica was harmony the regular order of things. Nicaragua and Honduras continued to suffer and by 1930 the malady reached Guatemala. In each of these cases final settlement was in a large measure determined by the attitude and force of the United States, but the support of one faction by that government was accompanied by a corresponding distrust felt by other factions. Under such conditions separatism thrived, and there was little likelihood of another attempted union.

A decisive split in Central America occurred over the problem of recognition of the new Hernández Martínez regime in El Salvador in 1931. That government and Costa Rica alleged adherence to the Estrada Doctrine, proclaimed first by Mexico. This was the belief that *de facto* recognition was less conducive to revolts and less interventionist in nature than the legitimist recognition policy that had been proclaimed in the Washington discussion. Applied to Central America the latter course was still supported by the United States, Guatemala, Nicaragua, and Honduras. The issue was muddied by the fact that between 1930 and 1933 the United States recognized *de facto* regimes in several other instances in Latin America, while

Hernández Martínez was recognized by some twenty-three European and Latin American states but not by the United States. The obvious result was confusion, and the situation was in many ways unfair to the administration as well as to the people of El Salvador. Declaring that the treaty of 1923 had failed to live up to expectations and that the recognition requirements were unrealistic, the Costa Rican government gave the necessary year's notice and denounced the treaty as of January, 1934. The government of El Salvador promptly followed suit.

For the second time an attempt to create a "Washington system" for Central American affairs had met failure. The denunciations brought out into the open a need for a change in the rules. The Central Americans were now ready to start over again—without any help from the United States.

Chapter X

Latter-day Proposals

HAVING definitively discarded the 1923 Treaty of Peace and Amity, the Central American states determined to replace it with a work that would be their own and would not bear the imprint of the United States. In this aim they were greatly assisted by the fact that a new administration and the new Latin American policy of Franklin D. Roosevelt meant to the Central Americans that the United States would not interfere in the affairs of Central America. For the first time in thirty years these little republics felt that they could ignore the attitude of Uncle Sam.

The impact of this realization was felt in many spheres, but in none more than in the confederation story. The next conference among the states was held in Guatemala City instead of Washington; it was called by President Jorge Ubico of Guatemala instead of the United States Secretary of State. No representative of the United States was in attendance even as an observer. Delegates of the five nations met on March 15, 1934, and remained in session nearly a month. On April 12 they completed their work by signing a Treaty of Central American Fraternity and a Convention of Extradition of Fugitive Criminals. The treaty provided for the compulsory pacific settlement of all international disputes, it recognized the principle of nonintervention in each other's affairs, and it outlawed war among the five countries. More specifically pertinent to our story, the signatories agreed as usual that a political union of all of Central America was their supreme aspiration. The treaty, the delegates declared, was a step in that direction.

The number of protocols, conventions, and treaties was unimposing when compared to the grist of the two Washington conferences, but the delegates felt satisfied that they had re-established friendly relations among themselves based upon the full sovereignty of independent states. Although the Bryan-Chamorro Treaty was still in existence, United States political interference in Central America was being reduced to a minimum, and at Buenos Aires in 1936 the United States formally denied for itself the right to intervene in the affairs of any Latin American state.

The Buenos Aires declaration confirmed for Central Americans what the "Good Neighbor" practice appeared to be. Rarely after that time was the Bryan-Chamorro Treaty mentioned as an obstacle to union, and just as rarely was the United States branded as a reason for failure. The Central Americans thus returned to the nineteenth-century pattern of seeking confederation—and finding failure—through their own exclusive efforts. Into numerous recent constitutions many provisions were written to the effect that the people concerned would always be willing to join all or any of the others in a confederation when the situation permitted. During and since World War II a number of preliminary as well as actual plans of federation were discussed.

In September, 1942, the Central American Ministers of Education met at San José, Costa Rica, to devise steps for the promotion of educational unity. No plan was put into effect, but the conference was unique in that delegates from Panama were invited and specifically referred to as part of the Central American family. Panama previously had played no part in confederation measures. In colonial times it had never been under the jurisdiction of the captaincy general at Guatemala City and since independence, with brief exception, had been a part of the republic of Colombia. Presumably their inclusion at this one conference was merely an aberration, for the act has not since been repeated.

Back to more traditional fashion the Unionists soon took advantage of an anniversary to raise the banner of Central Americanism. This time the event was the centenary of the death of Francisco Morazán, chief symbol of confederation. The Central American Union party called a convention for San José, Costa Rica, to commence September 15, 1942. The question immediately arose as to why the party chose as a site the town where Morazán was put to death. Some Costa Ricans looked upon the selection as a sly reproach for that republic's part in the execution one hundred years before. The Union party's leader, Salvador Mendieta, quickly did his best to reassure the Costa Ricans that the choice was an honor, that it was the best city in Central America to illustrate the virtues of liberty, democracy, and the protection of citizens' rights.

What Mendieta did not mention was that in 1942 Costa Rica was the only one of the five states not controlled by a dictator, and dictators knew from the experience of Estrada Cabrera the danger of the Union party. Every one of the presidents except Costa Rica's Rafael Angel Calderón Guardia had extended his term of office beyond the constitutional limitation, and all but Calderón were generals. This coincidence of military leaders in a time of international war against Germany, Italy, and Japan gave the Unionists a ready-made plank, and they adopted an "anti-fascist" theme in their program when it got under way on the magic date of September 15.

The specific platform when hammered out proved to be ambitious. The party recommended: (1) full amnesties to political fugitives, (2) complete restoration of civil rights where they had been abridged, (3) immediate freedom to political prisoners, (4) positive electoral guarantees, (5) abolition of *continuismo* and any constitutional reform which would legalize it, (6) more democratic elements in government.[1] While some of the aims were vague, the attack upon the office-holding proclivities of four of Central America's presidents was all too apparent. These goals were considered intermediate, to clear the atmosphere for a more specific campaign which would advocate a common currency, one flag, a customs union, a federal army, and a federal congress. President Anastasio Somoza of Nicaragua was quoted as saying that he would resign his office if his action would facilitate formation of the union. Until the time of his assassination in 1956 Somoza had not yet deemed the step advisable.

In broadening the party's base to make it anti-Fascist as well as pro-Union, the organization acquired support from some individuals who were to prove embarrassing in the anti-Communist campaigns following World War II. One of these men was Mexico's Lombardo Toledano, President of the Confederación de Trabajadores de la América Latina, soon to be branded as Communist dominated. And when a Unionist daily proposed a slate of possible presidents for a united Central America, one of

1. Varios, *Por qué lucha Centro América* (México, 1943), p. 13, a publication of the Central American Unionist party.

the firm believers who was so nominated was Manuel Mora Valverde, then secretary general of Costa Rica's Communist party. Another Tico Communist, Carlos Luis Sáenz, was also suggested as a candidate.[2] No permanent harm was done, however, for there has been no serious charge that unionism is another "Red" menace.

While the "continuist" presidents were in office, Central American confederation stood little chance of success. Even the usual discussions by presidents or foreign ministers were not attempted. It was not until 1945 that the overthrow of two of these dictators permitted the resumption of such talks. Guatemala's new chief executive, Juan José Arévalo, initiated the action shortly after the inauguration in March of El Salvador's President Salvador Castañeda Castro. The two men met at Santa Ana, El Salvador, and appointed a temporary federal council with technical committees to work out details for cooperative action of the states. For a beginning they planned economic coordination with political unity to come later.

The first steps to implement the presidents' avowals were to remove customs barriers, to eliminate restrictions on immigration, and to combine the two banking, monetary, and educational systems. In the normal fashion, the other states were invited to participate in the agreements. The president of Honduras, cool because of a recent invasion of his soil by exiles in Guatemala, declared that he had no official report of the proposal. In Nicaragua, Somoza, alternately reported as favoring and resisting the proposal, did nothing at all about it. Straddling the issue, as was the tradition among Costa Rica's politicians, President Teodoro Picado Michalski stated that he would support his nation's entrance into the new super-state if public opinion so desired. He added suggestively that he was not

2. *El Mundo Libre* (San Salvador), September 19, 1942.

sure what his people wanted. The government of El Salvador urged Costa Rica to adhere to the pact in any event. Picado's reply was that the idea was progressive and beneficial. He asked his cabinet to consider the possibility of holding a plebiscite to determine Tico opinion. No plebiscite was held, and the question disappeared from the Costa Rican public eye.

In June of 1945 the governments of Guatemala and El Salvador announced the full political merger of their five million people, more than half the population of all Central America.[3] The agreement was solemnized by being deposited with the United Nations as Unionists rejoiced, and Salvador Mendieta affirmed his party's intentions of lending its support to this forward step.[4]

But the rejoicing was not unanimous. The Honduran Conservative, Carías Andino, in his twelfth year as president, became concerned with the new confederation and viewed it as a threat against Nicaragua as well as his nation. He thereupon sent an emissary to Managua to see Somoza, apparently to formulate plans to counter the Guatemalan–El Salvadorean Republic. The trip received too much publicity, and keeping his own counsel as usual, "Tacho" Somoza refused to see Carías' representative. The latter returned to Honduras without success.

Nevertheless, the threat, if such it were, vanished. Although the two chief executives of Guatemala and El Salvador were reported ready to resign so that they might be replaced by mere governors under one unified administration, affairs never reached that stage of consummation.[5] Throughout the summer of 1945 Castañeda Castro occupied himself with a number of internal disturbances

3. *El Diario* (San José), June 5, 1945.
4. *La Nueva Prensa* (Managua), May 26, 1945.
5. New York *Times*, June 7, 1945.

in El Salvador which were partly based on food shortages and partly based on factionalism. In October, Arévalo faced the first of more than twenty uprisings in his six years of office, and so the two lands were forced to ignore the active phases of the merger.

As the following September was the 125th anniversary of the independence of Central America, new proposals for confederation were not long in coming. The president of the International Court of Justice, an ardent internationalist named José Gustavo Guerrero, invited the five Central American states to send representatives to his home at Santa Ana, El Salvador, to consider a plan. Castañeda and Arévalo attended in person. Honduras and Nicaragua took no notice of the proceedings, partly because of recent Union party attacks on their regimes and partly because of the ill-feeling existing between Guatemala and Honduras over the activities of refugees. Costa Rica's government was represented by Foreign Minister Julio Acosta. Amid denials by Arévalo that Guatemala had any intention of using force to obtain the adherence of any other state, Santa Ana was proclaimed the capital of Central America.[6] When Arévalo gratuitously added that it was a time for firm decision and not "half-baked plans," Acosta, who had so far agreed only to a system of Central American travel cards, decided that the remark was intended for Costa Rica and quickly departed from the conference.

Unrest in El Salvador meanwhile reached the extreme of a general strike which brought on a state of seige and the closing of the Guatemalan border. The Guatemalan press reported in unsympathetic fashion on these proceedings in her tiny neighboring state, and the resulting tension again swept aside plans for a confederation.

6. *El Diario* (San José), September 15, 1946.

For the next several months the threat of war hung continually over Central America although actual hostilities were uncommon. In 1948 there was civil war in Costa Rica over the election of a successor to President Picado. Protesting illegal electoral procedures a victorious rebellion was carried out by José Figueres, leading a band that the United States' press referred to as the Caribbean Legion. The old problem of *emigrados* then arose to upset Nicaraguan–Costa Rican relations. Former President Picado took a position in the Finance Ministry of Nicaragua, and his ally, former President Calderón Guardia, also received asylum in that land. There were rumors that the legion was dedicated to the overthrow of all dictators in the area, specific targets being Somoza, Carías, and Trujillo. Each of these men strengthened his forces in preparation for the attack that never came.

Apparently unconcerned by the prospect of a general war, President Figueres announced the dissolution of the Costa Rican army (transformed into a military-looking *guardia*). About the same time, December, 1948, Costa Rica was invaded by Calderonistas armed and supported by Nicaraguans. Costa Rica blamed her neighbor for the aggression and asked the Organization of American States to investigate. This body quickly sent representatives from the United States, Brazil, Colombia, and Mexico to sift the charges. Meanwhile, Castañeda Castro was overthrown in El Salvador by a clique whose leader was Major Oscar Osorio. Immediate recognition of this *junta* by Guatemala and Costa Rica gave credence to the belief that the three states were solidified against Nicaragua and Honduras.[7]

The expected internal uprising in Costa Rica failed to occur to aid the insurgents; and when the Organization of American States' agents acted promptly and decisively

7. New York *Times,* December 19, 1948.

in assessing the mutual responsibility of Nicaragua and Costa Rica, the threat of war disappeared.

The result of all these disturbances was the existence for many months of such suspicion and ill-will that precluded any proposals for union. As time passed and regimes changed much of the antagonism eased, and by 1951 the states were once again ready to consider confederation.

President Osorio of El Salvador acted as host for a series of meetings that began October 8, 1951, in the city of San Salvador. The agenda was "mutual problems." All of the Central American nations participated and sent their foreign ministers; Manuel Galich of Guatemala, Oscar Sevilla Sacasa of Nicaragua, Mario Echandi of Costa Rica, and José Edgardo Valenzuela of Honduras. The chairman was the Salvadorean minister, Roberto Canessa.

First reports were to the effect that the conferees did not intend a plan of union but sought practical steps for the promotion of closer economic, political, and cultural ties. But as seems inevitable in a Central American consultation, the dream of Morazán was offered as a substitute for the business at hand. In the opening address President Osorio told the men present that some type of union was needed to solve their principle problems: "primitive agriculture, incipient commerce and industry, illiteracy, misery, malnutrition and a thousand others."[8]

The Nicaraguan delegate made a formal motion for the immediate "reconstruction" of the federal union, but it was voted to postpone action for further study. More enthusiastically received were the proposals of Guatemala and El Salvador to create an Organization of Central American States as the first effective move toward isthmian solidarity. A commission was named to define the statutes

8. San Francisco *Examiner,* October 10, 1951.

of this body and make it acceptable to all five of the states.[9] Other committees were appointed to study means of introducing a customs union, to standardize education throughout the region, and to create a Central American university.

There were other signs of solidarity. For example, Sevilla of Nicaragua urged that the talks should be followed by a reunion of the five presidents. Galich secured declarations from the group that Belice was a problem of their common concern, and sympathy was sent to the Peoples' United party of Belice in their campaign to keep from being incorporated into a single colony with other British possessions in the Caribbean. El Salvador was reported ready to contribute half the costs of construction for a Honduran highway to Puerto Cortés on the Gulf of Honduras. Then the five republics agreed to inaugurate a fleet of merchant vessels for coastwise trade in the fashion of the Grand Colombia Merchant Marine of Colombia, Venezuela, and Ecuador.[10]

By far the most significant result of the 1951 San Salvador talks was the establishment of the Organization of Central American States. This agency was based upon eighteen articles drafted by the foreign ministers into a document called the "Charter of San Salvador." The major terms of this pact include: an intention to carry on mutual consultations to promote and maintain peaceful relations and help solve Central American problems; a reiteration of the five states' adherence to the United Nations and the Organization of American States; proclamation of the ideals of juridical equality and nonintervention; the acceptance of the five foreign ministers as the main body of the organization, meeting at least once a year and functioning by unanimous decision. A special invi-

9. *La Prensa* (New York), October 12, 1951.
10. New York *Times,* October 15, 1951.

tation was sent to Panama permitting that nation to join in the covenants if it desired. (It did not.)

In the preamble of the charter the delegates repeated in the usual language that the five republics were disintegrated portions of a single nation attempting to coordinate their efforts for the re-establishment of the old unity and to break down the artificial barriers holding the people apart.[11]

Although the republics ratified the charter promptly,[12] ODECA (Organización de los Estados Centroamericanos) did not really begin to function until 1955. In that year the foreign ministers chose José Guillermo Trabanino of El Salvador to be the secretary general for a four-year term ending in August, 1959. His office in a mansion was declared international territory and was provided by the government of El Salvador. The five states contribute to a budget of $125,000 a year.[13]

ODECA is too young to be judged fairly. In the political realm disappointments have been frequent. In 1957 a boundary dispute between Honduras and Nicaragua was referred to ODECA for settlement, but both nations refused its good offices and the issue was passed on to the Organization of American States and finally to the International Court of Justice. Many months passed before a successor to Trabanino could be chosen, the distinguished Costa Rican, Marco Tulio Zeledón. Meanwhile, Guatemala, withdrew from ODECA in 1954 because of Salvadorean charges that Central America was being infiltrated by Com-

11. Ricardo Gallardo, *Las Constituciones de la República Federal de Centro-América* (Madrid, 1958), II, 1232-58 includes the text of the charter as well as the final act of the ministers.

12. *La Prensa* (New York), October 15, 1951; New York *Times,* December 13, 1951.

13. New York *Times,* October 25, 1959; *Américas,* VII (October, 1955), 3.

munists through Guatemalan influence. Guatemala then renewed its membership after the successful revolution of the same year brought Carlos Castillo Armas into the presidency. While the Communist issue is obviously a new one in Central American relations, it served to point out the traditional ease with which these republics slip in and out of organizations intended to bring about "permanent union."

Measures taken in the economic field look much brighter. Cooperating closely with the United Nations' Economic Commission for Latin America (ECLA), ODECA has helped create a climate of economic cooperation rarely seen in Latin America. Some measures were ODECA's own; others were promoted by businessmen encouraged by the fresh attitude and imaginative opportunities.

Which projects will succeed cannot, of course, be predicted here, but a sample of their breadth will give an idea of the vision and optimism prevalent in Central American commerce and industry today.

The goal is the "economic integration" of the isthmus, to be achieved by measures such as more liberal travel policies, elimination of quota restrictions, tariff reductions (or abolition), and the creation of integrated industries. A complete customs union within ten years was the stated aim.[14] In 1958 the five states agreed upon and signed a "Multilateral Treaty of Free Commerce." As of 1960 Costa Rica had not yet ratified the treaty, but the plan was considered in effect after three states indorsed it in 1959. A similar treaty, but presumably simpler and quicker to initiate, was drawn up in early 1960, but again Costa Rica, plus Nicaragua, refused ratification.

Specifically, not a great deal has yet been done in

14. *El Imparcial* (Guatemala), August 22, 1956; *Américas*, X (October, 1958), 19.

the direction of a customs union. Some tariffs have been reduced substantially and a number of items are on the free list, but no uniform tariff policy toward non-Central American states has been evolved. Presumably this is near-ly impossible without the unanimous agreement of the five states.

It would appear that greatest progress is being made in the establishment of integrated or regional industries. Certain industries are too costly to justify their existence with only one small republic as the entire marketing area. ODECA, therefore, has encouraged—and individually ap-proved—creation of factories with region-wide investment and has then guaranteed them a tariff-free monopoly for the entire Central American market. Such projects can provide the republics with badly needed, fundamental commodities. In varying stages there are plans for a pulp and paper plant in Honduras, a paint and varnish factory in Costa Rica, a tire and rubber factory in Guatemala, and a chemical fertilizer works in El Salvador.[15]

Central Americans have reason to feel optimistic about these industrial strides. Regional trade is improving, and the expensive reliance upon imports from the United States must decline. Local businessmen seem anxious to partici-pate in future manufactories, and it should be noted that investors from outside Central America have already de-veloped plans for complementary industries. Such labor can do more for the people of Central America than a handful of conventions to draw up another constitution for the five states. One word of caution must be added: as so often before, the Costa Rican congress has decided to watch and wait. It has not ratified either major treaty

15. New York *Times,* June 12, 1960; Vincent Checchi and asso-ciates, *Honduras, a Problem in Economic Development* (New York, 1959), p. 84.

that would lead to a customs union or common market. Lack of such adherence might not prevent participation in some of the regional industries (and this is certainly not clear), but it will prevent more positive steps in the complete economic integration so needed and so sought.

One should note, finally, that basic to much of this hopeful economic activity is the belief that this is but a new bridge to the inevitable confederation. At times this wish was placed in the official record of the proceedings; on other occasions the press quoted delegates that the real objective was a unified government which would make unnecessary such stopgap measures.[16]

And so, in the middle of the twentieth century, proposals for some sort of Central American unity continue to burgeon just as they have for more than one hundred years. Is there any more reason to expect success today than in the past? It might prove useful to make a final analysis of the reasons for such steadfast effort and consistent failure and to venture a guess for the future of the movement.

16. *La Hora* (Guatemala), August 17, 1956; New Orleans *Times Picayune,* July 13, 1958.

Chapter XI

A Judgment

THREE years after securing independence from Spain, the five provinces of Central America in November, 1824, promulgated a constitution and set into operation the Federal Republic of Central America. This union clearly failed by 1838, and the individual states seceded and went their separate ways. From 1842 until the present writing the idea of re-establishing the Federal Republic has never completely disappeared from the Central American mind. On at least twenty-five different occasions formal and official steps were taken to reconstitute the states into some single form of government. No attempt lasted more than a few months, nor included all five of the nations. There has never been anything resembling success. With so much devotion to an ideal, with so much effort and, at times, blood expended for so many years, why has confederation always failed, and why is there none today? There might be scores of reasons, but to make the study of any significance it is necessary to reduce their number to a few of the most basic.

At the outset it should be stressed that obstacles or reasons for the failure of Central American confederacy are fundamental; the reasons why *individual* attempts collapsed might be very superficial, as indicated in earlier chapters, and will not be repeated here.

1. The failure of Central American confederation is basically the failure of representative government in Central America. The cliché is too well suited to be omitted— one can not learn to run until one learns to walk. Central American republics are just beginning to walk. The federal form of government as generally contemplated is complex. It necessitates an informed electorate and many qualified office-holders. Both of these criteria have been lacking in Central America. Costa Rica, for example, coming the closest to meeting these requirements, has shied from federation on the grounds that the other states lack these virtues.

Central America was the scene of some of the longest and most vicious dictatorships the world has known, too often relieved only by brief anarchy. They gave no training in self government. Then, mistakes in judgment exacted their penalty; in the success of the United States, early Central American statesmen thought they saw their image. They copied the United States constitution and form of government without realizing their inapplicability to a Latin American society. Later in the nineteenth century, Central Americans misunderstood what they saw happening in Germany and Italy. They observed modern nations being formed by the use of force and justified its use at home if it would lead to the same end, but in Central America only Guatemala was strong enough to dominate one or two others, and even that state lacked the military might to subjugate four enemies. So there could result only a stalemate at best when power was employed. In the early twentieth century the United States would not permit domination of the rest of Central America by one state. Today peace regularly prevails among the states, and it can be hoped that the Organization of Central American States will act promptly and decisively to prevent future political difficulties. It seems a safe conclusion that a federation by force is no longer possible.

But, given the character of Central American self-government, is not a more peaceful union possible from one of the numerous conferences held for that purpose? There is little reason for cheer. Consider the nature of elections under such circumstances. Party lines would form easily—the Liberals of Honduras would have much in common with the Liberals of El Salvador, for example. But would other states accept the ballots cast in a republic dominated by an Estrada Cabrera or, more recently, a Somoza, or any of a dozen like them? Such despots, with complete or nearly complete control of the electoral processes would be rightfully suspected by the governments which at that moment were enjoying a measure of democracy. Customs unions or similar economic cooperation might be attainable, but while one of the republics remains in the grip of political serfdom, there can be no true federation. Today it is Nicaragua, but in the later 1960's it could be another, for the pendulum swings both ways, and even Costa Rica interspersed her freer eras with regimes such as those of Tinoco and Guardia. Time and the maturity of time can bring about the changes which will make democracy work in Central America. Democracy can help create a federation, but federation cannot take the time to develop democracy. Central America is politically adolescent still. The masses yet lack the training to rise above indifference. To these people federation is a slogan belonging with "Viva la Constitución" or "Death to the Serviles." It is meaningless on their lips and valueless in their minds. When representative government in any one state can be trusted by the representative governments in all of the other four states, only then will a representative government of the whole have a chance for success.

2. Another major reason for the failure of federation in Central America is nationalism. Obviously this is a characteristic of all states everywhere, but in Central America it has been exceptionally aggravated. A century ago the chances for a single government were probably brighter than they are today because the citizens of that time were all born under one flag (Spain's or Central America's) and had not yet thought of themselves as members of individual states. But even then strong jealousies existed. Provincial distrust antedated independence, and it was particularly aimed at Guatemala for its larger population, power, and wealth. In fact, one of the chief reasons for the type of government structure adopted in 1824 was the fear of little El Salvador that Guatemala would swallow her in a more centralized government.

These jealousies, though put aside when a stronger interest temporarily dictated, have generally continued unabated. As late as 1946 Guatemala's president felt constrained to declare that his union plans did not include the use of force. The recent regimes of Figueres in Costa Rica and Somoza in Nicaragua were notoriously ill-tempered toward each other. The revolution which installed Castillo Armas into Guatemala's presidency was mounted in Honduras. Honduras fears the population pressure exerted upon it by crowded El Salvador. And so on. Chief executives are often personal friends or enemies. They know full well the opportunities and temptations put in the path of the presidency by plotting *emigrados*. Each state is too much aware of the affairs of its neighbors.

Thus the proximity of Central American peoples to one another is a mixed blessing: their close ties demand efforts to confederate, but these same ties have brought about the familiarity that breeds mistrust.

Now, on the foundation of provincial rivalry, there is built more than a century of nationalistic development. Two dozen and more abortive confederations have not served to pull the states together. For several generations the people of El Salvador, for example, have thought of themselves as Salvadoreans even though their constitution may declare that they are the "separated fragments of the Federal Republic of Central America."

Nationalism has further thrived upon a diet of almost perpetual boundary disputes even along such natural borders as the Río San Juan. Not until 1936 did Guatemala, Honduras, and El Salvador agree upon a single mountain peak as the common point of contact of the three nations. Honduras disputes with Nicaragua the ownership of a region comprising 20 to 30 per cent of the accepted area of either of these two republics. Nicaragua still claims Costa Rica's Guanacaste province, and Guatemala seeks the support of all of Central America for the "return" of British Honduras. Often these issues concern significant portions of land and are of grave importance as shibboleths. They perpetuate ranklings that in no wise contribute to the success of a confederation movement.

3. The next most important obstacle to the restoration of the Federal Republic is the isolationism of Costa Rica. This strong, consistent policy bears characteristics that clearly distinguish the attitude from the nationalism of the other four states. Largely basing their judgments upon economic motivation, Costa Rican leaders of late colonial times concluded that this weak province must chart a very

careful course in Central American affairs. The commercial pull from Colombia and Panama was greater than that from Central America, and Costa Rican merchants saw the advantages of balancing one region against the other.[1] The picture was not changed in republican times as first Great Britain and then the United States became the chief markets of Costa Rican products. Never has Costa Rica's Central American trade been primary.

Furthermore, located on the geographical fringe of Central America, Costa Ricans were to find abstention from the affairs of the others highly advantageous and easily achieved. As separation continued, the Ticos concluded that it was the major factor in their nation's more stable political development.

Federation has never been of great importance in Costa Rica, as a consequence. No plebiscite has ever been held on the matter, and it has never been seriously considered in a presidential campaign. Some degree of this lack of interest can be measured by her participation in conferences called to discuss Central American confederation. Since 1842 there have been about two dozen meetings of that nature. While El Salvador and Honduras participated in virtually every one, and Guatemala and Nicaragua in just a few less, Costa Rica sent delegates to a scant one-third of the conventions called. Furthermore, with rare exception, her congress refused to ratify the occasional commitments that her diplomats made. Theirs was largely a policy of inactivity. Not always have Costa

1. It is my belief that a Central American federation must cope with the force of nationalism in all five of the republics, but Costa Rica presents an attitude that has had social, economic, and religious origins leading to a feeling that must be called isolationism. I have attempted to explore this in two articles: "La Norma de Conducta de Costa Rica," in *Revista de los Archivos Nacionales de Costa Rica,* XVII (Julio-Diciembre, 1953), 266-72, and "The Origins of Costa Rican Federalism," in *The Americas,* XV (January, 1959), 249-69.

Rican statesmen been as outspoken as former President Otilio Ulate, who declared in 1951 that Costa Rica could not consider confederation until the rest of Central America attained the cultural and democratic level reached by Costa Rica.[2] More often the tactic is to affirm support of various plans but postpone action until the "times" are more propitious. Public opinion has ever seemed to support this policy.

The Costa Rican smugly believes that his schools are the best, his literacy rate the highest, and his elections the most democratic in Central America. He does not wish to jeopardize his accomplishments by too much intercourse with states that he considers more backward. Then, as Costa Rica is the only predominantly white nation in Central America, he quietly concludes that the Indians and *mestizos* in the other lands are unstable, untrained, and poor political partners who would outnumber the Costa Rican in any representative body. In sum, the idea of federation is not dead in Costa Rica, but it is too weak to surmount anything resembling the constitutional requirement of a two-thirds majority in congress, plus a two-thirds majority of a special assembly called for that purpose.

While the absence of a single state should not necessarily be fatal to a union of the other four, it does destroy the homogeneity of the isthmus and sets in motion consonant feelings of separatism in the remaining republics. The others rarely consider a union without Costa Rica.

Many other factors explaining the failure of Central American confederation might be cited, such as the varying debt structures and the competitive nature of the five

2. Victoria Bertrand, "Pentagonal Portrait," *United Nations World,* V (September, 1951), 37.

economies, but these are lesser factors and can be over-come.

Considering the long history of failure, why are con-federation proposals still made? Why is the subject still of interest to the Central American governments? The an-swer is easily found in the correspondence exchanged by officials before each meeting and still reported enthusias-tically in the press as each generation discovers for itself the blessings of union. A typical summary was made by Alberto Lleras Camargo while secretary general of the Pan American Union. The distinguished Colombian wrote that if the people of Central America had their way, there would be four fewer republics in Latin America. In their stead would be a new, enlarged nation of about eight million people and an area of about 187,000 square miles. It would be midway among American states in commercial importance. He listed other advantages, some perhaps less real, but there is implicit belief that a sharp increase in size alone would be beneficial to Central America.[3] Lleras Camargo, surely less concerned with invasion than earlier writers, nevertheless echoed the region's chronic fear of invasion and intervention. International respect would be enhanced by increased population, more extensive com-merce, and a stronger army. There would be greater in-ternal security because the enemies of a regime would no longer find a friendly neighbor state in which to hide.

Central Americans have frequently declared that by combining efforts they could have much wider diplomatic representation in the world. They would expect tax savings because there would be one president instead of five, one supreme court instead of five, and so on. The theoretical economies would be substantial. Credit would be firmer,

3. Alberto Lleras Camargo, "Toward Central American Union," *Américas,* IV (April, 1952), 3.

hence industry and agriculture would develop more rapidly, and trade would be multiplied. Cultural ties so important to Latin Americans would be enhanced by the merging and consolidating of educational systems, and there are many lesser benefits that Unionists speak of. The more ardent Unionists claim that *all* of the problems of Central America would disappear if only the five states could become one. In sum, federation to many Central Americans is the short cut to good government.

What factors exist that might yet bring such advantages about? The apparent similarities have been examined in the first chapter—language, race, religion, culture, common interests, and location. To these must be added the strong tradition that the states once were joined and therefore ought to be joined. Are these reasons sufficient to surmount the obstacles to confederation? Compelling as they may seem, they do not alter the conditions that have always brought failure and which still exist to plague present-day confederation movements. While it may be hoped that the Central American states will gradually broaden their democratic bases, it must be recognized that nationalism is getting stronger through the decades. As for Costa Rica its separatism is nourished by continued Central American misgovernment.

On the optimistic side are the rapid improvements in communications during the past decade and the probable role of the United States. The former is obvious and readily measured. The latter needs analysis.

Throughout the nineteenth century the course of the United States was to foster union movements in Central America. This was not altruism. In first place the United States viewed the Central American experiment as an attempt at imitation. It was flattering and gave a proprietary interest to the North American. Europeans might tend to look upon the two areas as similar in political philosophy, and if the one failed, it was a reflection upon the system of the other. Secondly, it was normally held in Washington that a federation would make Central America stronger and would help to prevent incursions such as those by the British and those rumored by the Spanish and French.

From the dissolution of the Federal Republic until the end of the nineteenth century, United States policy toward Central American confederation can be traced in the instructions from the State Department to ministers residing abroad. With but one exception the order was repeated at least once every decade that United States diplomats should help the cause of unity by advice and counsel and by aid within legitimate bounds.[4]

Nevertheless, the belief spread in Central America that the United States was a threat to federation. This not unreasonable conclusion arose out of the destruction of the Central American Court of Justice by the refusal of the United States (and its protectorate, Nicaragua) to observe the court's verdict concerning the Bryan-Chamorro Treaty of 1916. The United States interpretation of the pact was a serious political and juridical error which could easily have been avoided, but the decision was one of pure self-interest and was not designed as an attack upon Central Americanism. Any damage to that already feeble ideal was not only slight, but unintentional and incidental to other purposes.

4. Secretary Seward informed the minister in Guatemala that the United States did not know enough about Central American affairs to advise the people whether federation was best for them or not. One can wonder if it is mere coincidence that the only secretary of state who was unsure regarding federalism was the official who held that post during the American Civil War. William H. Seward to Elisha O. Crosby, October 9, 1862, Diplomatic Instructions, XVI, 255.

In more recent years there has been little reason for Central Americans to fear that the United States would act to prevent their confederation. State Department expressions indicate that if a Nicaraguan canal is ever built by the United States, benefits would accrue to the rest of Central America as well as to Nicaragua. If the five republics should succeed in unifying themselves, the impact upon the United States would scarcely be of much significance today. As long as there is no great turbulence, Central America is surely secure from future Yankee intervention. If there exists a United States policy for Central America in the middle of the twentieth century, it appears to be one that favors stability and prosperity unless a Communist threat appears. In the absence of that danger, the Yankee dollar shines beneficently upon the entire Caribbean area, oligarchic, democratic, despotic alike. There is no reason to believe that the United States, now or in the immediate future, would not be pleased to see the reconstruction of the Central American Republic.

With the "foreign menace" gone and communications sharply improving, can the Central American ideal overcome the several obstacles that still remain? This writer has difficulty concealing his pessimism. While it is easy to envision a customs union or some other form of economic cooperation so popular today, any significant political step seems most unlikely. Nothing has occurred to promise a sudden reversal of a long history of disappointments. The failures serve a function; they provide an excuse for inactivity or error in administration, and what can be the possible consequences of some twenty-five failures in the past century and a quarter? No lessons seem to be learned; the same methods are used; the same language is used; the same agreements are made. Are not Central American diplomats aware of these facts when they make their regular treks to Santa Ana or Antigua to rake over the old coals?

Is it not possible that Central Americans have grossly exaggerated the grass-roots strength of the confederation feeling? There are no mass movements, no popular demonstrations, no confederationist candidates. The historic Central American goal has been reduced to a literary exercise. Few, indeed, must be the diplomats who expect success at their confederation conferences and who can remain very serious about the prospects of their work. If the issue were ever to be settled, something exciting would disappear from Central American affairs. As a substitute for achievements, as a trick when things are dull, as a serviceable red herring, the question of Central American confederation is perfect.

In conclusion it should be made clear that confederation is, of course, possible. It *could* be attained in the next few decades with ease, but on any historical basis one must conclude that Central Americans would do well to realize that a federated republic should not be an end itself. The goal should be Central American welfare, not a form of government. Other tiny nations in the world have thrived, educated their children, and met the responsibilities of government. These aims are real and attainable. They warrant some of the money, effort, and blood which have gone into the elusive dream, wasted in a century of failure.

Bibliography

1. MANUSCRIPT COLLECTIONS

Costa Rica. Archives, Ministerio de Relaciones Extranjeros. Useful for *Informes* and diplomatic correspondence especially between 1880 and 1925. San José, Costa Rica.

————. Archivos Nacionales, San José, Costa Rica. Several thousand items, 1821-1942.

Great Britain. Foreign Office records relating to Central America, 1825-52, series 15, microfilm in library of Middle American Research Institute, Tulane University.

Guatemala. Archivo Nacional, Guatemala City. Several thousand items, 1818-1951.

United States. Records of the Department of State. Diplomatic Instructions, American States. 1833-1906. Microfilm in library, Stanford University.

2. PRINTED GOVERNMENT DOCUMENTS

A. FOREIGN DOCUMENTS

Central America, Corte de Justicia. *Anales*. San José, Costa Rica, 1911.

————, Gobierno Federal. *Gazeta*. San Salvador, 1834.

————, Tercer Congreso. *Pacto de unión provisional*. Managua, Nicaragua, 1889.

Costa Rica, Secretaría de Educación Pública. *Documentos históricos posteriores a la independencia, 1821-1836*. San José, 1923.

————, Secretario de Estado. *Informes del Secretario de Estado al Congreso Constitucional, 1848-1925.* San José, 1848-1925.

————, Secretario de Estado. *Revista de Costa Rica en el siglo XIX.* San José, 1902.

El Salvador, Asamblea Nacional. *Diario de las sesiones de la Asamblea Nacional.* San Salvador, 1890.

————, Ministerio de Relaciones Exteriores. *Anuario diplomático del Salvador.* San Salvador, 1885.

————, Ministerio de Relaciones Exteriores. *Libro Rosado.* San Salvador, 1921.

————, Secretario de Estado. *Documentos y datos históricos y estadísticos de la república de El Salvador.* San Salvador, 1926.

Great Britain, Foreign Office. *British and Foreign State Papers, 1903-04.* London, 1908.

Guatemala, Gobierno Superior. *Documentos de la Capitanía General de Guatemala.* 2 vols. Guatemala, no date.

————, Ministerio de Educación Pública. *Escritos del Doctor Pedro Molina.* 3 vols. Guatemala, 1954.

————, Ministerio de Relaciones Exteriores. *Circular dirijido a los gobiernos de las repúblicas del Salvador, Honduras, Nicaragua y Costa Rica.* Guatemala, 1875.

————, Secretario de Estado. *Guatemala Independiente. Documentos después de la independencia de Centro América.* Guatemala, 1932.

————, Secretario de Estado. *Memoria de la Secretaría General de Estado sobre todos los ramos.* Guatemala, 1837.

Mexico, Secretaría de Relaciones Exteriores. *La Anexión de Centro América á México.* 2 vols. Mexico, 1924 and 1927.

B. UNITED STATES DOCUMENTS

Congressional Globe, 23rd-42nd Congresses, 1833-73.

Congressional Record, 43rd-82nd Congresses, 1873-1950.

Foreign Relations of the United States, 1873-1922.

House of Representatives Documents Relative to Central American Affairs. Washington, 1856.

House of Representatives Executive Documents, 47th Cong. 2nd sess., no. 2090, Washington, 1883.

Monthly Consular and Trade Reports, 1895.

Register of Debates in Congress, 1824-1837.

Senate Executive Documents, 31st Cong., 1st sess., no. 43, and 66th Cong., 1st sess., no. 77, Washington, 1851 and 1919.

3. NEWSPAPERS

Crónica de Costa Rica, 1859. San José.

Daily National Intelligencer, 1829-30. Washington.

El Costaricense, 1848. San José.

El Diario, 1919-53. San José.

El Federalista, 1833. Guatemala.

El Imparcial, 1956. Guatemala.

El Mentor Costarricense, 1842-46. San José.

El Mundo Libre, 1942. San Salvador.

El Salvador Rejenerado, 1846. San Salvador.

Honduras Observer and Belize Gazette, 1845. Belice.

La Gaceta de Nicaragua, 1876. Managua.

La Hora, 1956. Guatemala.

La Nueva Prensa, 1945. Managua.

La Prensa, 1951-52. New York.

La Prensa Libre, 1889-1951. San José.

La República, 1908. San José.

La Tertulia, 1834-35. San José.

La Tribuna, 1909-47. San José.

Le Moniteur Universal, 1830. Paris.

New Orleans *Times Picayune,* 1958.

New York *Times,* 1913-60.

Noticioso Universal, 1833-35. San José.

Reconciliación, 1925-28. Tegucigalpa, Honduras.

San Francisco *Chronicle,* 1948-52.

San Francisco *Evening Bulletin,* 1885.

San Francisco *Examiner,* 1951.

4. PERIODICALS AND MAGAZINES

American Historical Review, 1899. New York.

Américas, 1949-59. Washington.

Business Week, 1947. New York.

Contemporary Review, 1921. London.

Current History, 1922, 1934. New York.

Harper's Magazine, 1858, 1942. New York.

Hispanic American Historical Review, 1920-60. Baltimore.

Inter-American, 1944-45. New York.

International Conciliation, 1923. New York.

Nation, 1887. New York.

Newsweek, 1945. New York.

Niles' Weekly Register, 1811-49. Baltimore.

North American Review, 1828. Boston.

Outlook, 1908. New York.

Overland Monthly, 1875. San Francisco.

Pan American Union Bulletin, 1934, 1935, 1942. Washington.

Review of Reviews, December, 1922. New York.

Revista de la Academía de Geografía e Historia de Nicaragua, 1930-44. Managua.

Revista de los Archivos Nacionales de Costa Rica, 1936-50. San José.

Revista del Archivo y Biblioteca Nacionales, 1942. Tegucigalpa.

Time, 1942, 1946. Chicago.

Travel, 1944. New York.

United Nations World, 1951. New York.

World Peace Foundation Pamphlet, 1917. Boston.

5. COLLECTED DOCUMENTS, LETTERS, AND WORKS

Barrios, Modesto, ed. *Memoria del General Manuel José Arce.* San Salvador, 1903.

Bolivar, Simón. *Cartas del Libertador.* Vols. VIII, IX, X. Caracas, 1930.

Bowring, John, ed. *The Works of Jeremy Bentham.* Vols. IX, X, XI. Edinburgh, 1843.

Fernández, León. *Colección de Documentos para la historia de Costa Rica.* 10 vols. Barcelona, 1881-1907.

García, Genaro. *Documentos inéditos ó muy raros para la historia de México.* Vol. XXXV. Mexico, 1911.

Iglesias, Francisco María, ed. *Documentos relativos a la independencia.* San José, 1899.

Lecuna, Vicente, and Bierck, Harold A., eds. *Selected Writings of Bolívar.* New York, 1951.

Manning, William R., ed. *Diplomatic Correspondence of the United States. Inter American Affairs.* Vols. III and IV. Washington, 1933, 1934.

―――. *Diplomatic Correspondence of the United States Concerning the Independence of the Latin American Nations.* 3 Vols. New York, 1925.

Molina, Pedro. *Escritos,* Editorial del Ministerio de Educación Pública. Guatemala, 1954.

Moore, John Bassett, ed. *The Works of James Buchanan.* Vol. VIII. Philadelphia, 1909.

Pacheco Cooper, Federico. *Costa Rica en 1842.* San José, 1904.

Picado Michalski, Teodoro, and Fournier Quirós, Ricardo. *Unión Centro-americana.* San José, 1921.

Richardson, James D., ed. *A Compilation of the Messages and Papers of the Presidents.* 10 vols. Washington, 1897.

Vallejo, Antonio R. *Compendio de la historia social y política de Honduras.* Tegucigalpa, 1926.

Varios. *Colección de varios folletos sociales.* London, 1893.

―――. *Costa Rica y Morazán.* San José, 1887.

―――. *El ideal latino americano.* México, 1919.

―――. *Por qué lucha Centro América.* México, 1943.

Valle, Rafael Heliodoro, ed. *La anexión de Centro América a México.* Mexico, 1924-27.

Webster, C. K., ed. *Britain and the Independence of Latin America.* Vol. I. London, 1938.

Zeledón, Marco Tulio, ed. *Digesto constitucional de Costa Rica.* San José, 1946.

6. AUTOBIOGRAPHIES, DIARIES, AND REMINISCENCES

Baily, John. *Central America.* London, 1850.

Barrios, Gerardo. *Manifiesto de Gerardo Barrios.* New York, 1864.

Barrios, Justo Rufino. *Carta.* Guatemala, 1883.

Belly, Felix. *A travers L'Amérique Centrale.* 2 vols. Paris, 1867.

Crowe, Frederick. *The Gospel in Central America.* London, 1850.

De Périgny, Maurice. *Les cinq republiques de L'Amérique Centrale.* Paris, 1914.

Dunlop, Robert G. *Travels in Central America.* London, 1847.

Filísola, Vicente. *La cooperación de México en la independencia de Centro América.* Mexico, 1911.

Froebel, Julius. *Seven Years' Travel in Central America.* London, 1859.

————. *Aus Amerika.* Leipzig, 1856.

Humboldt, Alexander von. *Personal Narrative of Travels to the Equinoctial Regions of America.* Vol. I. London, 1872.

Iglesias, Francisco María. *Pro Patria.* San José, 1900.

Roberts, Orlando. *Narrative of Voyages and Excursions on the East Coast and in the Interior of Central America.* Edinburgh, 1827.

Scherzer, Carl. *Travels in the Free States of Central America.* 2 vols. London, 1857.

Squier, Ephraim G. *Nicaragua, its people, scenery, monuments and the proposed interoceanic canal.* 2 vols. New York, 1852.

————. *The States of Central America.* New York, 1858.

Stephens, John L. *Incidents of Travel in Central America, Chiapas and Yucatán.* 2 vols. New York, 1841.

Thompson, George A. *Narrative of an Official Visit to Guatemala from Mexico.* London, 1829.

Trollope, Anthony. *The West Indies and the Spanish Main.* New York, 1860.

Wagner, Moritz and Scherzer, Carl. *La República de Costa Rica en Centro América*. Leipzig, 1856. Translated into Spanish, San José, 1944, by Jorge Lines.

Walker, William. *The War in Nicaragua*. Mobile, 1860.

Wells, William V. *Exploration and Adventures in Honduras*. New York, 1857.

7. BIOGRAPHIES

Anduray, M. Bertrand. *Dr. Paulino Valladares; in memoriam*. Tegucigalpa, 1927.

Burgess, Paul. *Justo Rufino Barrios*. New York, 1926.

Chamberlain, Robert S. *Francisco Morazán, Champion of Central American Federation*. Coral Gables, Florida, 1950.

Davis, Harold E. *Makers of Democracy in Latin America*. New York, 1945.

Díaz, Victor Miguel. *Barrios ante la posteridad*. Guatemala, 1935.

Durón y Gamero, Rómulo Ernesto. *Biografía de don Juan Nepomuceno Fernández Lindo*. Tegucigalpa, 1932.

Fernández Guardia, Ricardo. *Morazán en Costa Rica*. San José, 1943.

Greene, Laurence. *The Filibuster*. Indianapolis, 1937.

Martínez López, Eduardo. *Biografía del General Francisco Morazán*. Tegucigalpa, 1899.

Mejía Nieto, Arturo. *Morazán, presidente de la desaparecida república centroamericana*. Buenos Aires, 1947.

Moorehead, Max L. "Rafael Carrera of Guatemala." Unpublished doctoral dissertation, University of California, 1942.

Priestley, Herbert I. *José de Gálvez*. Berkeley, 1916.

Reyes, Rafael. *Vida de Morazán*. San Salvador, 1925.

Rosa, Ramón. *Biografía de Don José Cecilio Del Valle*. Tegucigalpa, 1943.

Sanabria, Víctor. *Bernardo Augusto Thiel, segundo obispo de Costa Rica*. San José, 1941.

Sanso, Aro. *Policarpo Bonilla*. Mexico, 1936.

8. PERIODICAL ARTICLES

Anderson, Luis. "The Peace Conference of Central America," *American Journal of International Law*, II (January, 1908), 144-51.

Bailey, Thomas A. "Interest in a Nicaraguan Canal," *Hispanic American Historical Review*, XVI (February, 1936), 2-28.

Bertrand, Victoria. "Pentagonal Portrait," *United Nations World*, V (September, 1951), 37.

Brown, Philip M. "American Diplomacy in Central America," *American Political Science Review*, VI (Supp. 1912).

Buell, Raymond Leslie. "The United States and Central American Stability," *Foreign Policy Reports*, VII (July 8, 1931), 161-86.

————. "The United States and Central American Revolutions," *Foreign Policy Reports*, VII (July 22, 1931), 187-204.

————. "Union or Disunion in Central America," *Foreign Affairs*, XI (April, 1933), 478-89.

Chapman, Charles E. "The Failure of the Central American Union," *Review of Reviews*, LXVI (December, 1922), 613-17.

"Conference on Central American Affairs," *International Conciliation*, No. 189 (August, 1923).

Dawley, Thomas R., Jr., "How the Central American Union Was Born," *Current History*, XV (January, 1922), 616-26.

Dozer, Donald. "Roots of Revolution in Latin America," *Foreign Affairs*, XXVII (January, 1949), 274-88.

Dulles, John Foster. "Conceptions and Misconceptions Regarding Intervention," *Annals of the American Academy of Political and Social Science*, CXLIV (July, 1929), 102-4.

Durón, Rómulo E. "José Cecilio Del Valle," *Pan American Bulletin*, LXIX (January, 1935), 39-45.

Emerson, Edwin. "The Unrest in Central America," *Independent*, LXVII (December 9, 1909), 1286-91.

"Fall of the Union Seen at Close Range," *Current History,* XVI (May, 1922), 287.

Fitzgibbon, Russell H. "Continuismo in Central America and the Caribbean," *The Inter-American Quarterly,* II (July, 1940), 56-74.

———. "Executive Power in Central America," *The Journal of Politics,* III (August, 1941), 297-307.

Frank, Willard. "The Central American Peace Conference," *Independent,* LXIII (December 12, 1907), 1406-9.

Gonzáles Víquez, Cleto. "Carrillo y Costa Rica ante la Federación," *Revista de los Archivos Nacionales de Costa Rica,* I (San José, Julio-Agosto, 1937), 492-521.

Griffith, William J. "El Puerto de Santo Tomás," *Anales de la Sociedad de Geografía e Historia de Guatemala* (forthcoming issue).

———. "Juan Galindo, Central American Chauvinist," *Hispanic American Historical Review,* XL (February, 1960), 25-52.

Hudson, Manley O. "The Central American Court of Justice," *American Journal of International Law,* XXVI (October, 1932), 759-86.

Karnes, Thomas L. "La Norma de Conducta de Costa Rica," *Revista de los Archivos Nacionales de Costa Rica,* XVII (Julio-Diciembre, 1953), 266-72.

———. "The Origins of Costa Rican Federalism," *The Americas,* XV (January, 1959), 249-69.

Lleras Camargo, Alberto. "Toward Central American Union," *Américas,* IV (April, 1952), 3.

Lockey, Joseph B. "Diplomatic Futility," *Hispanic American Historical Review,* X (August, 1930), 265-94.

Martin, Lawrence and Sylvia. "Four Strong Men and a President," *Harper's Magazine,* CLXXXV (September, 1942), 418-27.

Michelin, Marcelle. "Suicide by Oil," *The Nation,* CLXXIII (October 27, 1951), 353-54.

Ogden, R. "The Proposed Central American Federation," *The Nation,* XLV (July 21, 1887), 47-48.

Perry, Edward. "Central American Union," *Hispanic American Historical Review,* V (February, 1922), 30-51.

Scott, James Brown. "The Central American Peace Conference," *American Journal of International Law,* II (January, 1908), 121-43.

Selva, Salomón de la. "On the Proposed Union of Central America," *Hispanic American Historical Review,* III (November, 1920), 566-70.

Slade, William F. "The Federation of Central America," *Journal of Race Development,* VIII (July and October, 1917), 79-150, 204-75.

Warner, Arthur. "Guatemala—our Blow at Pan Americanism," *The Nation,* CXIV (June 21, 1922), 745-46.

Williams, Mary W. "Ecclesiastical Policy of Morazán and other Liberals," *Hispanic American Historical Review,* III (May, 1920), 119-43.

9. MONOGRAPHS, GENERAL WORKS, AND REFERENCES

Appleton, D., and Co. *The American Annual Cyclopaedia,* XII and XVI. New York, 1873, 1877.

Ayón, Tomás. *Historia de Nicaragua.* 3 vols. Managua, 1882-89.

Badía Malagrida, Carlos. *El Factor Geográfico en la Política Sudamericana.* Madrid, 1919.

Bancroft, Hubert Howe. *History of Central America,* III. San Francisco, 1887.

Barrios Castro, Carlos. *Labor Americana.* San José, 1926.

Batres, Luis. *La Cuestión de la Unión Centro-Americana.* San José, 1881.

Bemis, Samuel Flagg. *The Latin American Policy of the United States.* New York, 1943.

Biesanz, John and Mavis. *Costa Rican Life.* New York, 1945.

Cardona, Jorge. *Convención Unionista de Santa Ana.* San José, 1921.

Castro, Angel Anselmo. *La Unión Nacional.* San José, 1889.

Chamorro, Pedro Joaquín. *Historia de la Federación de la América Central*. Madrid, 1951.

Checchi, Vincent, and associates. *Honduras, a Problem in Economic Development*. New York, 1959.

Coronado Aguilar, Manuel. *Influencia de España en Centro América*. Guatemala, 1943.

Cox, Isaac J. *Nicaragua and the United States*. Boston, 1927.

Crowther, Samuel. *The Romance and Rise of the American Tropics*. New York, 1929.

Curtis, William E. *The Capitals of Spanish America*. New York, 1888.

Elliott, L. E. *Central America*. London, 1924.

Facio, Rodrigo. *Trayectoria y Crisis de la Federación Centroamericana*. San José, 1949.

Fernández, León. *Historia de Costa Rica*. Madrid, 1889.

Fernández Guardia, Ricardo. *Cartilla Histórica de Costa Rica*. San José, 1949.

―――. *Historia de Costa Rica*. San José, 1941.

―――. *La Independencia y otros Episodios*. San José, 1928.

Figeac, José F. *Recordatorio histórico de la república de El Salvador*. San Salvador, 1938.

Gallardo, Ricardo. *Las Constituciones de la República Federal de Centro-América*. 2 vols. Madrid, 1958.

Gámez, José Dolores. *Historia de Nicaragua*. Managua, 1889.

García Calderón, Francisco. *Latin America, its Rise and Progress*. New York, 1913.

Grimaldo, Eladio. *En el Centenario del Congreso de Bolívar*. Panama, 1926.

Haring, C. H. *The Spanish Empire in America*. New York, 1947.

Herrarte, Alberto. *La Unión de Centroamérica*. Guatemala, 1955.

Holleran, Mary P. *Church and State in Guatemala*. New York, 1949.

Jones, Chester Lloyd. *Costa Rica and the Civilization in the Caribbean*. Madison, 1935.

―――. *Guatemala: Past and Present*. Minneapolis, 1940.

Juarros, Domingo. *Compendio de la Historia de la Ciudad de Guatemala*. 2 vols. Guatemala, 1808, 1818.

Levene, Ricardo. *Historia de América*, Tomo XI. Buenos Aires, 1941.

Lines, Jorge. *Libros y folletos publicados en Costa Rica durante los años 1830-1849*. San José, 1944.

Martin, Percy F. *Salvador in the XXth Century*. London, 1911.

Martineau, Harriet. *A History of the 30 Years' Peace*, Vol. II. London, 1877.

Marure, Alejandro. *Bosquejo histórico de las revoluciones de Centro América*. Guatemala, 1837.

————. *Efemérides de los hechos notables acaecidos en la república de Centro-América*. Guatemala, 1895.

Mecham, J. Lloyd. "The Origins of Federalism" in Conyers Read, ed., *The Constitution Reconsidered*. New York, 1938.

Mendieta, Salvador. *Alrededor del problema unionista de Centro-América*. Barcelona, 1926.

————. *Exposición presentada á la Asamblea Nacional Constituyente de la República de Centroamérica*. Managua, 1921.

————. *La Nacionalidad y el Partido Unionista Centroamericano*. San José, 1905.

Meza, Rafael. *Centro América, campaña nacional de 1885*. Guatemala, 1935.

Molina, Felipe. *Bosquejo de la república de Costa Rica*. New York, 1851.

Monge Alfaro, Carlos, and Wender, Ernesto J. *Historia de Costa Rica*. San José, 1947.

Montero Barrantes, Francisco. *Elementos de historia de Costa Rica*. San José, 1892.

Montúfar, Lorenzo. *Reseña histórica de Centro América*. 7 vols. Guatemala, 1878-88.

Montúfar, Manuel. *Memorias para la historia de la revolución de Centro América*. 5 vols. Guatemala, 1853.

Moreno, Laudelino. *Historia de las relaciones interestatuales de Centroamérica*. Madrid, 1928.

Munro, Dana G. *The Five Republics of Central America*. New York, 1918.

Naylor, Robert A. "British Commercial Relations with Central America, 1821-1851." Unpublished doctoral dissertation, Tulane University, 1958.

Nuñez, Francisco María. *Interpretación histórica del momento Morazánico*. San José, 1942.

Obregón Loría, Rafael. *Conflictos militares y políticos de Costa Rica*, San José, 1951.

Palmer, Frederick. *Central America and its Problems*. New York, 1910.

Peralta, Hernán G. *Agustín de Iturbide y Costa Rica*. San José, 1944.

Quijando Quesada, Alberto. *Costa Rica, ayer y hoy*. San José, 1939.

Rippy, J. Fred. *Rivalry of the United States and Great Britain over Latin America*. Baltimore, 1929.

Rodríguez, Manuel F. *El Centenario Negro*. Buenos Aires, 1939.

Rodríguez, Mario. *The Livingston Codes in the Great Crisis of 1837-1838*. Middle American Research Institute Publication, No 23, New Orleans, 1955.

Rodríguez Beteta, Virgilio. *Ideologías de la independencia*. Paris, 1926.

Ruhl, Arthur. *The Central Americans*. New York, 1928.

Sáenz, Vicente. *Cartas á Morazán*. Comayaguela, Honduras, 1922.

―――. *Centro América en pie*. México, 1944.

―――. *Norteamericanización de Centro América*. San José, 1925.

Salvatierra, Sofonías. *Contribución a la historia de Centroamérica*. 2 vols. Managua, 1939.

Sansón-Terán, José. *Universalismo y regionalismo en la sociedad interestatal contemporánea*. Barcelona, 1960.

Scroggs, William O. *Filibusters and Financiers*. New York, 1916.

Sociedad de Geografía e Historia de Costa Rica. *Las verdaderas causas de la caída y muerte del General don Francisco Morazán.* San José, 1941.

Soley Güell, Tomás. *Historia económica y hacendaria de Costa Rica.* San José, 1947.

Soto Hall, Máximo. *Un vistazo sobre Costa Rica en el siglo XIX.* San José, 1901.

Stanger, Francis M. "The Struggle for Nationality in Central America." Unpublished doctoral dissertation, University of California, 1930.

Stansifer, Charles L. "The Central American Career of E. George Squier." Unpublished doctoral dissertation, Tulane University, 1959.

Steinberg, S. H., ed. *Statesman's Year Book.* New York, 1951.

Stimson, Henry L. *American Policy in Nicaragua.* New York, 1927.

Stokes, William S. *Honduras, An Area Study in Government.* Madison, 1950.

Strobeck, Susan. "The Political Activities of Some Members of the Aristocratic Families of Guatemala." Unpublished master's thesis, Tulane University, 1958.

Stuart, Graham H. *Latin America and the United States.* New York, 1955.

Thompson, Wallace. *Rainbow Countries of Central America.* New York, 1926.

Ward, A. W., and Gooch, G. P., eds. *The Cambridge History of British Foreign Policy, 1783-1919.* Vol. II. Cambridge, 1923.

Wilgus, A. Curtis, ed. *The Caribbean Area.* Washington, 1934.

———. *The Caribbean Area.* Vol. VII. Gainesville, 1957.

Williams, Mary W. *Anglo-American Isthmian Diplomacy.* Washington, 1916.

Williams, Mary W., Bartlett, Ruhl J., and Miller, Russell E. *The People and Politics of Latin America.* Boston, 1955.

Winsor, Justin. *History of America.* Vol. VIII. Cambridge, Mass., 1889.

Zelaya, Ramón. *Mea Culpa Centroamericana.* San José, 1920.

Index

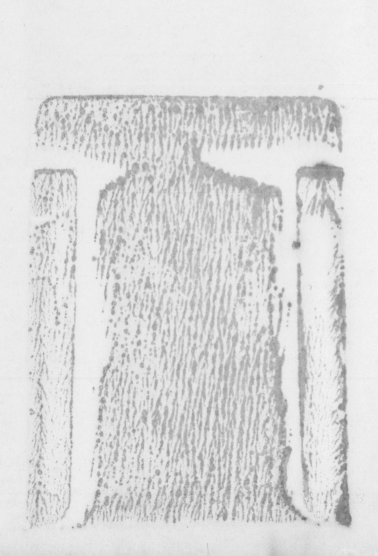